The English Georgic

*Ideas and Forms
in English Literature*

EDITED BY JOHN LAWLOR

The English Georgic
A study in the development of a form

John Chalker

London
Routledge & Kegan Paul

*First published in 1969
by Routledge and Kegan Paul Ltd
Broadway House 68–74 Carter Lane
London, E.C.4
Printed in Great Britain
by C. Tinling & Co. Ltd
London and Prescot
© John Chalker 1969
No part of this book may be reproduced
in any form without permission from
the publisher, except for the quotation
of brief passages in criticism*

SBN 7100 6645 7

Contents

	Introduction	1
One	Theory and Practice: Dryden's Translation of the 'Georgics' and Addison's 'Essay'	17
Two	The Formal Georgic: Philips, Dyer, Smart, Grainger	34
Three	Paysage Moralisé: Denham, Waller, Pope	66
Four	Thomson's 'Seasons'	90
Five	John Gay: 'Rural Sports' and 'Trivia'	141
Six	'The mob of gentlemen . . .'	180
	Conclusion	206
	Select Bibliography	213
	Index	217

Acknowledgements

I should like to thank Professor J. R. Sutherland and Professor Norman Callan for the generous help and encouragement that they have given me at all times. I am grateful also to the General Editor of the series, Professor Lawlor, whose penetrating reading of the manuscript led to many suggestions from which I profited. Part of Chapter Four appeared in an earlier version in *Studia Neophilologica*, and I am indebted to the editor, Professor H. W. Donner, for permission to make use of the material here. Finally, my thanks are due to the Loeb Classical Library, Harvard University Press and William Heinemann Ltd. for permission to quote from the following volumes in the Loeb series: Virgil *Eclogues, Georgics, Aeneid*, trans. H. R. Fairclough; Lucretius *De Rerum Natura*, trans. W. H. D. Rouse; Ovid *Metamorphoses*, trans. F. J. Miller; *Minor Latin Poets*, trans. J. W. Duff and A. M. Duff.

J.C.

Introduction

I

That eighteenth-century writers were great and conscious users of past literature is a commonplace. Whether it is Swift adapting a travel story, Pope writing Horatian epistles or Fielding producing his first novel 'in imitation of the manner of Cervantes', we are aware of literature as a process in which old ways of coming to terms with experience are adapted and made new by the transforming power of the writer. What this book does is to examine the transformations of a single form – the Georgic poem. The term means literally 'a poem about farming', and all examples of the genre derive from Virgil whose *Georgics*, written basically as a treatise on Italian agriculture, showed an extraordinary vitality in the eighteenth century, and inspired a number of important poems which were often remote from any practical purpose, although others were didactic in intention.

All students of English literature have heard about Philips' *Cyder* and Dyer's *Fleece* which belong to the second group. They figure in the literary histories, and they are generally assumed to be faintly absurd and sterile off-shoots of Augustan orthodoxy. So, in a sense, they are. Nobody can well pretend that these particular poems, however fascinating they may be to the antiquarian, will ever be resurrected as 'live' literature. But the study of Georgic writing leads to a fresh examination of works of abundant and continuing interest, among others Pope's *Windsor Forest*, Gay's *Trivia* and Thomson's *Seasons*. Once it is realized how greatly these radically different poems, as well as the more traditional Georgics, were indebted to the same Virgilian inspiration, it seems worth looking at the whole question of Georgic writing in the eighteenth century, and the way in which the Virgilian influence developed.

My initial interest was in matters of form, in discovering what formal concepts the term 'Georgic' implied and why the genre was so popular and evidently useful in the eighteenth century, but these questions could naturally only be answered by combining analysis of form with a thematic study. Eighteenth-century variations of the form occurred partly because Virgil's poem offered a view of life which was found to be significant and usable, partly because the form itself enabled poets to arrive at an interpretation of very varied experience. It is this interaction and the unexpected boldness and freedom of the resultant mutations that is discussed here.

I hope that the book will be useful, not only for its critical discussions of individual poems, but as a study of what eighteenth-century writers understood the process of 'imitation' to be.

2

In the *Epistle to Burlington* ('Of the Use of Riches')[1] Alexander Pope describes the ostentation of Timon's villa, a country house where good sense is sacrificed to fashionable display and theatrical effect. The grounds are a perversion of nature:

> With here a Fountain, never to be play'd,
> And there a Summer-house, that knows no shade....
>
> (121–2)

while the interior is an exercise in baroque flamboyance. The ceiling of the chapel is decorated with sensually painted figures who lie on 'gilded clouds' in 'fair expansion', the dining-room is set up with monstrously perverted bad taste:

> The rich Buffet well-colour'd Serpents grace,
> And gaping Tritons spew to wash your face.
>
> (153–4)

Pope sees the comic indecorum of all this, but he sees also the moral bankruptcy, and the fertility of his satiric images gradually develops a nightmare quality. But the apparently inexhaustible succession of Timon's vanities is not the end of the story. At the conclusion of the poem Pope looks to a time far in the future when Timon's villa will be destroyed, and the land on which it stands will revert to its natural use, which is not, significantly, to be a part of untamed nature, but to be absorbed into a prosperous agricultural landscape:

Introduction

> Another age shall see the golden Ear
> Imbrown the Slope, and nod on the Parterre,
> Deep Harvests bury all his pride has plann'd,
> And laughing Ceres re-assume the land.
>
> (173–6)

In these lines, and the contrast that they make with what has gone before, the reader comes most memorably close in English poetry to the spirit of Virgil's *Georgics*.

One of the most compelling images in Virgil's poem (and one which particularly impressed the imagination of later writers) is that of the battlefield of Philippi, the scene of an unnatural civil slaughter which will be only dimly remembered in the future by the farmer who turns up bones and rusty weapons – the relics of the battle – with his plough:

> ... the Emathian plains once more were strewed
> With Roman bodies, and just heaven thought good
> To fatten twice those fields with Roman blood.
> Then, after length of time, the labouring swains
> Who turn the turfs of those unhappy plains,
> Shall rusty piles from the ploughed furrows take,
> And over empty helmets pass the rake –
> Amazed at antique titles on the stones,
> And mighty relics of gigantic bones.
>
> (I, 659–67)[2]

I am not suggesting that Pope's lines in the *Epistle to Burlington* derive directly from a Virgilian reminiscence, but rather that the underlying values of the passages are parallel. In both Pope and Virgil we see the enduring patterns of agriculture contrasted with the turbulence and transitoriness of more fashionable and more public kinds of life.

It is the kind of country activity that is important. The *Epistle to Burlington* places the same emphasis upon prosperity and utility that had appeared early in Pope's work in *Windsor Forest* where, in the landscape that the poet sees, it is the 'fruitful fields' that are the focal point:

> ... 'midst the Desart fruitful Fields arise,
> That crown'd with tufted Trees and springing Corn,
> Like verdant Isles the sable Waste adorn ...

Introduction

> Here *Ceres*' Gifts in waving Prospect stand,
> And nodding tempt the joyful Reaper's Hand.
>
> (26–40)

Again the reader is brought very close to attitudes which are characteristically Virgilian, and in *Windsor Forest*, indeed, the influence of the *Georgics* is demonstrably at work guiding Pope's response to the countryside and its values. It is, as I shall hope to argue, precisely in the matter of the poet's response to experience that the primary influence of the *Georgics* is to be found; but before that can be examined in detail the nature of Virgil's poem needs to be discussed.

The Georgics were written between 37–30 B.C. and the four books make up a poem which is extremely complex despite Virgil's apparent simplicity of intention as he expresses it in the opening lines:

> What makes a plenteous harvest, when to turn
> The fruitful soil, and when to sow the corn;
> The care of sheep, of oxen, and of kine;
> And how to raise on elms the teeming vine;
> The birth and genius of the frugal bee,
> I sing . . .
>
> (I, 1–6)

The poem is certainly about agriculture and it gives a good deal of information that is useful to the farmer. Each of the four books takes as its subject a central aspect of farming – the first deals with crops, the second with trees, the third with cattle and the fourth with bees. But this bald statement of the poem's didactic purpose and subject-matter is a very inadequate summary of the whole. For although the sheer information takes up a good deal of space, the work is clearly a poem and not a treatise, and the information plays only one part in the final effect. The temptation for the critic is to say that Virgil ornaments his didacticism with digressions. He refers, for example, to topical events, praising Augustus and his conquests; he finds a chance in the fourth book to retell the story of Orpheus and Eurydice; he moves frequently outside his apparent subject in order to describe a disastrous plague or sing the praises of country life. Naturally he also takes the opportunity to describe the countryside, writing on Spring as a renewal of the Golden Age,

Introduction

or discussing the weather appropriate to various farming tasks. His book is very different from a *Complete Husbandry*, but to describe it as digressive gives a false idea of its structure. A more satisfactory way of putting it is the suggestion that 'Virgil wrote the *Georgics* in balanced masses, alternating practical instruction with passages of imaginative brilliance, which it is a bad mistake to call adornments'.[3] The most heterogeneous material is not yoked together arbitrarily or by violence but is carefully articulated to express a single imaginative vision.

Of the many kinds of expansive material it is perhaps the political references that are most unexpected and that seem to the modern reader the most obtrusive. One expects that a work about farming will have a timeless remoteness from topical events; but this is certainly not true of the *Georgics*. The poem is a response to the national and political situation of Rome in the period from the death of Julius Caesar to the Battle of Actium and it is prophetic of the Augustan peace. It springs from a time of great national disorder, recognises the need for stability and looks forward to the peace that is possible. In all this it is a pre-Augustan poem which expresses an ideal as yet unrealized.

Octavian received the title of Augustus from the Senate on 16 January 27 B.C., some two years after the completion of Virgil's work. This title marked the final recognition of the ruler's power and indispensability and it coincided with the establishment of peace and constitutional order within Italy. It was the culmination of a process which had begun with the assassination of Julius Caesar seventeen years earlier when Virgil was twenty-six years old. Octavian, Caesar's heir, was the ultimate victor in the long struggle for power which developed, but it was a struggle that was not settled until Antony's defeat at Actium in 31 B.C., and in the long intervening period it must often have seemed that the unity and stability of the Roman world was crumbling completely. Twice Octavian himself was involved in events of extraordinary cruelty. The formation of the triumvirate with Antony and Lepidus in 43 B.C. was inaugurated with the proscription of 2,000 men including Cicero, and although the proclamation naturally spoke of political necessity (the need to free Rome from subversives while war was waged against Brutus and Cassius across the sea), the desire to raise funds and satisfy personal vengeance was an even stronger motive, and horse-trading between the three rulers over

Introduction

the composition of the lists formed an ugly part of the business.⁴ At Antony's insistence Octavian was forced to agree to the proscription of Cicero, but he exacted the death of Antony's uncle and Lepidus's brother in return. Once the list was drawn up a high price was put on the heads of each of the condemned and the killings were carried out with conspicuous cruelty. After Cicero's death, for example, his head and hands were publicly exhibited above the rostra, 'a dreadful spectacle', says Plutarch, 'to the Roman people, who thought they did not so much see the face of Cicero, as a picture of Antony's soul.'

Antony may have been the force behind the proscription of 43, but three years later Octavian showed his talent for independent cruelty. After Philippi Antony went to the East while Octavian returned to Italy to settle 100,000 demobilized troops on the land, and this meant ejecting the original inhabitants and alienating the local populations. Antony's brother Lucius exploited the discontent and raised troops to oppose Octavian, but he was eventually besieged at Perusia, eight miles north-west of Rome, and forced to capitulate in the February of 40. Octavian was compelled by political necessity to treat Lucius himself with apparent generosity, but Perusia was shown no mercy. Its leading citizens were killed and the town itself pillaged and burned. Octavian at this time seems to have been determined to demonstrate his ruthlessness.

The violence of the proscription and of the destruction of Perusia underlines the essential instability of the times. During the next few years a facade of peace was more than once built up, but it was always a holding operation rather than a final settlement. At Brundisium in the October of 40 B.C. the triumvirs redefined their respective spheres of influence and sealed the treaty with the dynastic marriage between Octavia and Antony. But only three years later a radical realignment took place when Lepidus lost all power after an abortive attempt to assert his authority over Sicily. Similarly a pact was made in 39 B.C. with Sextus Pompeius, whose fleet controlled the seas around Italy and who could therefore interfere with the essential supplies of North African grain, and this agreement was supported by the marriage of Octavian to Scribonia, Sextus's father-in-law's sister. But again the stability was transitory. Sextus returned to his piracy. Octavian raised a fleet with the help of Antony and Sextus was defeated in the September of 36 B.C. Meanwhile it was clear that the uneasy

Introduction

alliance between Octavian and Antony could not last, and Antony's actions in Egypt gave Octavian every excuse for moving towards supreme power. Antony publicly acknowledged Cleopatra as his wife, attacked Octavian as Caesar's heir, asserted the legitimacy of Caesarion, Cleopatra's son by Julius Caesar, and made a will in which he directed that he should be buried beside Cleopatra in Alexandria. These actions made inevitable Octavian's campaigns against Antony which were decisively concluded at the Battle of Actium in 31 B.C.

But despite the ruthlessness and cruelty of the early stages of his rise to power Octavian began during the thirties to show a more sympathetic side to his character. Lepidus was defeated and removed from political life but he was not killed or banished: in fact he continued to be Pontifex Maximus until his death in 13 B.C. Octavian's leniency towards Lepidus, together with his public attitude towards the defeat of Sextus, shows a new side of his character. The defeat of Sextus was bound in itself to be welcome in Rome because it meant that the grain could once more flow unhindered into the city, but Octavian took the opportunity to make the occasion more significant than that. On his return to Rome he delivered a speech to the Senate in which he surveyed his achievements and proclaimed that a new era of peace and prosperity had begun. As a practical measure he cancelled some debts owed by individuals to the state and reduced taxation. The day on which Sextus had been defeated was declared an annual holiday, and, further to mark the significance of the victory, a gilded column, surrounded by the beaks of Sextus's captured ships, and surmounted by a statue of Octavian, was to be erected in the Forum. An inscription said that Octavian had re-established the peace which had long been disturbed on sea and land. H. T. Rowell comments that 'some years were to pass before the *pax Augusta* became a stable reality. But the seed of the idea which was later to play so large a part in the Augustan climate of thought was then sown in men's minds.'[5] In its military aspect the struggle against Antony was about to begin, but the vision of peace was clear, and events were moving towards the moment in January 29 B.C. when, to signify the advent of peace in the Roman world, the Temple of Janus was closed for only the third time in Roman history.

Contrasting with the cruelty of the times, the instability of the political situation and the constant danger before Actium that the Roman world might split into two separate empires, there is then, under the influence of Octavian, an emphasis also upon the ideas of peace, unity and nationhood. Virgil's *Georgics* is a work which reflects this political situation.

3

The immediate 'occasion' of the poem lies in the double effect of the political turmoil upon Italian farming. There had been some depopulation of rural areas as men were drafted to the wars, and this combined with the general disruption to make the farms less efficient and prosperous than they had been before. Then (after Philippi) this disorganization was aggravated by Octavian's policy of settling his discharged veterans on lands which were expropriated for the purpose by commissioners that he had appointed. Virgil's first *Eclogue* is a lament by a shepherd who had been evicted, presumably in this way, and there is a tradition (now regarded with some scepticism) that Virgil himself had been dispossessed of a farm near Mantua, and recovered it only after a personal appeal to Octavian.[6] Whether this is so or not, personal concern for the state of agriculture certainly lies behind the *Georgics*. There is a further tradition, however, which suggests a more specifically political prompting; namely that Maecenas, to whom the work is inscribed, requested Virgil to write a poem on agriculture in order both to instil a new enthusiasm for the subject amongst the upper classes, and to provide practical instruction for veterans newly settled in the country.

If these were the immediate motives they were certainly interpreted with a profound sense of the intrinsic significance of the subject, and a sympathetic understanding of the Augustan ethos which was, as we have seen, only then in the process of evolution. Virgil presents agriculture, and the order, fruitfulness and peace of country life, in strong contrast to the destructive turbulence of recent history. The conclusion of Book I is especially important. Since Julius Caesar's death, Virgil says, which was accompanied by prodigious upheavals in nature – volcanoes, earthquakes, comets and spectres – the world has seemed to be ruled by Mars, 'the god of unholy strife'. All control has been lost, as when the horses of a chariot break from their driver:

Introduction

> Nor reins, nor curbs, nor threatening cries, they fear,
> But force along the trembling charioteer.
>
> (I, 692–3)

Like the chariot the world has seemed to be running out of control, causing bloodshed which may, however, be expiating, Virgil suggests, a primal curse on the Roman nation. Now there is hope that enough blood has been spilt to make atonement:

> O! let the blood, already spilt, atone
> For the past crimes of cursed Laomedon.
>
> (I, 674–5)

If this prayer is granted it is Octavian who will 'save the sinking age' and re-establish order from chaos.

Octavian, the establisher of political and administrative order, is called upon to preside over the *Georgics*, and in doing this he is associated with the fundamental order of life, the rhythms of the seasons, the repeated patterns of ploughing, sowing and reaping. The thematic greatness of the poem depends very much on its sense, communicated through this invocation and its development at many points in the work, of the interplay between the life of the state, and the activity of the farmer – and of the essential need for order in both. In his opening invocation Virgil calls for aid first upon a succession of harvest gods, Bacchus and Ceres, Pan, Minerva ('inventor of the olive') and Triptolemus who discovered the plough, all the

> gods and goddesses, that wear
> The rural honours, and increase the year.
>
> (I, 26–7)

It is into this context that Octavian is introduced when Virgil extends the invocation to him as a man about to become a God. His precise sphere of influence is 'yet the business of the gods' debate', but, in speculating about Octavian's role, Virgil thinks of him first as 'the giver of increase and lord of the Seasons', wearing the myrtle crown sacred to Venus; and, in anticipation of this role, he is asked to 'pity the poet's and the ploughman's cares'. Virgil is establishing the ultimate priorities very clearly at the beginning of his poem, and, as in the reference to a future age when the ploughman will turn up rusty weapons on the battlefield of Philippi,

Introduction

he is setting state affairs in relation to what is truly permanent.

This perspective is present throughout the poem, but it is not exclusively insisted upon. Virgil recognizes and praises the success of Roman armies in maintaining and extending the Empire, and in a resonant passage in praise of Italy in the second book all the achievements of Roman civilization are catalogued. But the emphasis is always upon the approaching peace and the prosperity and renewal that will accompany it. At the end of the poem Octavian's triumphal progress through the East after Actium is thought of as the extension of law and Roman peace to a world willing to accept it:

> Thus have I sung of fields, of flocks, and trees,
> And of the waxen work of labouring bees:
> While mighty Caesar, thundering from afar,
> Seeks on Euphrates' banks the spoils of war;
> With conquering arts asserts his country's cause,
> With arts of peace the willing people draws. . . .
> (IV, 811–16)

It was entirely in the spirit of Virgil that Dryden added to the strict sense in his translation by making the next line read:

> On the glad earth the golden age renews.
> (IV, 817)

There is indeed a prevailing sense in the *Georgics* that the Roman state is moving towards a new Golden Age.

In this general framework of ideas the main material of the poem – practical instruction on farming – finds firm although unobtrusive support: the work of the farmer is seen both as the embodiment of permanence and as a foundation of peace and prosperity.

That a poem of this general character should have been popular in England during the century following the Restoration is not surprising, for the political situations of Rome and England had been sufficiently close for men to experience an instinctive sympathy with Virgil's ideals. His emphasis upon permanence and prosperity might be expected to appeal to an age which, looking back to the immediate past, saw the Civil War, the execution of Charles I, the Restoration and the disputes over the succession which culminated in the Revolution of 1688.

Introduction

One of the deepest awarenesses during the period is in fact that of the precariousness of civilization; and this is surely the great driving force behind Augustan satire. Much of the prophetic power of *The Dunciad* springs from the vision in the third book of the destruction of Roman civilization by the Vandals:

> How little, mark! that portion of the ball,
> Where, faint at best, the beams of Science fall:
> Soon as they dawn, from Hyperborean skies
> Embody'd dark, what clouds of Vandals rise!
> Lo! where Maeotis sleeps, and hardly flows
> The freezing Tanais thro' a waste of snows,
> The North by myriads pours her mighty sons,
> Great nurse of Goths, of Alans, and of Huns!
>
> (III, 83–90)[7]

What makes the threat of Dullness against England so ominous is the intensely realized knowledge that Roman civilization fell and when, in the great passage at the end of the poem, England succumbs to the 'uncreating word' of Dullness, and 'universal Darkness buries all', a pattern is felt to be repeating itself. England is joining Rome in a new barbarism. The *Dunciad* is the most extended expression of an apprehension that haunts the period, the fear that the civilizing power in man may be too weak to contain the forces ranged against it, and that the apparently solid framework of Augustan life may prove hopelessly unstable.

It is a fear that appears twenty-five years later in the work of Thomas Gray whose *Impromptu on Lord Holland's Seat* ends with a vision of the desolation which Gray claimed that Holland, the type of the corrupt statesman, had really wanted to produce.[8] 'If', the Peer is thought of as saying, 'our plans had been fulfilled, London itself would have been destroyed' –

> Purg'd by the sword and beautifyed by fire,
> Then had we seen proud London's hated walls,
> Owls might have hooted in St. Peter's Quire,
> And foxes stunk and litter'd in St. Pauls.

On one level this is satiric hyperbole, a grotesque caricature of Holland's intentions; but the extraordinary emotional power of the lines springs from Gray's Augustan sense that London is no more permanent than Rome, and that its churches could easily

Introduction

become the resting places of wild creatures. What distinguishes this Augustan sense, however, from the straightforward perception that life is transitory and all is vanity, is the further sense that man must strive to preserve what has been achieved and must constantly be on guard against attacks. It is not the inevitable transitoriness of life that Pope or Gray laments, but the avoidable transitoriness of civilization. To prevent man's acquiescence in his loss is the satirist's task:

> To rouse the Watchmen of the public Weal.

It is consequently a very strenuous and exacting moral world that the Augustans inhabit, and the keynote is man's responsibility to preserve what has been achieved, to be active in his own defence.

An age which showed such constant vigilance and continual awareness of the dangers which beset man's attempt to impose a civilized pattern upon experience was in a mood to respond fully to the demanding political and moral world of Virgil.

4

But the appeal of the *Georgics* in the eighteenth century is not to be explained solely in political and moral terms, important though they are. The emphasis upon man's responsibility which is peculiarly characteristic of the period sometimes took more mundane forms, and in one of the most spontaneous manifestations of the 'spirit of the age', the novels of Defoe, we find practical attitudes which are as relevant as *The Dunciad* to an understanding of Georgic writing in the period.[9] Defoe's heroes are solitary figures who confront their environment, often with no help beyond their own resources. Colonel Jacque is a typical figure: growing up as one of a gang of young beggars, he is given no formal education whatsoever, but makes up his social and moral ideas as he goes along, thinking at first that stealing is a trade like any other, yet making the most of experience and gradually establishing a workable life for himself. Robinson Crusoe does the same thing in purcly material terms on his island where he has to husband the small stock of goods that he rescues from the ship, and gradually increase his comfort and security by prudence and hard work, until eventually his desert island has become a kingdom to him. Always in Defoe's novels, man is placed

Introduction

in a hostile setting and is called upon to impose a pattern upon experience. *A Journal of the Plague Year* develops its compelling power because for Defoe the city becomes a symbol of man's success in overcoming his environment, and in the book we see the highly complex mechanism of the city being almost, but not quite, overcome by the power of the hostile, relentless forward movement of the plague. But man just survives: the living are always able to bury the dead, and as the plague passes the mechanism of the city is seen to be intact. Man has remained in control against the onset of a destructive force.

It is particularly striking that in Defoe this sense of human responsibility in the face of the environment should involve a meticulous concern for the minutiae of physical existence. His characters spend a great deal of time cataloguing their possessions or giving an exact account of their movements, and no detail of their practical life is too small to be remembered and set down. And without, of course, suggesting that there is any direct connection between Defoe and Virgil, it might well be said that a reading of Defoe and a consideration of the values that his novels express helps to explain aspects of the eighteenth-century climate of opinion that led the *Georgics* to become a seminal book. The superficial similarities are clear enough. In Book III, for example, Virgil explains how to pick out a particularly promising foal at an early age:

> Upright he walks, on pasterns firm and straight;
> His motions easy, prancing in his gait;
> The first to lead the way, to tempt the flood,
> To pass the bridge unknown, nor fear the
>   trembling wood;
> Dauntless at empty noises; lofty necked;
> Sharp-headed, barrel-bellied, broadly backed:
> Brawny his chest, and deep; his colour gray;
> For beauty, dappled, or the brightest bay:
> Faint white and dun will scarce the rearing pay...
> His horny hoofs are jetted black and round;
> His chine is double...
>
> (III, 121–37)

There is an impressive precision about every line which would make the passage a useful guide at a horse fair, and it is typical in this respect of all the practical advice in the poem. When Virgil writes on how to forecast rain he points to exact signs, among others that:

> The careful ant her secret cell forsakes,
> And drags her eggs along the narrow tracks
>
> (I, 522–3)

and when he tells how to discover whether a particular soil is acid the method is given with all practical details:

> For first an osier colander provide
> Of twigs thick wrought (such, toiling peasants twine,
> When through strait passages they strain their wine:)
> In this close vessel place the earth accursed,
> But filled brimful with wholesome water first;
> Then run it through; the drops will rope around,
> And by the bitter taste, disclose the ground.
>
> (II, 328–34)

There is an obvious affinity between Virgil's concern for precise practical details here and, say, Crusoe's account of how he made a pot or baked bread. Crusoe is amazed at 'the strange multitude of little things necessary in the providing, producing, curing, dressing, making and finishing' the one article of bread, and gives an exact account of how he overcame this host of difficulties. Of course, he has no oven, but he is able to improvise one by inverting a shallow pot that he has made on his hearth and covering it with hot embers:

> When the firewood was burned into embers, or live coals, I drew them forward upon the hearth, so as to cover it all over, and there let them lie till the hearth was very hot; then sweeping away all the embers, I set down my loaf, or loaves, and covering them with the earthen pot, drew the embers all round the outside of the pot, to keep in and add to the heat; and thus, as well as in the best oven in the world, I baked my barley loaves...

In both Virgil and Defoe there is an active, enquiring intelligence at work, facing up to the practical problems of life and intently seeking a solution to them.

5

Tentatively, then, at this stage, it can be suggested that the popularity of the *Georgics* in the eighteenth century derived from the fact that Virgil expressed, in unusual combination, attitudes which had a particular potency for the period. That the English reader can usefully approach the poem either from the standpoint of the *Dunciad*, Book III or that of *Robinson Crusoe* indicates the breadth of its appeal and its strength. On the one hand it promotes awareness of the instability of civilized values, and on the other the ethic of work, and of the need to build patiently by mastering the fundamental resources of life. Both ideas were of profound importance for the English Augustan age.

Notes

1. Pope's *An Epistle to the Right Honourable Richard Earl of Burlington* was published in 1731.
2. Verse translations of the *Georgics* are taken from Dryden's version unless otherwise stated. For a discussion of the translation and the view of Virgil's work that it implies see Chapter One.
3. W. F. Jackson Knight *Roman Virgil* (1944), p. 118.
4. See R. S. Conway *Harvard Lectures on the Virgilian Age* (1928), I 'The Proscription of 43 B.C.'.
5. H. T. Rowell *Rome in the Augustan Age* (1962), p. 37.
6. See H. J. Rose *The Eclogues of Virgil* (1942), Chapter III.
7. These lines formed part of the 1728 *Dunciad* and were retained unchanged in the later reorganization of the poem.
8. Gray wrote the *Impromptu* in 1768 and it was published (anonymously and without his permission) in 1769.
9. Defoe's *Life and Strange Surprising Adventures of Robinson Crusoe, of York, Mariner* was published in 1719; *Moll Flanders*, *A Journal of the Plague Year* and *Colonel Jacque* all appeared in 1722.

One

Theory and Practice: Dryden's translation of the 'Georgics' and Addison's 'Essay'

Although the *Georgics* began to affect English literature in important ways as early as Denham's *Cooper's Hill* (1642), the most significant phase of its influence did not come until after the turn of the century. An important factor in encouraging imitation was the publication in 1697 of Dryden's translation of the *Georgics*, prefaced by Addison's *Essay* on the Georgic kind. Both the translation and the essay were extremely influential, and it is appropriate to begin a study of eighteenth-century developments of the form with an analysis of these two works. They point rather interestingly to two different views of Virgil's achievement, both of which were important in subsequent writing.

Addison's *Essay on the Georgics* is a brief attempt to trace the relationship between Virgil and Hesiod, his most important model, and to distinguish the peculiar excellencies of the genre.[1] In form the *Essay* is modest enough, but its influence upon subsequent attitudes to the *Georgics* bore no relation to its size or scope. When discussing this type of didactic poetry both early and mid-century critics take Addison's dicta as their starting point, and often do little more than vary his phraseology. Joseph Trapp and Joseph Warton are the two most authoritative writers on didactic poetry; and as one reads these later critics it becomes clear that they see the *Georgics* through Addisonian spectacles, and that his critical attitude became the established one for some generations.[2]

The *Essay on the Georgics* is in two parts: first a 'short scheme of rules' for the Georgic kind, and then a comparison between Hesiod and Virgil as the chief exponents of that kind. Addison says that the rules of the kind have not previously been drawn up, that most critics have either passed the *Georgics* over in silence or put them in the same category as pastoral, 'a division by no means proper'. It is by no means proper because, whereas the pastora poet is engaged in imitation – in producing the 'voice of the shepherd' – the Georgic poet delivers the precepts of husbandry in his own person. There is no attempt at imitating the voice of the farmer dramatically. The *Georgics* has affinities, not with pastoral verse, but with other instructive and preceptive poetry, with Lucretius and Aratus. But the poet who writes on agricultural topics has great advantages over the moral and philosophic poet in that his subject matter 'addresses itself wholly to the imagination ... and has the most delightful part of nature for its province'. Inevitably his work will be full of pictorial images. Addison now shapes his definition of a Georgic:

> A Georgic therefore is some part of the science of husbandry put into a pleasing dress and set off with all the beauties and embellishments of poetry.

In enlarging on this definition Addison makes it clear that for him the greatest skill of the Georgic poet lies in his application of ornament, and that ornament may be thought of as either structural or stylistic. Structural ornamentation is seen in the juxtaposition of precepts and in the handling of transitions:

> They should all be so finely wrought together in the same piece, that no coarse seam may discover where they join, as in a curious brede of needlework, one colour falls away by such just degrees, and another rises so insensibly, that we distinguish the variety without being able to see the total vanishing of the one from the first appearance of the other.

Above all, the distinctive quality of the didactic poet is seen in his oblique presentation of material. For the skilful poet does not give his precepts to the reader directly: indeed, to speak straightforwardly is the province of the prose writer. The poet can use narration, can select and emphasize his facts in such a way that he does not appear to be preceptive at all. And it is 'wonderfully diverting to the understanding, thus to receive a precept, that enters as it were through a bye-way, and to apprehend an idea that draws a whole train after it'. The reader is charmed into knowledge unawares.

Next the poet should be careful to develop opportunities for digression. Here some relevance to the main theme is obviously to be looked for, but Addison's conditions are not stringent. All he lays down is that digressions 'ought to have a remote alliance at least to the subject, that so the whole poem may be more uniform and agreeable in all its parts'.

Granted that the instruction should be indirect and varied, it is time for Addison to turn to stylistic matters. The problem here is that the 'lowness' of his subject matter may debase the poet's style and 'betray him into a meanness of expression'. Addison's discussion of this question shows a preoccupation with levels of experience and language that was to become increasingly important in the eighteenth century, especially under the influence of associationist psychology. Thus Dr. Johnson made memorable use of the concept of 'lowness' in condemning some lines in which Lady Macbeth, before the murder of Duncan, calls upon night to surround the deed with total blackness,

> That my keen knife see not the wound it makes,
> Nor Heaven peep through the blanket of the dark,
> To cry, 'Hold, hold!'
>
> (I, v, 52–4)

Johnson argues, too rigorously for most modern readers, that the fearful sentiment of the speech 'is weakened by the name of an instrument used by butchers and cooks in the meanest employments; we do not immediately conceive that any crime of importance is to be committed with a *knife*'. In reading the speech, Johnson asks, 'who does not, at last, from the long habit of connecting a knife with sordid offices, feel an aversion rather than a terror'?[3] Associations derived from 'sordid offices' debase the higher kinds of poetry and lead to a ludicrous and unavoidable descent from the elevated to the commonplace. In *Peri Bathous, or the Art of Sinking in Poetry*, Pope ironically catalogued techniques for producing bathos, advising the author to 'form his thoughts by familiarizing his mind to the lowest objects, to which it may be added that vulgar conversation will greatly contribute', and suggesting that lowness, or bathos, is peculiarly the province of modern writers who fail to understand the sublime.[4]

Addison anticipates discussions of this kind when he suggests that in order to maintain 'the pomp of numbers and dignity of words' the poet must banish all conversational words and phrases from his work. Words which recall everyday life will give the poem 'too great a turn of familiarity' and destroy the dignified impression that the poet is striving to produce. Similarly the 'low phrases and terms of art that are adapted to husbandry' must be banished and more elevated circumlocutions sought out. These will give the verse 'greater pomp and preserve it from sinking into the plebian style'.

This is as far as Addison goes in laying down laws for the Georgic kind, but he now considers Hesiod and Virgil in their light. Hesiod has the praise due to an originator, but he lacks surprise and variety and is everywhere 'bent on instruction'; moreover he suffers, in Addison's opinion, from an inappropriate homeliness. 'Thus', Addison says after a brief quotation, 'does the old gentleman give himself up to a loose kind of tattle, rather than endeavour after a just poetical description'. His power of selection is inadequate and precepts follow one another so thick and fast that 'they clog the poem too much'. Hesiod, in brief, shows 'the plainness of a downright countryman', but in Virgil we see 'something of a rustic majesty, like that of a Roman dictator at the plough-tail'. This judgement is rounded off with the memorable sentence:

> He delivers the meanest of his precepts with a kind of grandeur; he breaks the clods and tosses the dung about with an air of gracefulness.

Addison then gives some general praise to characteristic beauties in each book, says that he would point out the poem's imperfections if it had any, and concludes with a general panegyric:

> I ... shall conclude this poem to be the most complete, elaborate and finished piece in all antiquity. The Aeneis, indeed, is of a nobler kind, but the Georgic is more perfect in its kind. The Aeneis has a greater variety of beauties in it, but those of the Georgic are more exquisite. In short, the Georgic has all the perfection that can be expected in a poem written by the greatest poet, in the flower of his age, when his invention was ready, his imagination warm, his judgement settled, and all his faculties in their full vigour and maturity.

To a modern reader the foundations of this resounding judgement look a little insecure. Addison makes it clear that for him there is a fundamental incongruity in the *Georgics*: there is 'lowness' of subject matter coupled with dignity in the total effect, and he concludes that the poet is raising his subject – mainly by linguistic means – to a more elevated position than it would normally hold. It is quite explicitly a matter of dressing up, putting a dustman in ducal robes. The subject is not to appear 'in its natural simplicity and nakedness . . . but in the pleasantest dress poetry can bestow upon it'.

The best way to test Addison's general attitudes is by reference to his judgements on individual passages. He says of one of the digressions in the third Book, for example, that 'the force of love is represented in noble instances, and very sublime expressions'. But the point of Virgil's long passage on the loves of the beasts is surely rather different. The following lines describe the turbulence of mind that is supposedly brought about in a bull by the sight of a cow:

> carpit enim viris paulatim uritque videndo
> femina, nec nemorum patitur meminisse nec herbae
> dulcibus illa quidem inlecebris, et saepe superbos
> cornibus inter se subigit decernere amantis.
>
> (III, 215–18)

> For the sight of the female slowly inflames and wastes his strength, nor indeed does she, with her soft enchantments, suffer him to remember woods or pastures; oft she drives her proud lovers to settle their mutual contest with clash of horns.[5]

A bull is certainly a noble, a sublime animal ('noble instances and very sublime expressions') and it is part of Virgil's purpose to express the universality of sexual passion. But the universality of female coquetry is just as important a theme, and the tone of the passage in, for example, the phrase *dulcibus inlecebris* adds mockheroic to the sublime. The account of the loves of the beasts implies a comment upon the loves of men and points to the complexity of experience.

Dryden's translation emphasizes and indeed develops this mockheroic element:

> With two fair eyes his mistress burns his breast:
> He looks, and languishes, and leaves his rest,

> Forsakes his food, and, pining for the lass,
> Is joyless of the grove, and spurns the growing grass.
> The soft seducer, with enticing looks,
> The bellowing rivals to the fight provokes.
>
> (III, 333–8)

Here one world is constantly interpreted in terms of another, and the opportunities for irony are continuously used. The single addition *pining for the lass* introduces a degree of sophistication that is at variance – and consciously at variance – with the apparent subject and provokes a re-examination of it. There is a good deal of artificial elevation in the lines, in, for example, the construction *joyless of the grove* as well as in the interpretation of the cow in terms of a sophisticated coquette. But the function of the elevation is not merely decorative. It contributes to an ironical probing of experience, through the juxtaposition of the animal and human kingdoms, and it is this which provides the central justification of the passage as a whole. It is because the juxtaposition is purposive and meaningful that the disparity between lowness of subject ('a cock and a bull') and elevation of diction ('Is joyless of the grove and spurns the growing grass') is immediately acceptable. If it were simply a matter of dressing up farming the pleasure would surely be a very transitory one. As it is, the passage says something important about life, about the universality of experience, and says it with great ease of manner and a good deal of incidental satire.

The tendency towards development of the mock-heroic overtone, which is clearly to be detected in this passage, is characteristic of Dryden's translation. The following lines, taken again from the section on the loves of the beasts, seem, for example, to be predominantly descriptive in Virgil, with very little of the mock-heroic about them:

> tempore non alio catulorum oblita leaena
> saevior erravit campis, nec funera volgo
> tam multa informes ursi stragemque dedere
> per silvas; tum saevus aper, tum pessima tigris.
>
> (III, 245–8)

> At no other season doth the lioness forget her cubs, or prowl over the plains more fierce; or the shapeless

bear spread death and havoc so widely through the forest; then savage is the boar; then most fierce the tiger.

But Dryden has seized upon a mock-heroic potential and exploited it:

> 'Tis with this rage, the mother lion stung,
> Scours o'er the plain, regardless of her young;
> Demanding rites of love, she sternly stalks,
> And hunts her lover in his lonely walks.
> 'Tis then the shapeless bear his den forsakes;
> In woods and fields, a wild destruction makes:
> Boars with their tusks; to battle tigers move,
> Enraged with hunger, more enraged with love.
>
> (III, 381–8)

It is in the third line that one becomes aware of something other than plain statement. 'Demanding rites of love' has no sanction in Virgil; as it stands it has slight overtones of Milton's 'Nor *Eve* the Rites Mysterious of connubial love refused'[6] – at least its connotations are those of order, calmness and mystery – so that there is a tension between the phrase and the picture of the lioness 'stung' by sexual desire. But there is a genuine tension. It is not that the brute passion of the lioness has been dressed up until it becomes suitable for a polite audience. In effect it puts the question how far the 'rites of love' of civilized society alter or express something different from the instincts of animal creation. Again the reader is compelled to make a comparison between society and brute nature; he is put into a position where judgement and evaluation must inevitably be brought into play, just as he is by the last line of the extract:

> Enraged with hunger, more enraged with love ...

where the proposition that love is a hunger is put provocatively, in a manner that compels further attention. The noble instances and sublime expressions are used as a means of questioning established ways of thought: they have a genuinely mock-heroic function in that the effect of the lines depends upon consciously playing-off one kind of experience against another. The truth about love is not to be found either in the sophisticated, mannered style of the passage ('demanding rites of love') or in the aggressive desire of the lioness, but in some middle ground that will comprehend them both.

Oscillation between the heroic and the mundane is characteristic of the *Georgics*. It is easy to forget how much of the poem is epic in scope and manner, and how widely the heroic passages range. There are, as we have seen, for example, those sections of the poem which are nationalistic or patriotic in character. Early in the *Georgics* Virgil looks forward to the apotheosis of Augustus Caesar and asks for his semi-divine aid in writing the work, and in making such an appeal he immediately gives the *Georgics* a dimension greater than that of a straightforwardly preceptive poem. The opportunity which Virgil takes of speculating on the sphere in which Caesar will choose to exercise his divinity (will he be the guardian of Rome, or of the crops, or of seafarers?) is expansive and provides scope for a wide and exotic range of reference:

> tibi serviat ultima Thule,
> teque sibi generum Tethys emat omnibus undis ...
> (I, 30–1)

> farthest Thule owns thy lordship and Tethys with the
> dower of all her waves buys thee to wed her daughter

The agricultural subject of the poem is related straightway to a wide political and mythological context. This kind of reference is repeated in Book III where Virgil dedicates his poem allegorically as a temple to Augustus. In Dryden's translation the lines read:

> I, first of Romans, shall in triumph come
> From conquered Greece, and bring her trophies home,
> With foreign spoils adorn my native place,
> And with Idume's palms my Mantua grace.
> Of Parian stone a temple will I raise
> Where the slow Mincius through the valley strays ...
> Full in the midst shall mighty Caesar stand,
> Hold the chief honours, and the dome command.
> (III, 15–24)

In passages like this the *Georgics* are thought of as subserving a broadly political purpose, the maintenance and glorification of the Empire.

Theory and Practice

This nationalistic, partially political, purpose is allied to the more general but profoundly important patriotic motive which becomes explicit in the great passage in praise of Italy in Book II, lines which made a great appeal to eighteenth-century English poets.

Similarly, many of the most memorable descriptive passages in the *Georgics* are on an epic scale. The description of the tempest, for example, in the section on the signs of the weather in Book I, is of a catastrophe vast in its size and in its effects. Virgil deliberately takes the reader beyond natural description and provides a storm of epic magnitude:

> saepe etiam immensum caelo venit agmen aquarum
> et foedam glomerant tempestatem imbribus atris
> collectae ex alto nubes; ruit arduus aether,
> et pluvia ingenti sata laeta boumque labores
> diluit ... (I, 322–6)

> Often, too, there appears in the sky a mighty column of waters, and clouds mustered from on high roll up a murky tempest of black showers: down falls the lofty heaven, and with its deluge of rain washes away the gladsome crops and the labours of the oxen ...

Other examples of this epic use of natural description are found in the account of the plague amongst the animals in Book III where, in lines largely derived from Lucretius, Virgil gives an extended account of a time when 'ghastly Tisiphone rages, and, let forth into light from Stygian gloom, drives before her disease and dread ...' (551–2); or one can refer to the account of the Scythian winter, also in Book III, a description which, for the Northern reader, has its moments of near comic exaggeration – when, for example, 'everywhere brass splits, clothes freeze on the back, and with axes they cleave the liquid wine' (363–4) – but whose general tone is that of serious heroic description.

This epic tone appears constantly in details of the poem. It is very marked, for example, in a description of the Calabrian serpent occuring in an otherwise unremarkable passage on the danger of snakes:

> est etiam ille malus Calabris in saltibus anguis,
> squamea convolvens sublato pectore terga
> atque notis longam maculosus grandibus alvum ...
> (III, 425–7)

> There is, too, that deadly Serpent in Calabria's glades, wreathing its scaly back, its breast erect, and its long belly mottled with large spots.

This is a truly heroic creature, fit to be placed beside Milton's equally colourful figure:

> Crested aloft, and Carbuncle his Eyes;
> With burnisht Neck of verdant Gold ...
> *(Paradise Lost,* IX, 500–1)

The most extended epic passages are found in the fourth Book. Dryden notes that

> Virgil has taken care to raise the subject of each Georgic. In the first he deals only with dead matter. In the second, he just steps on the world of life, and describes that of vegetables. In the third, he advances to animals; and in the last, he singles out the bee, the most sagacious of them, for his subject.

The last Book is far less preceptive than the first three. It opens with a long mock-heroic treatment of the bees and ends with the fully developed epyllion of the Aristaeus/Orpheus/Eurydice story, an episode which, since it ends the poem, plays a very important part in guiding the reader's response to the work as a whole. The final Book also contains the idealized pastoral figure of the 'old Corycian swain ... lord of few acres, and those barren too' who achieves contentment through work on his own estate. 'As he planted herbs here and there among the bushes, with white lilies about, and vervain, and slender poppy, he matched in contentment the wealth of kings, and returning home late in the evening would load his board with unbought dainties'. (IV, 130–3)

This old Corycian swain is in a sense the true heroic figure of the Georgics. The view of life which emerges from Virgil's poem springs from the passage in Book I in which the poet contrasts the indolence of the Golden Age with the laborious existence which is necessary in life as we know it. Jove has decreed that men should work, but through work arts are developed and the world can be conquered. Good may therefore spring from the curse of work.

> labor omnia vicit
> improbus et duris urgens in rebus egestas.
> (I, 145–6)

Theory and Practice

> Toil conquered the world, unrelenting toil, and want that pinches when life is hard.

Life is a condition dominated by the fact that

> The sire of gods and men, with hard decrees,
> Forbids our plenty to be bought with ease.
>
> (Dryden, I, 183–4)

There is a continual struggle between Man and Nature, a struggle which is seen through Virgil's contrast between unfallen and fallen man. In the Golden Age 'Men made gain for the common store, and Earth yielded all, of herself, more freely, when none begged for her gifts'. The contest between Man and Nature is one of heroic dimensions, calling for the exercise of virtues heroic in quality.

To balance these manifold heroic implications there is obviously a good deal of the poem which is concerned entirely with mundane affairs: when to plant, how to test soil, how to graft, what to do about sheep-scab, how to deal with a swarm of bees. There is no lack of practical information in Virgil's poem. And the link between the mundane and the heroic, the mode which enables them both to be seen as part of a single pattern, is the mock-heroic attitude which has already been touched upon in connection with the passages on the loves of the beasts.

The only piece of formal mock-heroic in the *Georgics* is found in the opening section of Book IV, the section dealing with bees. Here the mode is made quite clear from the beginning, in the mock-heroic invocation. Virgil again asks for the approval of Maecenas, this time while he shows 'the wondrous pageant of a tiny world: chiefs great-hearted, a whole nation's character and tastes and tribes and battles ... Slight is the field of toil; but not slight the glory, if adverse powers leave one free, and Apollo hearkens unto prayer'. (IV, 3–7)

Addison comments upon the mock-heroic passages in the fourth Book:

> But Virgil seems no where so well pleased as when he has got among his bees in the fourth Georgic; and ennobles the actions of so trivial a creature, with metaphors drawn from the most important concerns of mankind. His verses are not in a greater noise or hurry in the battles of Aeneas and Turnus, than in the engagement of

the two swarms. And as in his Aeneis he compares the labour of his Trojans to those of bees and pismires, here he compares the labours of the bees to those of the Cyclops. In short, the last Georgic was a good prelude to the Aeneis; and very well showed what the poet could do in the description of what was really great, by his describing the mock-grandeur of an insect with so good a grace.

Here again one feels that Addison is considerably understating his case: the excellence of the mock-heroic sections is made to depend on their 'grace', on the delicacy with which the epic parallels are handled, on the evidence which they provide of highly developed poetic tact. And this is undoubtedly an important quality of the fourth *Georgic*. A good deal of enjoyment derives from the disparity in size between the bees and mankind and the caricature of human attitudes and emotions that this disparity encourages. The two opposed bee-princes give this sort of pleasure:

> ipsi per medias acies insignibus alis
> ingentis animos angusto in pectore versant,
> usque adeo obnixi non cedere, dum gravis aut hos
> aut hos versa fuga victor dare terga subegit.   (IV, 82-5)

> In the midst of the ranks the chiefs themselves, with resplendent wings, have mighty souls beating in tiny breasts, ever steadfast not to yield, until the victor's heavy hand has driven these or those to turn their backs in flight.

As one would expect Dryden has a splendidly delicate translation:

> With gorgeous wings, the marks of sovereign sway,
> The two contending princes make their way;
> Intrepid through the midst of danger go,
> Their friends encourage, and amaze the foe.
> With mighty souls in narrow bodies prest,
> They challenge and encounter breast to breast;
> So fixed on fame, unknowing how to fly,
> And obstinately bent to win or die ...   (IV, 120-7)

The essential source of pleasure in these lines is the humorous discrepancy between the solemnity of the language – *sovereign sway, intrepid, amaze, mighty souls,* – and the tiny insect that is being described. There is also some implied satire against the pride of princes, an indication that their stateliness is as insecurely founded as that of the bees, but this seems comparatively unimportant. The reader laughs at the bee rather than at the prince, and, as Addison says, is pleased by the skill with which the contrast has been handled.

But the reaction is not always so straightforward as this. In the following lines the comedy of contrast is a much less important element in the total experience:

> Sin autem ad pugnam exierint – nam saepe duobus
> regibus incessit magno discordia motu;
> continuoque animos volgi et trepidantia bello
> corda licet longe praesciscere; namque morantis
> Martius ille aeris rauci canor increpat et vox
> auditur fractos sonitus imitata tubarum ...
> (IV, 67–72)

Dryden's version reads:

> But, if intestine broils alarm the hive
> (For two pretenders oft for empire strive),
> The vulgar in divided factions jar;
> And murmuring sounds proclaim the civil war.
> Inflamed with ire, and trembling with disdain,
> Scarce can their limbs their mighty souls contain.
> With shouts, the coward's courage they excite,
> And martial clangours call them out to fight.
> (IV, 92–9)

Here the comic image of the diminutive bee warriors is not important so much for its own sake as in its human application. *Nam saepe duobus regibus incessit magno discordia motu* (for often strife with terrible turmoil hath fallen on two kings) is a statement which Virgil must surely have interpreted in contemporary political terms. The tendency of Dryden's translation is to emphasize the civil character of the war (*intestine broils; proclaim the civil war*) and when one reads his translation the wider frame of reference is provided by *Absalom and Achitophel* or *The Medal*:

> All other errors but disturb a state
> But innovation is the blow of fate ...
> (*Absalom and Achitophel*, 799–800)

or

> The sober part of Israel, free from stain,
> Well knew the value of a peaceful reign;
> And, looking backward with a wise affright,
> Saw seams of wounds, dishonest to the sight:
> In contemplation of whose ugly scars
> They curs'd the memory of civil wars.
>
> <div align="right">(<i>Absalom and Achitophel</i>, 69–74)</div>

The mock-heroic is effective because of the heroic implications which the verse contains, implications which concern man as a social and political being. From this point of view the value of the mock-heroic is not that it 'ennobles the actions of so trivial a creature with metaphors drawn from the most important concerns of mankind', but that it provides a vehicle for the oblique expression of a political interpretation of life. Addison's account of Book IV leaves one with an impression of triviality and mere playfulness that is critically damaging to the reputation of Virgil's poem, but the style and tone of Dryden's translation demands a more serious reading.

In fact a serious justification of the Georgic kind cannot rest upon the reasoning that Addison puts forward. The poem is more than a collection of 'low' precepts embellished with exalted diction, elegant figures and dignified digressions. Nor is the style merely decorative. It is a way of saying something that could not be said with the same economy in any other way. In the mock-heroic passages that have been discussed so far this is quite clear. Particularly in Book IV the invocation sets the tone and prepares the readers for ironic parallels. The only question is how seriously the parallels will have to be taken. At what level will they work?

Dryden's attitude towards this problem can be judged to some extent by the specimens of his translation which have already been analysed. But one final extract will help to complete the argument. There are many passages in the poem which, although they cannot satisfactorily be labelled as mock-heroic, cannot be thought of, either, as straightforwardly preceptive. The function of such passages is not simply to convey information (although they certainly do that). It is also to convey an attitude to the subject. An example occurs in Book I when Virgil is discussing the different kinds of soil and their treatment:

> at si non fuerit tellus fecunda, sub ipsum
> Arcturum tenui sat erit suspendere sulco:
> illic, officiant laetis ne frugibus herbae,
> hic, sterilem exiguus ne deserat umor harenam.
> Alternis idem tonsas cessare novalis
> et segnem patiere situ durescere campum . . . (I, 67–72)

but should the land not be fruitful, it will suffice, on the eve of Arcturus' rising, to raise it lightly with shallow furrow – in the one case, that weeds may not choke the the gladsome corn; in the other that the scant moisture may not desert the barren sand. In alternate seasons you will also let your fields lie fallow after reaping, and the plain idly stiffen with scurf.

Dryden's translation reads:

> But, if the soil be barren, only scar
> The surface, and but lightly print the share,
> When cold Arcturus rises with the sun;
> Lest wicked weeds the corn should over-run
> In watery soils; or lest the barren sand
> Should suck the moisture from the thirsty land.
> Both these unhappy soils the swain forbears,
> And keeps a sabbeth of alternate years,
> That the spent earth may gather heart again,
> And, bettered by cessation, bear the grain.
> (I, 100–9)

What Dryden has done is to emphasize the sense – already present in Virgil – of the dignity and patterned rhythm of agricultural activities. The passage begins with a versified precept in a poetically neutral tone. There are no 'low' words, nothing offensive to a fastidious taste, but at the same time there is nothing euphemistic in the vocabulary. The slight feeling of elevation is produced by the 'poetic' form *but lightly,* and perhaps by the slightly unusual use of the words *scar* and *print* to describe the marks made in ploughing. This touch of elevation is increased a little in the next couplet through the conventional image of 'cold Arcturus' and the pathetic fallacy implicit in the adjective *wicked* – 'Lest wicked weeds the corn should over-run'. Here Dryden has simply transferred the pathetic fallacy from the corn in Virgil (*laetis herbae*) to the weeds. In the sixth and seventh lines he has added his own touch of personification in the phrases: the *thirsty* land and the *unhappy* soil. The eighth line marks a change of tone which is scarcely justified by the original but which is in keeping with Dryden's translation as a whole. 'And keeps a sabbath of alternate years' is entirely remote from ordinary speech and all the associations of *keeps a sabbath* tend towards solemnity. This new and loftier tone is maintained in the last line with the abstract phrase *bettered by cessation*. At first sight these four lines seem appropriate, linguistically to the theme of *Religio Laici* or *The Hind and the Panther*, but less suitable for a poem on farming. But this simplified view of appropriateness can only be maintained if one assumes that the sole function of the poem is to offer practical advice. If one approaches the lines from the opposite direction and asks, not whether the lines fulfil some external criterion of appropriateness, but what effect the shift in tone produces, then Dryden's purpose becomes clearer.

What happens in these lines is that, by a gradual elevation of tone, the simple precepts about ploughing and the reasons for ploughing in a particular way are merged in the larger considerations of the change of seasons and the fertility of the earth. Advice on how to break the ground is seen as part of a far larger pattern. The details of husbandry may be low – the dung, the pig-sty, the pole-axe. But husbandry itself, the harnessing of nature to man's purpose, is one of the noblest of subjects, and reverence for this great theme provides the unifying mood of the *Georgics*. One of the problems is how to reconcile practicalities – digging and dunging – with idealization of the unchanging and essentially fruitful cycle of the seasons. Stylistic variation of the kind to be seen in this passage is a means of doing that, of bringing together the earthy and the ideal. It is not that the associations produced by the first two lines are true and that those of the 'sabbath of alternate years' are sentimental or strained. They are both true and they complement each other.

This brief examination of Dryden's translation and Addison's *Essay on the Georgics* reveals two attitudes to Virgil's poem and two attitudes which are often opposed to each other. Dryden stresses the complexity and sophistication of Virgil's work, sometimes, as has been shown, tending to exaggerate these elements beyond the limits of a strict translation, but not, it could be argued, beyond the spirit of the poem as a whole. Virgil's attitude to his subject is complex, the range of subject extensive and the preoccupations far wider than would be found in a merely preceptive agricultural poem. Addison's attitude is much simpler. For him the chief interest of the *Georgics* is stylistic: namely in seeing how Virgil has elevated his low subject, how he has dressed his precepts in becoming and elegant fashions.[7]

Clearly these are both possible ways of looking at Virgil's poem, and the writers who developed an English Georgic tradition were influenced by both of them. The next chapter will be concerned with the attitude to the Georgic kind of four writers who attempted serious and straightforward imitations of Virgil: John Philips, John Dyer, Christopher Smart and James Grainger.

Notes

1. For an account of Virgil's treatment of his sources see E. K. Rand *The Magical Art of Virgil* (1931).
2. Joseph Trapp *Praelectiones Poeticae*, Two Volumes, 1711–15. *The Oxford Lectures on Poetry*, translated into English by W. Clarke and W. Bowyer (1742). Joseph Warton *A Discourse on Didactic Poetry* (1753).
3. *Rambler*, 168, published on 25 October, 1751.
4. Pope's *Peri Bathous, or the Art of Sinking in Poetry*, although it originated in the meetings of the Scriblerus Club in the last years of Queen Anne's reign, was not published until 1728. There are modern editions by E. L. Steeves (1952) and by Bertrand A. Goldgar (1965). For the section quoted see Chapter VII.
5. *Virgil*, edited with an English translation by H. Rushton Fairclough. The Loeb Classical Library. (Rev. Ed. 1935).
6. *Paradise Lost*, IV, 742–3.
7. For discussions of Dryden as translator see H. M. Hooker 'Dryden's translation of the *Georgics*' *Huntington Library Quarterly* (1945); W. Frost *Dryden and the Art of Translation* (1955) and Leslie Proudfoot *Dryden's Aeneid and its Seventeenth-Century Predecessors* (1960).

Two

The Formal Georgic: Philips, Dyer, Smart, Grainger

The concept of 'imitation' as a form of writing distinct from translation became important in the seventeenth century, especially with the publication of Cowley's versions of Pindar and Oldham's adaptation of Horatian satire to contemporary abuses.[1] In a Preface to his first two Pindariques, Cowley said that he was 'not so much enamoured of the name translator, as not to wish to be something better, though it want yet a name', and he drew a rather suspect analogy from painting to support the freedom of his versions. The attempt to copy nature exactly is 'a vile and unworthy kind of servitude, incapable of producing anything good or noble':

> I have seen originals both in painting and poesie, much more beautiful than their natural objects; but I never saw a copy better than the original, which indeed cannot be otherwise; for men resolving in no case to shoot beyond the mark, it is a thousand to one if they shoot not short of it.

Realizing that 'if a man should undertake to translate Pindar word for word, it would be thought that one mad man had translated another', Cowley attempts instead to capture the spirit of his author and to find an English equivalent for 'his way and manner of speaking'. Oldham acknowledged similarly that in his translation of Horace he had not been 'over-nice in keeping to the words of the original', but that he had put Horace 'into a more modern dress than hitherto he has appeared in, that is by making him speak as if he were living and writing now'. Consequently, he has altered the scene from Rome to London and used English names of men, places and customs 'where the parallel would decently permit'.

By the time Dryden came to write his Preface to *Ovid's Epistles, Translated by Several Hands* (1680),[2] he felt it necessary to define

The Formal Georgic

this new approach to 'Englishing' the classics. He distinguishes three kinds of translation. The best method, which he calls *paraphrase* and which has Horatian authority, is where the translator keeps close to the author's meaning and alters the word order and manner of expression only as may be necessary to conform to the spirit of a different language. Dryden approves of this and declares that 'the sense of an author ... is to be sacred and inviolable'. He reinforces his point by rewording Cowley's painterly comparison:

> ... when a painter copies from the life, I suppose he has no privilege to alter features and lineaments, under pretence that his picture will look better; perhaps the face which he has drawn would be more exact, if the eyes or nose were altered, but 'tis his business to make it more resemble the original.

But in order to do full justice to the sense it may be necessary for a translator to treat the expression with some freedom, 'for every language is so full of its own proprieties, that what is beautiful in one is often barbarous, nay nonsense, in another'.

It is because languages differ in their nature that the second method, *metaphrase*, or word by word translation, is impossible in practice. Dryden likens the difficulties of this method to 'dancing on ropes with fettered legs: a man may shun a fall by using caution, but the gracefulness of motion is not to be expected'. He is equally suspicious, however, of the third method, that adopted by Cowley and Oldham, which he calls *imitation*. This he defines, with Cowley's practice in mind, as a kind of writing where

> the translator (if now he has not lost that name) assumes the liberty not only to vary from the words and sense, but to forsake them both as he sees occasion; and taking only some general hints from the original, to run divisions on the ground-work, as he pleases.

The translator in this style takes his author only 'as a pattern ... to write, as he supposes that author would have done, had he lived in our age and in our country'.

Clearly the dispute is not so much over translation in the normal sense as over the relative value of translation proper and 'imitation' considered as a new kind of creative writing. As

Dryden himself said: 'to state it fairly, imitation of an author is the most advantageous way for a translator to show himself', and writers became increasingly interested in attempting this 'advantageous way' so that by the eighteenth century the 'imitation' had established itself as a new form, recognized in its own right, in which 'the ancients are familiarized by adapting their sentiments to modern topics'.[3]

Horace and Juvenal provided the most obvious sources for imitation, especially since their work could be made to give authoritative sanction to satire of contemporary events. As Pope said in the Advertisement to *The First Satire of the Second Book of Horace Imitated*,[4] in which he replies to attacks on the fourth *Moral Essay*, 'an answer from Horace was both more full, and of more dignity than any I could have made in my own person'. Pope clearly enjoys the feeling that there is a continuity between his own work and that of the Augustan poet and that this helps to establish the validity of what he is doing. More than most poets the satirist needs a moral backing for his work. But the methods of imitation can be applied to any form, and the Georgic, for social and political reasons that have already been considered, suggested important continuities in human experience which poets were eager to explore. Georgic imitation was of many types, varying from attempts to recreate the complete Georgic 'kind' in English terms, to burlesque imitations of single features of Virgil's poem. In this chapter it is what may be termed formal Georgics – those which deal with some aspect of husbandry and are conscious attempts to reproduce the essential structural features of the Georgic – that will be discussed. The four most important examples of the genre are John Philips' *Cyder* (1708); Christopher Smart's *The Hop-Garden* (1752); John Dyer's *The Fleece* (1757) and James Grainger's *The Sugar-Cane* (1764). These poems are all seriously didactic: the advice that they give derives from contemporary farming manuals and the authors are clearly interested in practical agricultural matters. But they also have a strong literary motive, and emphasize frequently the 'imitative' aspect of their work.

It was suggested in the last chapter that one way of reading Virgil's *Georgics* is to look upon it as a poem containing both epic and mundane elements with mock-heroic acting as a mediator between the two. The four works to be discussed in this chapter

The Formal Georgic

can best be considered from this point of view. They are not great poems, but they are interesting because they show representative minds at work, and demonstrate how widespread was the inclination to use the derived form to juxtapose, and by implication to evaluate, different attitudes to experience.

The poems all contain passages which are clearly epic in manner: in particular there are both digressive narrative episodes, justified by reference to Virgil's use of the Orpheus and Eurydice legend, and also patriotic passages similar to the praise of Italy in the second *Georgic*. Precepts are obviously an essential part of their subject-matter, and clear mock-heroic is found in all these works.

The practical purpose of *Cyder* is to give information on the cultivation of apples and the making of cider, and, as we shall see, Philips' advice is down-to-earth. But he also makes many opportunities for elevated digressions. The central epic episode is an account of the destruction by earthquake of Ariconium (I, 179ff), a legendary town, which is parallel to Virgil's account of the omens that foretold the death of Caesar (I, 461ff). In both Virgil and Philips the transition which links the epic episode to the rest of the poem is provided by lines on the sun. Virgil's discussion of the signs of the weather ends with the indications that can be gained from the sun, and he then modulates very skilfully into the heroic passage:

> solem quis dicere falsum
> audeat? ille etiam caecos instare tumultus
> saepe monet fraudemque et operta tumescere bella.
>
> (I, 463-5)
>
> Who dare say the the Sun is false? Nay, he often warns us that dark uprisings threaten, that treachery and hidden wars are upswelling.

Philips gives an account of a heat-wave which, he says, encourages 'maladies of various kinds and names unknown'; this leads him to reflect on the death of a girl from smallpox, and then, having heightened the tone, he modulates (very clumsily, when compared with Virgil) into the epic digression:

> But if it please the sun's intemp'rate force
> To know attend, whilst I of ancient fame
> The annals trace, and image to my mind
> How our forefathers ... etc.
>
> (I, 167-70)

He then develops in a tapestry of Miltonic and Virgilian echoes the fable of a spacious city which was destroyed by an earthquake. The full rumbustiousness of the derived Miltonic style is well enough adapted to the earthquake itself:

> Sulphur and nitrous spume, enkindling fierce
> Bellow'd within their darksome caves, by far
> More dismal than the loud disploded roar
> Of brazen enginery, that ceaseless storm
> The bastion of a wellbuilt city deem'd
> Impregnable ...   (I, 193–8)

The subject – a mythical earthquake – allows a style which would be flatulent if applied to most other topics (its humorous potentialities were, of course, recognized by Philips and had already been exploited in *The Splendid Shilling*),[5] but here the elevated vocabulary – *disploded* (cf. *Paradise Lost*, VI, 605) and *enginery* (cf. *Paradise Lost*, VI, 553) – and the extended, somewhat orotund rhythms are used with serious intention. The Miltonic echoes are appropriate to the subject, and the lines present an heroic picture, a set-piece of unambiguous description. They can be dismissed only if one dismisses all Miltonic imitation as inherently lifeless; but in this passage there is no lack of vigour. A little later the Miltonic style is used appropriately again to describe the panic which follows the first tremors of the earthquake:

> The thronging populace with hasty strides
> Press furious, and too eager of escape
> Obstruct the easy way; the rocking town
> Supplants their footsteps; too and fro they reel
> Astonish'd, as o'ercharg'd with wine ...
>   (I, 222–6)

The vocabulary is generally straightforward, despite the Miltonic use of *supplant* ('to trip up') and the form of the adverb *furious*, and the syntax, although Miltonic in its compression, is not inflated, as it is in the few lines on the earthquake quoted earlier. Philips, in other words, varies his epic style even within a single brief episode, and he is not mastered by the more obvious and exaggerated Miltonisms. The greatest danger of accidental burlesque springs from melodramatic personification:

> Horror stalks around
> Wild staring, and his sad concomitant
> Despair, of abject look ...   (I, 219–21)

This kind of thing has an air of Grand Guignol, but Philips obviously intends his Miltonic manner to suggest the scope and elevation of a genuine epic experience.

The Virgilian note is heard most unmistakeably at the end of the episode, where Philips says that no trace of Ariconium now remains

> save coins and mould'ring urns,
> And huge unwieldy bones, lasting remains
> Of that gigantic race, which as he breaks
> The clotted glebe the ploughman haply finds
> Appall'd.   (I, 238–42)

Virgil as we saw has the same image: Caesar's battlefields will revert to the plough and the ploughman wonder at the massive relics he turns up in the earth:

> Then, after length of time, the labouring swains
> Who turn the turfs of those unhappy plains,
> Shall rusty piles from the ploughed furrows take,
> And over empty helmets pass the rake –
> Amazed at antique titles on the stones,
> And mighty relics of gigantic bones.
>   (Dryden *Georgics*, I, 662–7)

But Philips, in a manner entirely typical of his age, goes on to make explicit the idea of agriculture as an all-enduring, fundamental activity which survives the decay of rulers and the destruction of cities:

> Upon that treach'rous track of land
> She whilom stood; now Ceres in her prime
> Smiles fertile, and with ruddiest freight bedeck'd
> The Appletree ...   (I, 242–5)

And from this passage (this time in an entirely satisfactory manner) he returns to his ostensible subject, the growing of cider apples.

The function of the heroic passage is expansive and, as it were, perspective. By temporarily going beyond his bucolic subject-matter to the wider world of a lost heroic age, and by setting his 'humble' subject against that extensive background, Philips deliberately encourages the reader to consider the value of the activities which are the subject of the poem. And the conclusion must surely be that 'Ceres in her prime' symbolizes a way of life that is more permanent and probably more valuable than the life of heroic action. At all events the question has been posed in a way that makes it far from absurd.

To play off against the heroic element in *Cyder* there are, as in the *Georgics* themselves, mock-heroic passages. But there is a preliminary difficulty which hinders discussion at this point, and that is how to distinguish between mock-heroic and what might be called playfulness. Philips has occasion to write, for example, of manuring, and he says:

> There are who fondly studious of increase
> Rich foreign mould on their illnatur'd land
> Induce laborious, and with fatt'ning muck
> Besmear the roots in vain. The nursling grove
> Seems fair a while, cherish'd with softer earth,
> But when the alien compost is exhaust
> Its native poverty again prevails.
>
> (I, 119–26)

Ideally one would like to read these lines 'with the same spirit that the author writ', but it is hard to know what that spirit was. At one moment it seems that Philips is being entirely serious, that the lines are a misguided attempt to handle a difficult subject in a genteel manner, so as not to offend the susceptibilities of an over-fastidious audience, ('Tossing the dung about with an air of gracefulness' which Addison might approve). At other moments they seem to be a deliberate burlesque in which heroic dignity is comically imposed upon an entirely inappropriate subject. But neither supposition is adequate. Philips is certainly writing a poem which is fundamentally serious (there is no possibility of burlesque, for example, in the passages of local patriotism discussed below). And since he is a writer of considerable skill, very much aware of problems of style, one cannot seriously believe him to have written

> and with fatt'ning muck
> Besmear the roots in vain . . .

without being aware of the potentially comic contrast between the 'low' word and the elevation of the surrounding style. He had, after all, published *The Splendid Shilling*. His probable attitude towards lines like these seems to me to be suggested by Addison's essay, *The Spectator*, 418,[6] one of the series on *Pleasures of the Imagination*:

> ... the description of a dunghill is pleasing to the Imagination, if the image be represented to our minds by suitable expressions; though, perhaps, this may be more properly called the Pleasure of the Understanding than of the Fancy, because we are not so much delighted with the Image that is contained in the Description, as with the aptness of the description to excite the image.

This distinction between the Pleasure of the Imagination and the Pleasure of the Understanding is a vital one in a critical consideration of Philips or indeed of most Georgic writers in the period, and it applies directly to the lines under discussion. Philips is interested in dunging; he is also interested in the literary problem of how to discuss dunging in an elevated poem. A satisfactory solution of the problem, which involves a measure of ironical detachment, the ability of the poet to stand aside and take pleasure in his own skill, gives intellectual pleasure. In other words an essential ingredient in one's response to

> But when the alien compost is exhaust
> Its native poverty again prevails ...

is awareness of the author's own sense of achievement, a mutual and slightly conspiratorial delight in having overcome an intransigent problem. There is a joint satisfaction in perceiving 'the aptness of the description to excite the image'.

A similar passage occurs in Philips' description of a cure for a plague of wasps:

> let ev'ry bough
> Bear frequent vials, pregnant with the dregs
> Of moyle or mum, or treacle's viscous juice;
> They by th'alluring odour drawn in haste
> Fly to the dulcet cates, and crowding sip
> Their palatable bane. Joyful thou'lt see

> The clammy surface all o'erstrown with tribes
> Of greedy insects, that with fruitless toil
> Flap filmy pennons oft' to extricate
> Their feet, in liquid shackles bound, till death
> Bereave them of their worthless souls. Such doom
> Waits luxury and lawless love of gain.   (I, 425–32)

'The Pleasure of the Understanding' is obviously very strong here in phrases like 'pregnant with the dregs ... palatable bane ... in liquid shackles bound'. The passage is a lighthearted piece of parody. What gives it point and makes it worthwhile is the skill with which Philips succeeds in establishing a sort of retrospective irony through the exaggerated solemnity of the final line and a half:

> Such doom
> Waits luxury and lawless love of gain.

Philips' obvious self-amusement does away with the danger that readers may take the ponderous mock-Miltonisms too seriously.

The attitude behind these lines is obviously different from that of the following passage on the redstreak, regarded by Philips as the noblest of apples:

> Let ev'ry tree in every garden own
> The redstreak as supreme, whose pulpous fruit,
> With gold irradiate and vermilion shines
> Tempting, not fatal, as the birth of that
> Primeval, interdicted plant that won
> Fond Eve in hapless hour to taste and die ...
>   (I, 512–17)

Here the lines work through associations with the apple of *Paradise Lost*, 'of fairest colours mixt, Ruddie and Gold'. We are intended to remember the appearance of Milton's apple together with its other qualities, its 'savorie odour blow'n, grateful to appetite'. The solemnity which surrounded the forbidden fruit helps to suggest the seriousness with which Philips approaches his theme. At the same time there is a nice contrast between Eve's hapless situation and that of her more fortunate successors in eighteenth-century Herefordshire. Philips uses the Miltonic reference, in itself after all grotesquely exaggerated, to express his own sense of good fortune. The lines are mock-epic in the most serious sense of the term: that is they bring ordinary life into relationship with the set of values provided by heroic reference or epic structure. The reference to the Garden of Eden reveals at once both the limitations and the excellencies of country life in Augustan England.

The passage is paralleled a little later in the poem:

> Now turn thine eye to view Alcinous' groves,
> The pride of the Phaeacian isle, from whence
> Sailing the spaces of the boundless deep
> To Ariconium precious fruits arriv'd,
> The pippin, burnisht o'er with gold, the moyle,
> Of sweetest honey'd taste, the fair pearmain,
> Temper'd like comeliest nymph with red and white.
>
> (I, 457–63)

The quality of Philips' feeling for the orchards of Shropshire can be expressed only through heroic echoes and by association with prelapsarian, paradisal experience, in one case that of the Garden of Eden and in the other with the Gardens of Alcinous. And in responding to the landscape in this way Philips is, of course, imitating his model. Virgil as we saw had spoken of Italy in similar terms:

> Perpetual spring our happy climate sees:
> Twice breed the cattle, and twice bear the trees ...
>
> (Dryden, *Georgics*, II, 204–5)

The distinction between these last two passages and the lines on the 'fatt'ning muck' or 'the greedy insects' is that here the element of parody and burlesque is entirely lacking. The tone introduces no hints of comedy – on the contrary, the associations are potentially tragic and they are not in any sense mocked.

The sense of good fortune suggested by the Garden of Eden parallel is found also in the pervasive patriotism of Philips' poem. This is clear first of all in the poet's pride as he surveys the Shropshire countryside:

> Lo! how the arable with barley-grain
> Stands thick, o'ershadow'd, to the thirsty hind
> Transporting prospect ...   (I, 554–6)

a pleasure which extends also to the less useful natural landscape:

> Nor are the hills unamiable, whose tops
> To heav'n aspire, affording prospect sweet
> To human ken... (I, 563–5)

But this simple sensuous pleasure leads on to a more positive, nationalistic kind of patriotism. Indeed the lines on the redstreak introduce a patriotic comparison between England and the Continent. Cider is superior to all foreign vintages: it 'far surmounts'

> Gallick or Latin grapes, or those that see
> The setting sun near Calpe's tow'ring height.
> Nor let the Rhodian nor the Lesbian vines
> Vaunt their rich must, nor let tokay contend
> For sov'reignty: Phanaeus' self must bow
> To th'Ariconian vales. (I, 536–41)

These lines are parallel to a passage in the second Georgic where Virgil praises the 'Aminnean vines, soundest of wines, to which the Tmolian and the royal Phanaean itself pay homage' (II, 97–98), and they are perhaps no more than a conventional exercise in which Philips is aware of the extent of the exaggeration. A more down-to-earth comparison is made a little later:

> Why should the Chalybes or Bilboa boast
> Their harden'd iron when our mines produce
> As perfect martial ore? Can Tmolus' head
> Vie with our saffron odours? or the fleece
> Baetick or finest Tarentine compare
> With Le'm'ster's finest wool? (I, 580–5)

These lines are presumably intended as a conscious challenge to Virgil's

> haec eadem argenti rivos aerisque metalla
> ostendit venis atque auro plurima fluxit. (II, 165–6)

> Yea, and this land has shown silver-streams and copper-mines in her veins, and has flowed rich with gold.

In manner it is almost a reversal of the preceding passage. There the effect depended on exaggeration and there was a slight undertone of comedy. Here Philips can afford to press his case seriously: in the matter of iron and wool he is not afraid of competition. But the exaggerated idealization and the serious challenge both express genuine patriotic feeling.

From praise of England's products Philips is able to move easily to praise of her men:

> Where shall we find
> Men more undaunted, for their country's weal
> More prodigal of life? (I, 585-7)

and from there to praise of his own patron Harley. General patriotism and political feeling are intermixed. Later, for example, there is specific praise for the condition of England under Queen Anne. Philips' starting point is an account of the Civil War when 'the mad headlong rout ... Apostate, Atheist rebels ... defy'd their prince to arms'. The present age, he suggests, forms a complete contrast:

> Now we exult, by mighty Anna's care
> Secure at home, while she to foreign realms
> Sends forth her dreadful legions, and restrains
> The rage of kings ... (II, 525-8)

This discussion of some of the central features of *Cyder* (the first attempt at a formal English Georgic) shows how complete Philips' attempt to imitate Virgil's poem was. He is not dominated by a single feature, either as regards subject-matter or style. He attempts to give in English terms something of the complexity of his original and to include in a single poem a view of life which comprehends farming, the countryside and government as well as life seen in its heroic aspect. The appeal of the form seems to lie for Philips in its many-sidedness, and the peculiar blend of political and patriotic and agricultural interests which characterizes the original evidently makes it congenial to him. In this form he can express some of the dominant preoccupations of his own age. As will be seen in subsequent discussions of Gay, Pope and Thomson the publication of *Cyder* was followed by the appearance of many works which were very significantly influenced by the Georgic tradition. *Windsor Forest*, *Rural Sports*, *Trivia*, and *The Seasons*, to name the most important Georgic poems of the twenty years after the publication of *Cyder*, all stem directly from Virgil, yet none of them is a straightforward imitation in the sense that Philips' poem is. As we shall see they all select from their source and modify the shape and character of Virgil's poem, and they produce very diverse and original works. But for some time no attempt was made to imitate the *Georgics* as directly as Philips had done. In the mid-century, however, formal Georgic imitation became something of a fashion, and a number of poems appeared which follow the pattern of *Cyder*. One of the first, by the author of *A Song to David* and *Jubilate Agno*, was published in 1752.

Christopher Smart's *The Hop-Garden* begins with a thoroughly Virgilian statement of purpose:

> The land that answers best the farmer's care,
> And silvers to maturity the Hop ...
> I teach in verse Miltonian. (I, 1-7)

and it is throughout a highly self-conscious poem. Smart acknowledges his debt to Hesiod, Virgil, Milton and Philips, and displays in a short Georgic of approximately 800 lines a wide variety of styles and attitudes.

The dominant *motif* of *The Hop-Garden* is local patriotism, the celebration of Kent. It includes a tribute to Sidney as a county poet who

> from court retir'd
> In Penshurst's sweet Elysium sung delight,
> Sung transport to the soft-responding streams
> Of Medway, and enliven'd all her groves ...
> (I, 12-15)

and the pastoral note of these lines is strongly marked also in the passage which follows, a modest refusal on the poet's part to sound

> the loud larums of the braying trump (I, 28)

and acceptance of 'the lawns ... the silver wave ... and the hopland shades' of his native county instead. After a preceptive passage the patriotic theme returns in a description of the Kent countryside which uses pastoral Miltonic echoes to produce an effect of mystery and solemnity:

> Here tow'ring spires
> First catch the eye, and turn the thoughts to heav'n.
> The lofty elms in humble majesty
> Bend with the breeze to shade the solemn groves
> And spread an holy darkness ... (I, 99-103)

The Formal Georgic

There are also suggestions of the Miltonic Garden of Eden, possibly owing something to Philips, in phrases like 'Flora's daedal hand' or in the picture of the 'pippin's palatable gold'. But this patterning of literary echoes is complemented by a purely English and observed picture

> Yet not even these – these ever varied scenes
> Of wealth and pleasure can engage my eyes
> T'o'erlook the lowly hawthorn, if from thence
> The thrush, sweet warbler, chants th'unstudied lays.
> (I, 116–19)

This leads directly to the concluding lines of this section of the poem, the statement that none of these images

> with half those charms
> Attract my eyes, as yonder hop-land close,
> Joint work of Art and Nature . . . (I, 126–8)

The passage is 'composed' (the painting term seems appropriate) of familiar motifs, and Smart is perhaps relying too heavily on stock responses, but it does effectively bring the Kentish countryside into relationship with literary and mythological settings. It expresses Smart's enthusiasm in literary terms and it prepares for and leads to a direct apostrophe some twenty lines later

> Hail, Cantium, hail!
> Illustrious parent . . . (I, 156–7)

and to a direct parallel with the Garden of Eden:

> Fav'rites of Heaven! to whom the general doom
> Is all remitted. (I, 170–1)

Smart now indulges in historical retrospection and introduces the first epic episode in the poem, the story of Hengist and Vortigern. This section poses all the problems of Miltonic pastiche, and it is by no means easy to decide what effect Smart intends to produce by lines such as those describing Roxena's seduction of Vortigern:

> lowly she bow'd
> Fawning insinuation bland, that might
> Deceive Laertes' son; her lucid orbs
> Shed copiously the oblique rays, her face,

47

> Like modest Luna's shone, but not so pale,
> And with no borrow'd lustre ...   (I, 235–40)

Clearly this is a serious passage intended in one sense to emphasize the importance of Kent by calling attention to its historic role. Equally clearly there is a degree of emphasis which cannot be adequately explained, however hard we press, on grounds of appropriateness. It seems probable that Smart is deliberately cultivating the element of pastiche and that as so often in this kind of Georgic writing the passage has both a serious and a comic intention. What happens is that the style (Miltonic pastiche) implies a commentary on the theme, or at least the use of the theme in this particular context. What Smart is doing is to balance the serious justification for insertion of this epic subject (a justification which is partly literary, that is in terms of the Georgic tradition, and partly thematic, that is in its glorification of Kent) against a feeling that there is something inherently incongruous about the mixture of precept and epic that the poem contains. Both the seriousness and the sense of incongruity are valid and the style serves to bridge the two, putting them into a workable relationship with each other.

At the end of the passage the two aspects of the subject come together in one of the most popular Georgic images, found, as we have already seen, in both Virgil and Philips:

> Long did he reign: but all-devouring time
> Has raz'd his palace walls – Perchance on them
> Grows the green hop, and o'er his crumbled bust
> In spiral twines ascends the scancile pole.   (I, 251–4)

Again one of the difficulties posed by *The Hop-Garden* is its range of conventions, the ease with which Smart moves, in a way alien to the modern reader, from preceptive writing to other modes. This could be fully illustrated only by extensive analysis, but indications can be given by examining some sixty lines from Book I (ll. 281–345). The passage is basically preceptive, and there is a good deal of advice, no doubt well-founded, about the treatment of hops:

> To every root three joints indulge, and form
> The quincunx with well regulated hills ...   (I, 286–7)

or
>The shovel next must lend its aid, enlarge
>The little hillocks, and erase the weeds.
>>(I, 335–6)

But there is certainly much more than versified precept. We find, for example, an extreme of elevated personification in descriptions of natural processes. When the young shoots are long enough they begin to climb the stakes in an elaborately emblematic manner. To speak of the 'marriage' of vines and elms was a commonplace, and Smart develops this traditional sexual imagery:

>   Their heads
>Thy young plants will uplift, their virgin arms
>They'll stretch, and, marriageable, claim the pole.
>>(I, 288–90)

They must then be tied up

>Else soon, too soon their meretricious arms
>Round each ignoble clod they'll fold and leave
>Averse the lordly prop . . .   (I, 322–4)

In lines like these the precept is an excuse for indulging a semi-allegorical interest. Rather similarly, but less elaborately, Smart gives a mythological account of natural events:

>When Phoebus looks thro' Aries on the spring . . .
>>(I, 281)

uses somewhat ponderous Miltonisms deriving from *L'Allegro*:

>   jolly Mirth,
>And fat Good-nature with her honest face . . .
>>(I, 292–3)

and falls back on passages of Miltonic/Thomsonian pastoralism:

>When smiling June in jocund dance leads on
>Long days and happy hours . . .   (I, 331–2)

These varying styles and tones all spring from the ostensible subject – hop-growing – but many lines are more remote in their implications. Contemplation of Kentish oaks, for example, leads Smart (by an almost inevitable eighteenth-century transition) to thoughts of the Navy and to a brief patriotic outburst. Finally, a reference to August introduces a short meditation on Augustus:

> Sovereign of science! master of the muse!
> Neglected genius' firm ally! of worth
> Best judge, and best rewarder ...
> (I, 339–41)

These sixty lines work through comparison and contrast of the various elements that have been isolated here. No single strand is dominant, and the success of the passage as a whole is greater than seems possible from a reading of any single section.

> And vernal flowers promise dulcet fruit ...
> (I, 282)

for example, is a line which can easily be mocked for the conventionality of *vernal* and the too easy Miltonism of *dulcet*. But in context these objections are not felt nearly so strongly as they are when the line is isolated. It is not a description that Smart wants to give: he is concerned with the implications of the scene in front of him, and as the starting-point for an examination of those implications he gives an idealized picture of actuality in the Kentish hopfields. This idealized picture (with its pastoral/ paradisal qualities) is an appropriate and neutral base, as it were, for the varied implications and the modal complexities that are to follow.

Fully developed mock-heroic is rare in *The Hop-Garden*. The most important episode is that of the hop-pickers in Book II. A woman, says Smart, can sometimes be found who will make a successful foreman of the hop-pickers:

> And yet I've known them own a female reign,
> And gentle Marianne's soft Orphean voice
> Has hymned sweet lessons of humanity
> To the wild brutal crew. Oft her command
> Has sav'd the pillars of the hop-land state,
> The lofty poles from ruin, and sustain'd,
> Like Anna, or Eliza her domain
> With more than manly dignity.   (II, 88–95)

Again one experiences a curious duality of response. The 'pillars of the hop-land state' are important and are thought of seriously by Smart; but the comparison with *Anna or Eliza* is absurdly far-fetched and *gentle Marianne's soft Orphean voice* is in ridiculous contrast to the presumably strident tones of the actual forewoman. Here it is the deliberate exaggerations of the mock-heroic mode

The Formal Georgic

which provide an implicit (entirely oblique) comment upon the idealization of the hop-gardens which is the staple of the poem. A similar effect is aimed at, but more crudely and with a more straightforwardly comic result, in lines like the following:

> Soon as bright Chanticleer explodes the night
> With flutt'ring wings, and hymns the new-born day
> The bugle-horn inspire, whose clam'rous bray
> Shall rouse from sleep the rebel rout, and tune
> To temper for the labours of the day ...
>
> (II, 149–53)

The result is largely comic inappropriateness, akin to that of the burlesque passages in Fielding's work.

But the presence of these mock-heroic passages gives us a clue to the way in which some of the Miltonic sections earlier in the poem should be read. One may easily feel at first sight that the opening of *The Hop-Garden* is simply an example of flatulent, humourless Miltonic imitation:

> The land that answers best the farmer's care,
> And silvers to maturity the Hop:
> When to inhume the plants; to turn the glebe;
> And wed the tendrils to th'aspiring poles:
> Under what sign to pluck the crop, and how
> To cure, and in capacious sacks infold,
> I teach in verse Miltonian.   (I, 1–7)

It is only in the light of the mixture of styles, and use of clear mock-heroic later in the poem that the attitude behind these lines can be understood. But in the context of the poem as a whole, and in the context of the tradition that Smart inherited, it is clear that his attitude to the style here is sceptical and experimental and that the exaggerations have the function of allowing him, many different viewpoints towards the subject of the work. Within the Georgic mode it is possible for Smart to handle his subject. Without it he would lack a vehicle to express the variety of his attitudes. The intransigence of the subject-matter would defeat his purposes.

The next important 'true' Georgic, following Smart's poem after a gap of only five years, is John Dyer's *The Fleece*, a more ambitious work in form than either *Cyder* or *The Hop-Garden*: it is in four

The English Georgic

books and this suggests a more complete attempt to emulate Virgil. Once again we find a strong impulse towards an heroic treatment of the subject, an impulse which is expressed most simply (if to the twentieth century reader rather over-confidently) in the final lines of Book III:

> What bales, what wealth, what industry, what fleets!
> Lo, from the simple Fleece how much proceeds!
>
> (III, 631–2)

The didactic element in *The Fleece* is by no means unimportant, but the glorification of his subject, a stressing of what seems to him its true significance, a commercial significance, is an equally important influence behind Dyer's work. And this glorification constantly moves towards an epic scale.

Book II opens with straightforward didactic passages, but Dyer soon begins a long historical and mythological digression:

> There was a time
> When other regions were the swain's delight,
> And shepherdless Britannia's rushy vales,
> Inglorious, neither trade nor labour knew ...
>
> (II, 191–4)

A survey of celebrated pastoral lands leads to an abbreviated account of the story of Jason which is entirely heroic in manner:

> And now the Thracian Bosphorus they dare,
> Till the Symplegades, tremendous rocks!
> Threaten approach; but they unterrify'd,
> Thro' the sharp-pointed cliffs and thund'ring floods
> Cleave their bold passage ...   (II, 260–4)

The point of the story in the general pattern of the poem is to introduce, in a suitably lofty manner, the moral and patriotic material which forms the rest of the Book. Even in the Jason section there is the hint of a moral attitude and this later assumes great importance. When Jason arrives at Colchis he finds 'nothing ... but luxury and crowds/Sunk deep in riot'. The King 'proud Aëtes' has begun

>   to slight
> The shepherd's trade, and turn to song and dance.
>
> (II, 288–9)

The Formal Georgic

Because of this lawless luxury (and without the traditional trials) Jason and the Argonauts are able to seize the golden fleece and make their prosperous return. The effect upon Colchis was disastrous and showed itself in commercial terms:

> Thus Phasis lost his pride ...
> The trade ship left his streams, etc.
> (II, 302–3)

From this point trade is the dominating topic of the Book:

> To censure Trade,
> Or hold her busy people in contempt,
> Let none presume ...   (II, 617–619)

And this leads Dyer to the rather clumsy patriotic point that England, unlike Colchis, is not 'sunk deep in riot', has a proper respect for trade and consequently prospers.

The vision of the poem is one which depends upon trade. The development of this theme and its relationship with the *Georgics* themselves will be discussed in subsequent chapters.[7] In Dyer we see the apotheosis of an attitude which had been maturing for a century and which was soon to disappear. But Dyer is still free from doubts; indeed he is intoxicated as he reflects on the benefits which commerce will bring in its train. He rejoices that the 'stately Thamis' should be

> ever checkered o'er
> With deeply-laden barges ...
> (III, 623–4)

just as he rejoices at the 'ruddy roofs and chimney tops'

> Of busy Leeds, up-wafting to the clouds
> The incense of thanksgiving ...
> (III, 309–10)

and

> Th'increasing walls of busy Manchester,
> Sheffield and Birmingham, whose reddening fields
> Rise and enlarge their suburbs.   (III, 338–40)

London 'where lofty Trade,/Amid a thousand golden spires enthron'd,/Gives audience to the world' is the centre-piece of a picture of national diligence and prosperity. Everything is made to subserve this picture. Whereas in Virgil the exotic images, like that of the Scythian winter, exist primarily as a contrast to the ideal land which is Italy, in Dyer the whole world (and especially the exotic world) has been subdued to the necessities of English trade:

> Why to the narrow circle of our coast
> Should we submit our limits, while each wind
> Assists the stream and sail, and the wide main
> Wooes us in every port? (III, 546–9)

It is a complete expression of a bourgeois and puritan ideal.

But for all his intensity, which one feels to be exceptionally strong, Dyer is also capable of effects which, within the context of the Georgic tradition, seem clearly to contain a saving element of self-mockery. When he invokes England in the following words he is either being accidentally bathetic or achieving a deliberate effect:

> Hail, noble Albion! . . .
> Rich queen of Mists and Vapours!
> (I, 152–8)

Dyer, for all his faults, was a man 'whose mind', said Dr. Johnson, 'was not unpoetical', and Gray, for his part, repeats the praise: 'Mr. Dyer has more of poetry in his imagination than almost any of our number'. Akenside regarded a liking for *The Fleece* as a touchstone of poetic taste. For Johnson, Gray and Akenside to agree in calling a man a poet must mean that they considered him to have a thorough understanding of the significance and use of varied poetic styles in the different kinds.[8] Accidental bathos would hardly have been expected, and it seems likely that Dyer is deliberately producing an air of comedy in these lines. He praises England in the noblest terms, but no-one can deny that England is foggy. By using his most elevated style on this particular subject Dyer makes his attitude quite clear and does so in the most economical manner. The preceding few lines are of similar stylistic interest:

> Those slow-descending showers,
> Those hovering fogs, that bathe our growing vales
> In deep November, (loathed by trifling Gaul,
> Effeminate) are gifts the Pleiads shed,

> Britannia's handmaids: as the beverage falls
> Her hills rejoice, her vallies laugh and sing.
>
> (I, 146-51)

The 'trifling Gaul, Effeminate' is an elaborate figure. By appearing in burlesque Miltonic dress his foppishness is appropriately emphasized, and his denigration of the stalwart British undermined; on the other hand, the sheer exaggeration of the description (it is, after all, reasonable enough to dislike fogs) turns him into a sympathetic figure. The comedy reflects on Dyer. An attack and a counter-attack are achieved through the same phrase; but it is, of course, only a careful control of styles that enables Dyer to write in what is, in these lines, an extremely concentrated way.

James Grainger's West Indian Georgic *The Sugar-Cane* is more obviously and seriously didactic than the three poems that have so far been considered in this chapter. Not that *Cyder*, *The Fleece* and *The Hop-Garden* are lacking in precepts or that the advice, so far as one can judge, is ill-founded, but Philips, Dyer and Smart do not go to Grainger's lengths in stressing the usefulness of their work by adding notes to explain technicalities and expand information which is inadequately developed in the body of the poem. Grainger asserts the utility of *The Sugar-Cane* in the Preface. 'I have often been astonished', he says,

> that so little has been published on the cultivation of the sugar-cane, while the Press has groaned under folios on every other branch of rural economy . . . and yet, except some scattered hints in Pere Labat, and other French travellers in America; an essay by Colonel Martyn of Antigua, is the only piece on plantership I have seen deserving a perusal.

But, although the preceptive side of the poem is of importance, and Grainger obviously felt that his work would be helpful to intending planters, he is not merely writing a handbook. He defends himself, for example, against a possible charge of using awkward and ugly-sounding 'terms of art' by reference to the established poetic authorities:

> It must be confessed that terms of art look awkward in poetry; yet didactic compositions cannot wholly dis-

pense with them. Accordingly we find that Hesiod and Virgil, among the ancients, with Philips and Dyer (not to mention some other poets now living in our own country) have been obliged to insert them in their poems.

He has very strong literary as well as didactic preoccupations, as may be seen, for example, not only in the Preface but also in passing references to his sources:

> Though lofty Maro (whose immortal muse
> Distant I follow, and submiss adore)
> Hath sung its properties ...   (II, 132-4)

The staple style of the poem is one of considerable elevation, and this is marked by frequent use of epic similes. The following lines are typical:

> As art transforms the savage face of things,
> And order captivates the harmonious mind,
> Let not thy blacks irregularly hoe
> But, aided by the line, consult the site
> Of thy demesnes and beautify the whole.
> So when a monarch rushes to the war,
> To drive invasion from his frighted realm
> Some delegated chief the frontier views
> And to each squadron and brigade assigns
> Their order'd station ...   (I, 266-75)

Much of Book II, especially passages on hurricanes and earthquakes has epic associations and the theme which draws together the diverse elements of the Book is itself epic in its implications – the struggle of man against the afflictions of nature:

> 'Gainst such ferocious, such unnumber'd bands,
> What arts, what arms shall sage experience use?
>   (II, 238-9)

The Book begins with an account of 'low' pests, monkeys, rats and insects. Here mock-epic is used both to elevate the subject and also, once more, to establish the poet's attitude towards it. Advising the use of dogs against monkeys Grainger writes:

> faithful dogs,
> Of nose sagacious, on their footsteps wait.
> With these attack the predatory bands;
> Quickly th'unequal conflict they decline,
> And chattering fling their ill-got spoils away.
>
> (II, 50–4)

The crucial line is *Of nose sagacious on their footsteps wait*. One of its functions, no doubt, is simply to give the dogs a dignified appearance – instead of being sharp at scent they are *of nose sagacious* – but there is obviously a mock-element which makes the elevation acceptable, reduces the danger of over-solemnity. The tone is the only appropriate one in which this particular subject could be satisfactorily treated. The same is true of the celebrated passage on rats:

> Nor with less waste the whisker'd vermin race,
> A countless clan, despoil the low-land cane . . .
>
> (II, 62–3)

Boswell's account of the original version of these lines is well known:[9]

> Having talked of Grainger's *Sugar-Cane*, I mentioned to him Mr. Langton's having told me, that this poem, when read in manuscript at Sir Joshua Reynolds', had made all the assembled wits burst into a laugh, when, after much blank verse pomp, the poet began a new paragraph thus:
>
> 'Now Muse, let's sing of *rats*
>
> And what increased the ridicule was, that one of the company, who slily overlooked the reader, perceived that the word had originally been *mice*, and had been altered to *rats*, as more dignified.
>
> This passage does not appear in the printed work. Dr. Grainger, or some of his friends, it should seem, having become sensible that introducing even *Rats* in a grave poem, might be liable to banter. He, however, could not bring himself to relinquish the idea; for they are thus, in a still more ludicrous manner, periphrastically exhibited in his poem as it now stands:

The English Georgic

> Nor with less waste, the whisker'd vermin race,
> A countless clan, despoil the low-land cane.

The anecdote is an entertaining one often used to illustrate the eighteenth-century fondness for elevation of diction; but for our present purpose Boswell's note to the passage gives the incident a particular interest. According, says Boswell, to the Bishop of Dromore (Thomas Percy):

> The passage in question was originally not liable to such a perversion; for the author having occasion in that part of his work to mention the havock made by rats and mice, had introduced the subject in a kind of mock-heroic, and a parody of Homer's battle of the frogs and mice, invoking the Muse of the old Grecian bard, in an elegant and well-turned manner. In that state I had seen it; but afterwards, unknown to me and other friends, he had been persuaded, contrary to his own better judgement, to alter it, so as to produce the unlucky effect above-mentioned.

Boswell comments:

> The above was written by the Bishop when he had not the Poem itself to recur to; and thought the account given was true of it at one period, yet as Dr. Grainger afterwards altered the passage in question, the remarks in the text do not now apply to the printed poem.

While it is true that the Bishop's remarks about the parody of Homer's battle of the frogs and mice do not apply to Grainger's poem in its present form, the account of the author's mock-heroic intention is valuable and is relevant to the poem as we have it.

> Now Muse let's sing of rats

would be broadly comic, burlesque, in its effect, but

> Nor with less waste the whisker'd vermin race

is far more delicate in its methods. It avoids the rather crude contrast of *Muse* and *rats* yet maintains the contrast obliquely. The Bishop of Dromore's evidence is valuable because it suggests that the effect is calculated, that Grainger is not (as the original anecdote suggests) simply striving for the dignified only to achieve the bathetic, but is deliberately cultivating a mock-heroic attitude towards his subject. With this evidence in mind it is possible to discuss more confidently than would otherwise be the case, some lines a little later on which deal with the unpromising subject of rat poison:

> With Misnian arsenic, deleterious bane,
> Pound up the ripe Cassada's well-rasp'd root,
> And form in pellets; these profusely spread
> Round the cane-groves, where skulk the vermin-breed:
> They greedy, and unweeting of the bait,
> Crowd to th'inviting cates, and swift devour
> Their palatable death ... (II, 83–9)

The passage is obviously analogous to Philips' advice on manure or Dyer's defence of English weather. Again much of the pleasure lies in seeing a man discover a way of handling a subject, and come to terms with material which is in itself intransigent. Nothing could be more inherently unpoetic than rat-poison. A reader's first reaction is similar to that provoked in Dr. Johnson by Dyer's *The Fleece*:

> The subject, Sir, cannot be made poetical. How can a man write poetically of serges and druggets.

or, as he said of *The Sugar-Cane* itself

> What could he make of a sugar-cane? One might as well write the 'Parsley-bed, a Poem' or 'The Cabbage-garden, a Poem'.

It is natural to sympathize with Dr. Johnson (and often dangerous not to) yet the tendency of his remarks is surely suspect. Most readers would feel, in theory at least, that a subject is not in itself poetic or unpoetic. The important thing is not the subject itself, but what it has become. And the first necessity, before anything can be made of a subject, is for the author to put himself into such a relationship with it that he can manipulate it, control it and not be dominated by it. When Grainger writes of

> Misnian arsenic, deleterious bane ...

he has brought his subject under complete control, just as Pope has when he writes of the playing-cards in *The Rape of the Lock*.[10]

But he has done a little more than that, of course, because in choosing to bring it under control in this way, through the mock-heroic mode, he has hinted at an evaluation of the subject. There is, underlying this Book, the epic theme of Man's struggle against Nature, and sometimes this struggle manifests itself as one against rats. Such a struggle obviously lacks the external grandeur of epic, but it may still have implications of epic size.

> They greedy, and unweeting of the bait,
> Crowd to th'inviting cates

says something about these implications and keeps them at least in the reader's mind.

From this mock-epic mood Grainger can move easily to disasters of more obvious magnitude, and as he does so he moves into a straightforwardly epic mode. All the time it is Man in his contest with Nature that provides the theme:

> When may the planter idly fold his arms
> And say, 'My soul take rest?' Superior ills,
> Ills which no care nor wisdom can avert
> In black succession rise. (II, 194–7)

The epic episodes in the latter half of the Book centre upon a hurricane and earthquake and end with a pathetic fable in the Thomsonian manner. In describing a hurricane, epic comparisons are clearly permissible on grounds of simple appropriateness and Grainger does not miss the opportunity:

>   The muse hath seen
> The pillar'd flame, whose top hath reach'd the stars;
> Seen rocky, molten fragments, flung in air
> From Aetna's vext abyss; seen burning streams
> Pour down its channell'd sides; tremendous scenes!
> Yet not vext Aetna's pillar'd flames, that strike
> The stars; nor molten mountains hurl'd on high;
> Nor ponderous rapid deluges, that burn
> Its deeply-channell'd sides; cause such dismay,
> Such desolation. (II, 275–84)

The comparison has elements of gratuitous exaggeration, and part of Grainger's poetic satisfaction seems to lie in his working up of the scene, the opportunity that it offers for the Miltonic imagery of *pillar'd flames*, *molten fragments* and *burning streams*. But the Miltonisms are there to emphasize the magnitude of the hazards faced by the sugar-planter, and the central comparison (*not vext Aetna's pillar'd flames . . . cause such dismay*) is an entirely serious one. There is no hint of mock-heroic here. Grainger is asserting that the life of the planter is sometimes epic in stature.

One would not want to make far-reaching claims for the poetic merit of this section of Grainger's poem. The style is often windy, and lines like

>> Grim desolation tears the shrieking isle,
>> Ere rosy morn possess th'ethereal plain . . .
>>   (II, 359–60)

are simply bad. But while it is true that individual lines and even longer passages may be strident and over-emphatic the overall effect of the section on the hurricane and the earthquake is by no means unsatisfactory. Its success is due to Grainger's skill in relating the 'poetic' imagery and associations to the actual West Indian scene. The lines quoted above are followed, for example, by plain advice to the householder:

>>   well, with massy bars,
>> Thy doors and windows guard . . .

and this is not, as it well might be, an example of the art of sinking in poetry, but an idea which relates the purple passage directly to the basic themes of the poem. The same relevance is apparent in the following account of the signs of the weather, one of the stock passages of Georgic imitation. When a hurricane is brewing,

>>   . . . the mid-day sun looks red; strange burs
>> Surround the stars, which vaster fill the eye.
>> A horrid stench the pools, the main emits.
>>   (II, 314–16)

This is, as it were, the domestic realization of the horrors that have already been seen in an elevated and personified form. The hurricane presents itself in this fashion. Similarly we are given the lightning as it strikes a house, and the dead tropical calm as it affects the sailor:

> Who, heart-fainting, eyes
> The sails hang idly, noiseless from the mast.
>   (II, 374–5)

The earthquake is similarly man-centred:

> Can the poor, brittle, tenements of man
> Withstand the dread convulsion?
>   (II, 399–400)

It is an ironic reversal in effect of Thomson's 'Man superior walks amid the glad creation'. Further, the picture of men who huddle together waiting in horror for the eruption of the earthquake, who

> on the open plain
> Appal'd, in agony the moment wait,
> When, with disrupture vast, the waving earth
> Shall wealm them in her sea-disgorging womb
>   (II, 402–5)

is complemented by an account of the terrors that afflict 'the bestial kind'. The picture is one of the instability of human fortune and the inadequacy, even pitifulness, of human effort when set against the vast attacking power of natural forces.

One other passage may be distinguished for the contribution it makes to the distinctively 'Georgic' nature of the poem, the account of Montano in Book I. Montano has been driven by persecution to settle in the West Indies, and at first he is a parallel figure to Virgil's 'old Corycian swain' in the fourth Georgic:

> At first a garden all his wants supplied
> (For temperance sat cheerful at his board)
> With yams, cassada, and the food of strength,
> Thrice wholesome tanies ...   (I, 594–7)

But the difference between Virgil's ideal and Grainger's is seen clearly in the conclusion of the story. The point about the old Corycian swain is that he contentedly makes the most of his situation, unpromising though it is on the surface:

> For, late returning home, he supped at ease,
> And wisely deemed the wealth of monarchs less:
> The little of his own, because his own, did please.
>   (Dryden, *Georgics*, IV, 201–3)

The Formal Georgic

Montano, in a more colonial spirit, prospers by his own labour, becomes rich and dies, an example of national benevolence. But this notable difference apart, Montano has the same sort of function in *The Sugar-Cane* as the Corycian swain in the fourth *Georgic*. He is a single idealization of a way of life that the poet finds admirable, a wholly typical figure.

The patriotic motive, which has been shown to be of importance in the other Georgics considered in this chapter, is strongly marked also in *The Sugar-Cane*, but inevitably it is more complex since the poet experiences patriotic feelings towards both England and the West Indies. The West Indian patriotism is first of all directed at the beauty of the countryside, its exotic quality and its fertility:

> the delighted eye expatiates wide
> O'er the fair landscape; where in loveliest forms,
> Green cultivation hath array'd the land.
> (III, 523-5)

But mingled with this there is the nostalgia of the exile for his native land:

> my native land,
> Whose sweet idea rushes on my mind,
> And makes me 'mid this paradise repine.
> (I, 302-4)

The double note of patriotism is united in the final invocation to 'old father Thames':

> All hail, old father Thames! though not from far
> Thy springing waters roll; nor countless streams,
> Of name conspicuous, swell thy watery store;
> Though thou no Plata, to the sea devolve ...
> Vast humid offerings; thou art king of streams:
> Delighted commerce broods upon thy wave;
> And every quarter of this sea-girt globe
> To thee due tribute pays; but chief the world
> By great Columbus found, where now the muse
> Beholds, transported, slow vast fleecy clouds,
> Alps pil'd on Alps, romantically high,
> Which charm the sight with many a pleasing form.
> The moon, in virgin-glory gilds the pole,
> And tips yon tamarinds, tips yon cane-crown'd vale,

> With fluent silver; while unnumber'd stars
> Gild the vast concave with their lively beams...
>
> (IV, 635–50)

This tribute of the new world to the old is united, quite naturally with a note of political patriotism in the concluding lines of the poem:

> The British George now reigns, the Patriot king!
> Britain shall ever triumph o'er the main.
>
> (IV, 680–1)

The 'British George' is no doubt ill-cast in the role of Augustus, but that is exactly the function that Grainger's poem makes appropriate for him.

The examination of these poems shows how persistently certain themes and stylistic methods recur in the serious Georgic, and how there was a typically Georgic attitude to experience and to the art of making poetry out of it. The imitation of Virgil's poem was not simply a mechanical, academic or literary exercise. Virgil's particular blend of patriotic, political and social themes was evidently felt to echo the preoccupations of these Georgic poets. With Philips the impulse was perhaps primarily literary; with Smart it was a local patriotism; with Dyer a politico-commercial interpretation of life; with Grainger the epic aspect of Man's struggle against Nature. But, whatever the immediate impulse, the Georgic form was welcome because it allowed the poet to develop a large range of implications and to place his central preoccupation in a wide literary, social and historical context. The Georgic is by its nature an expansive rather than an intensive form and the opportunity to expand, to dilate on the ramifications of a given theme was one that these poets enjoyed, and made the most of.

Notes

1. The Preface to the *Pindarique Odes* was first 'published in Cowley's *Poems* (1656). See *The English Writings of Abraham Cowley*, Volume I: *Poems*, edited by A. R. Waller (1905), pp. 155–6. For Oldham's comments on imitation see the Advertisement to his version of Horace's *Art of Poetry* (1681). A fuller discussion will be found in Harold Brooks' 'The "Imitation" in English Poetry, Especially in Formal Satire, Before the Age of Pope', *Review of English Studies*, 1949.

2. The Preface to *Ovid's Epistles, Translated by Several Hands* (1680). See John Dryden *Of Dramatic Poetry and Other Critical Essays*, edited with an Introduction by George Watson, Two Volumes (1962), Volume I, pp. 262–73.
3. Samuel Johnson *Lives of the English Poets*, edited by George Birkbeck Hill, Three Volumes (1905). Volume III, p. 176.
4. *The First Satire of the Second Book of Horace Imitated* (1733).
5. *The Splendid Shilling*, a short Miltonic burlesque which established Philips' reputation, was published in 1703.
6. *The Spectator*, edited with an Introduction and Notes by Donald F. Bond, Four Volumes (1965), Volume III, pp. 566–7.
7. See Chapter III, pp. 67–71, and Chapter IV, pp. 99–109.
8. See Johnson *op. cit.*, Volume III, p. 346 where Akenside's opinion is also quoted. Johnson's condemnation of *The Fleece* was severe, but was directed above all at the choice of subject – 'the irreverance habitually annexed to trade and manufacture, sink him under insuperable oppression'. For Gray's opinion see *Correspondence of Thomas Gray*, edited by Paget Toynbee and Leonard Whibley (1935), Volume I, p. 295.
9. See *Boswell's Life of Johnson*, edited by George Birkbeck Hill, revised by L. F. Powell (1934), Volume II, p. 353.
10. *Rape of the Lock*, III, 37–44.

Three

Paysage Moralisé: Denham, Waller, Pope

So far we have been concerned with poems where the Virgilian influence has been continuous and unmistakable. John Philips or James Grainger assume that the reader of *Cyder* or *Sugar-Cane* will be familiar with Virgil, and that he will recognize and enjoy the details of the imitation. In the descriptive poems to be discussed in this chapter Virgilian influence is not explicit to the same degree and it might be – indeed often is – ignored by the casual reader. Nevertheless it is of great importance both structurally and, even more, thematically. The principal poems in question are Denham's *Cooper's Hill*[1] and Pope's *Windsor Forest*.[2]

Denham's *Cooper's Hill* was published as early as 1642, and in parts it is very typically seventeenth-century in its moral preoccupations, imagery and verse movement. This strain is clearest in a passage where Denham contrasts periods of religious sloth and religious zeal, and asks whether a *via media* is quite impossible:

> Is there no temp'rate region can be known,
> Betwixt their frigid, and our torrid zone?
> Could we not wake from that lethargic dream
> But to be restless in a worse extreme?
> And for that lethargy was there no cure
> But to be cast into a calenture? (139–44)

The end-stopping, the emphatic, frequently monosyllabic, rhymes, the medical and geographical basis of the imagery have something of the economy and precision that one associates with Marvell's octosyllabics in, for example, *Upon the Hill and Grove at Bilborow*:[3]

> See how the arched Earth does here
> Rise in a perfect Hemisphere!
> The stiffest Compass could not strike
> A line more circular and like;
> Nor softest Pensel draw a Brow
> So equal as this Hill does bow.

> It seems as for a Model laid,
> And that the World by it was made.

This highly ratiocinative and emblematic argumentative manner is an important element in the poem.

But what is new, and what impressed eighteenth-century critics, is the discursiveness with which Denham treated his subject. It was this that Dr. Johnson pointed to:

> *Cooper's Hill* is the work that confers upon (Denham) the rank and dignity of an original author. He seems to have been, at least among us, the author of a species of composition that may be denominated local poetry, of which the fundamental is some particular landscape, to be poetically described, with the addition of such embellishments as may be supplied by historical retrospection, or incidental meditation.[4]

Denham's originality is seen if one compares *Cooper's Hill* with an earlier 'local' poem – Jonson's *To Penshurst*.[5] The difference is that Jonson is so much more local and concentrated than Denham. Everything in Jonson's poem forms part of a panegyric to Penshurst: above all, nature offers abundant gifts to the house and its owner:

> And if the high swolne Medway faile thy dish,
> Thou hast thy ponds, that pay thee tribute fish,
> Fat, aged carps, that runne into thy net.
> And pikes, now weary their owne kinde to eat,
> As loth, the second draught, or cast to stay,
> Officiously, at first themselves betray.

Here and in succeeding lines all externals are seen in relation to the house itself and by means of a prolonged conceit derive their meaning from it. In *Cooper's Hill* the scene itself is a focal point, certainly, but more important it is a starting-point for extensive meditation on topics suggested by the view of Windsor. Denham writes on the pleasures of retirement, praises famous men, meditates on religious conflict, considers trade and colonization, and finally gives an account of a stag hunt which allegorizes the fall of Strafford. Contrasted with *To Penshurst*, *Cooper's Hill* is an outward-turning poem with a wide range of implications of a social and political kind, and in this respect it became a model for the nature poetry of the eighteenth century.

In his development of these preoccupations Denham was mindful at several points of the *Georgics* although his reminiscences of Virgil's poem are occasional and, even cumulatively, are insufficient to suggest that he was attempting an imitation in the eighteenth-century sense of the term.[6] The section on retirement and the praise of national heroes owes a general debt to commonplace Virgilian themes, but it is in lines on the Thames (ll. 160ff) that the most significant, and the most interestingly developed, Georgic parallel occurs. Denham's praise of the Thames begins indeed with an image that has a conventional emblematic quality:

> Hasting to pay his tribute to the sea,
> Like mortal life to meet eternity.   (163–4)

but the next couplet has a Georgic echo which, exotic in itself, is used to introduce a more mundane emphasis:

> Though with those streams he no resemblance hold,
> Whose foam is amber, and their gravel gold,
> His genuine and less guilty wealth t'explore,
> Search not his bottom, but survey his shore,
> O'er which he kindly spreads his spacious wing,
> And hatches plenty for th'ensuing spring . . .
>   (165–70)

Denham is clearly echoing Virgil's passage in praise of Italy ('nor beauteous Ganges, nor Hermus thick with gold can vie with Italy's glories'), and, like Virgil, he prefers the fruitfulness of his own country to the more luscious and exotic (and dangerous) charms of foreign lands. This is traditional and might be expected; but, very interestingly from the point of view of later developments in nature poetry, Denham now develops this patriotic attitude to include praise of commerce and colonization:

> Nor are his blessings to his banks confined,
> But free and common as the sea or wind;
> When he, to boast or to disperse his stores,
> Full of the tributes of his grateful shores,
> Visits the world, and in his flying towers
> Brings home to us, and makes both Indies ours;

> Finds wealth where 'tis, bestows it where it wants,
> Cities in deserts, woods in cities plants;
> So that to us no thing, no place is strange,
> While his fair bosom is the world's exchange.
>
> (179–88)

This concern with the civilizing effects of exploration and colonization and the sense that the whole world is being brought into a new harmony by the expansion of trade is something that Denham adds to the Georgic attitudes that he had previously been expressing. But the directness of the last line makes his point unmistakably:

> While his fair bosom is the world's exchange.

There is obviously no feeling at all in Denham's mind that this use of the Thames might be looked upon as incongruous, no hint of the attitudes that were to lie behind Blake's phrase, 'the charter'd Thames'.[7] For Blake it is the nature of the Thames to be free and man has debased the river by exploiting it for commerce. It has lost its beauty and become associated with the 'marks of weakness, marks of woe' of man's fallen state. Denham's view on the contrary is man-centred and utilitarian. He assumes that man is right to subdue the Thames to his own purposes, and regards it as natural that the Thames should be used to develop trade, just as it is natural that the earth should be used to produce crops.

This was to be an influential attitude, and Denham's originality in associating it with traditional Georgic *motifs* is worth stressing. In a discussion which places Denham in the tradition of retirement poetry, Maren-Sofie Røstvig claims that 'Denham ... had shown nothing but scorn for the London merchants, associating them as a class with destructive religious enthusiasm and personal greed'.[8] Certainly this point of view is strikingly expressed earlier in *Cooper's Hill* where the City of London is thought of as a place where

> ... luxury and wealth, like war and peace,
> Are each the other's ruin and increase.
>
> (33–4)

But, to return to the passage under review, the Thames clearly cannot be used as 'the world's exchange' unless there are merchants to do business, and one's sense of Denham's overall attitude must be guided by both passages. There is no doubt that his view of the active commercial life was equivocal, and there is no reason why this should be reprehended. It is the nature of this kind of human activity to leave the onlooker in two minds; and it is the poet's achievement to leave him with a sense that the good and the bad are nicely balanced.

Denham seems to have been the first to associate the praise of trade with Virgilian patriotism, but some dozen years later Waller echoes him in *A Panegyric to My Lord Protector, Of the Present Greatness, and Joint Interest, of His Highness, and this Nation.* The association was evidently found to be congenial. Waller's passage begins with the Navy:

> Lords of the world's great waste, the ocean, we
> Whole forests send to reign upon the sea ...
>
> (41–2)

and passes easily to a picture of England as the recipient of the world's bounty:

> Our little world, the image of the great,
> Like that, amidst the boundless ocean set,
> Of her own growth hath all that Nature craves,
> And all that's rare, as tribute from the waves.
>
> (49–52)

From this point Waller moves quickly to England's superiority to more exotic lands: we enjoy the benefits but have none of the disadvantages of other countries, a neat development of Virgil's thought that 'ravening tigers are far away (from Italy), and the savage seed of lions':

> The taste of hot Arabia's spice we know,
> Free from the scorching sun that makes it grow;
> Without the worm, in Persian silks we shine;
> And, without planting, drink of every vine.
>
> (57–60)

It is now an easy modulation to praise of Englishmen, and from there back once more to praise of Cromwell:

> Things of the noblest kind our own soil breeds;
> Stout are our men, and warlike are our steeds;
> Rome, though her eagle through the world had flown,
> Could never make this island all her own.
>
> (65–8)

Paysage Moralisé

The pattern of attitudes and the extent of the literary reference is very similar to Denham's. More briefly and in passing we find the same imagery in Waller's Restoration poem *To the King, Upon His Majesty's Happy Return*. Charles's return is like the sun's:

> So the lost sun, while least by us enjoy'd,
> Is the whole night for our concern employ'd;
> He ripens spices, fruits, and precious gums,
> Which from remotest regions hither comes. (47–50)

By now the poetic treatment of trade seems to be well established. Only a few years later Dryden is writing extensively on the same subject in his account of the origins of the war at the beginning of *Annus Mirabilis*:

> Trade which like blood should circularly flow,
> Stopp'd in their channels, found its freedom lost:
> Thither the wealth of all the world did go,
> And seem'd but shipwreck'd on so brave a coast.
> (4–7)

And again we find the characteristic note of a luxurious emphasis on the exotic:

> For them alone the heavens had kindly heat;
> In eastern quarries ripening precious dew:
> For them the Idumaean balm did sweat,
> And in hot Ceylon spicy forests grew. (8–11)

As early as 1666, then, there is a clear tradition in the poetic treatment of commerce, stemming from Virgil and strongly emphasizing both patriotism and pleasure in the exotic. Denham's Virgilian preoccupations were fostered and became more obviously significant. The development is typified in Dryden's addition of a line in his translation of Virgil's passage in praise of Italy. Virgil's 'Shall I tell of the seas, washing the land above and below' becomes:

> Our twofold seas, that, washing either side,
> *A rich recruit of foreign stores provide* . . .
> (II, 217–18)

a significant addition which is entirely in the spirit of the times.

For Denham and Waller it was above all Virgil's praise of Italy that proved a valuable starting point, but poets naturally went on to explore the wider value of the *Georgics* as a generic model for descriptive poetry. In Pope's *Windsor Forest* the imitative element is of radical importance.

Many factors must have encouraged Pope to rely on Virgil as a model in *Windsor Forest*.[9] *Cooper's Hill* was likely to be a major source for topographical reasons, and as we have seen Denham had been very clearly influenced by Virgil, but the occasion of the final form of Pope's poem (the Peace of Utrecht) also made the twin themes of patriotism and peaceful development (involving trade and colonization) particularly congenial. Quite apart from the influence of Denham, Pope was probably affected by the flurry of interest in the *Georgics* that had taken place in recent years – Dryden's translation, Addison's extremely enthusiastic essay, Phillips' *Cyder*. He may also have known what form Gay was giving to *Rural Sports*,[10] another poem written in celebration of the Peace and greatly indebted to Virgil. Certainly he set out from the beginning to make the Virgilianism of his poem apparent.

The tone and character of the work is established completely in its first ninety-two lines. Indeed in the first couplet there is already the blend of local and political interest which is the groundwork of the whole:

> THY Forests, *Windsor*! and thy green Retreats,
> At once the Monarch's and the Muse's Seats.

The very location of the poem, Pope suggests, demands something more than 'pure description', and the alliteration on *Monarch's* and *Muse's* points forward to Pope's preoccupations. *Windsor Forest* will be concerned with government as well as with rural retirement. The political aspect is immediately reinforced by the dedication to Granville who had recently been given a peerage by Queen Anne in order to save the Tory Ministry. If, as Wakefield suggested, Pope consciously echoes the opening of Charles Hopkin's *The History of Love* (1695):

> Ye Woods and Wilds, serene and blest retreats,
> At once the Lovers, and the Muses seats:

then the effect must be by contrast to make the seriousness of his subject even more apparent.[11] There is obviously no intention of treating Anne and her Court ironically.

Paysage Moralisé

Following this brief invocation and statement of purpose, there is the most sustained piece of description in the poem as Pope contemplates *Windsor Forest* itself:

> The Groves of *Eden*, vanish'd now so long,
> Live in Description, and look green in Song:
> *These*, were my Breast inspir'd with equal Flame,
> Like them in Beauty, should be like in Fame.
> Here Hills and Vales, the Woodland and the Plain,
> Here Earth and Water seem to strive again,
> Not *Chaos*-like together crush'd and bruis'd,
> But as the World, harmoniously confus'd:
> Where Order in Variety we see,
> And where, tho' all things differ, all agree.
> Here waving Groves a checquer'd Scene display,
> And part admit and part exclude the Day;
> As some coy Nymph her Lover's warm Address
> Nor quite indulges, nor can quite repress.
> There, interspers'd in Lawns and opening Glades,
> Thin Trees arise that shun each others Shades.
> Here in full Light the russet Plains extend;
> There wrapt in Clouds the blueish Hills ascend:
> Ev'n, the wild Heath displays her Purple Dies,
> And 'midst the Desert fruitful Fields arise,
> That crown'd with tufted Trees and springing Corn,
> Like verdant Isles the sable Waste adorn.
> Let *India* boast her Plants, nor envy we
> The weeping Amber or the balmy Tree,
> While by our Oaks the precious Loads are born,
> And Realms commanded which those Trees adorn.
> Not proud *Olympus* yields a nobler Sight,
> Tho' Gods assembled grace his tow'ring Height,
> Than what more humble Mountains offer here,
> Where, in their Blessings, all those Gods appear.
> See *Pan* with Flocks, with Fruits *Pomona* crown'd,
> Here blushing *Flora* paints th'enamel'd Ground,
> Here *Ceres*' Gifts in waving Prospect stand,
> And nodding tempt the joyful Reaper's Hand,
> Rich Industry sits smiling on the Plains,
> And Peace and Plenty tell, a STUART reigns.
>
> (7–42)

The English Georgic

In the middle of this passage, when England is compared with other countries, there is a very distinct echo of the *Georgics*, a reference to the same section of Virgil's poem that Denham and Waller had found appealing: 'Let *India* boast her Plants ...' varies the opening of Virgil's passage in praise of Italy: 'Not Bactra, nor India, nor all Panchaea rich in incense-bearing sand ... can vie with Italy's glory' (II, 138-9), and gives an echo which will be heard again in *Windsor Forest*. Moreover, the literary reference is not isolated: it decisively affects the reader's attitude to the entire section and ultimately to the whole poem. It enables him to see, for example, that the earlier comparison between the 'Groves of Eden' and Windsor Forest is not a mere hyperbole. Placed within a traditional mode, artificiality and exaggeration have a clear meaning which is much more complex than it would be in a more 'realistic' form: with the help of the Georgic reference, which establishes a context of traditional values, one can see that the comparison between the prelapsarian scenery of Eden and that of eighteenth-century Windsor is not an empty extravagance. Virgil had claimed in his second book that Italy still experienced a Golden Age:

> Perpetual spring our happy climate sees:
> Twice breed the cattle, and twice bear the trees ...
> (Dryden, II, 205-6)

Similarly, Pope suggests that the beauty of Eden has been recreated in Windsor Forest. But in neither case is the statement as straightforwardly hyperbolical as it appears to be. In both the beauty of the external scene works in an almost emblematic way, as a sign or guarantee of Man's success in coming to terms with his environment. Virgil has already said in Book I that Jove destroyed the Golden Age in order that Man might, by his own labour, become master of the world and recreate his own paradise. A similar attitude underlies Pope's lines and accounts for the centrality of the harvest scene and the emphasis on trade, industry and political institutions. It is through work and trade and social organization that a Golden Age can be made to come again.

A sense of the ideal that is to be aimed at is conveyed through the balance of the scene. Earl R. Wasserman has shown how the concept of *concordia discors* operates throughout this opening description of the forest.[12] He argues that the harmonious confusion and the order in variety of the scene are felt to be emblematic of the balanced tensions which were known to exist in the heavens and which were regarded as a model for the organization of society. The scene that Pope sees before him is presented in terms of oppositions: 'Not *Chaos*-like ... But ... harmoniously confus'd; all things differ, all agree; part admit and part exclude; Nor quite indulges ... nor can quite repress; Here in full Light ... There wrapt in Clouds; Let *India* boast her Plants ... while by our Oaks; not proud *Olympus* ... more humble Mountains'. Each term is balanced by an opposite to suggest a state of equilibrium. The perfection of the balance is emphasized by the playfulness of the tone in some couplets, most notably in ll. 19–20:

> As some coy Nymph her Lover's warm Address
> Nor quite indulges, nor can quite repress.

The mock-heroic and mildly satirical flavour may seem at first to violate decorum, yet it contributes significantly to the overall tone of the paragraph. Its effect is to demonstrate the poet's complete assurance. Pope's willingness to pause and develop a rather bizarre simile through the length of a couplet acts as a guarantee of his imperturbability: it adds a special note of poetic confidence to the balance that is being both described and created.

By contrast there is a striking violence in the next section of *Windsor Forest*, which describes the desolation of the English countryside in the wake of the Norman invasion. Here everything is in extremes and there is no sense of restraining counterforces. The characteristic words are: 'Savage ... furious ... severe ... Wilds ... waste ... lawless ... Despotick ... bloody ... barb'rous', etc.

The vividly realized picture of a desolate civilization which is the focal point of this section is unmistakably Georgic in its inspiration:

> The Fields are ravish'd from th'industrious Swains,
> From Men their Cities, and from Gods their Fanes:
> The levell'd Towns with Weeds lie cover'd o'er,
> The hollow Winds thro' naked Temples roar;
> Round broken Columns clasping Ivy twin'd;

> O'er Heaps of Ruin stalk'd the stately Hind;
> The Fox obscene to gaping Tombs retires,
> And savage Howlings fill the sacred Quires.
>
> (65-72)

The lines derive from the account of a plague in the third book of the *Georgics* where the overturning of civilized order by a pestilence is expressed in images which Pope adapts to his own purpose. Virgil, for example, pictures wild animals, tamed by disaster, wandering through the houses:

> Timorous deer and shy stags now stray among the hounds and about the houses ... (III, 539-40)

and Pope imagines how,

> O'er Heaps of Ruins stalk'd the stately Hind.

In both passages it is a sense of the precariousness of civilization that is important, a premonition of the complete disaster that may be caused by a single shock, the total inversion of values. Here the inversion involves a change from fruitfulness to sterility, from 'fruitful Fields' and 'springing Corn' to a 'dreary Desert' and a 'gloomy Waste'. The ultimate monstrosity of the Norman reign, as it was seen by Pope, was in making the hunt more important than the harvest. The area of forest land was extended so much that,

> In vain kind Seasons swell'd the teeming Grain,
> Soft Show'rs distilled, and Suns grew warm in vain ...
>
> (53-4)

and this denial of the importance of the harvest leads to the desecration of all human institutions:

> The levell'd Towns with Weeds lie cover'd o'er;
> The hollow Winds thro' naked Temples roar.
>
> (67-8)

What we experience in the first ninety-two lines of the poem are two completely opposed visions of life. On the one hand there is a successful resolution of opposing forces to achieve a balance that is creative; on the other a state of sterile strife. In his development of this contrast Pope uses, as we have seen, a number of direct

Paysage Moralisé

Georgic parallels. The important thing, however, is not so much the individual echoes themselves, as the pointer which the echoes give to the Georgic character of the interpretation of life that Pope is expressing. The question is what man can make of a situation in which nature is often hostile and in which he has to rely on his own creative efforts to produce a life that is bearable. The possibilities both for success and failure are presented at the beginning of the poem, and in a manner which involves a characteristic blend of political, patriotic and descriptive *motifs*. The view is an exceptionally wide-ranging one.

The section which follows is far more difficult than the opening passage to interpret, partly because its literary antecedents are less clear. Here Pope describes contemporary hunting scenes with apparent enthusiasm, beginning in Autumn and taking the activities of each season in turn. It has been suggested that the first ninety-two lines of *Windsor Forest* should be interpreted in a Virgilian light. The hunting section also contains Georgic echoes, but they are less central to the meaning of the work. When Pope writes, for example,

> Thus (if small Things we may with great compare)
> When *Albion* sends her eager Sons to War . . .
> (105–6)

he must refer to Virgil's 'si parva licet componere magnis' (if we may compare small things with great) in the mock-heroic war of the bees in Book IV, but the reference seems to have little function beyond providing an easy transition to the comparison between hunting and war. There is, as in Virgil, a heightened self-awareness gained from pointing to an incongruity between the terms of a comparison (hunting and war; bees and cyclops); both Pope and Virgil are justifying their boldness, but Pope's use of the reference here does not go much further than that. Similarly, there is a clear echo when Pope writes of the death of some larks who are shot by fowlers:

> They fall, and leave their little lives in air (134)

As Warburton pointed out, this calls to mind

> praecipites alta vitam sub nube relinquunt
> (III, 547)

> They fall, leaving life beneath the clouds on high ...

and perhaps also the Aeneid, V, 517 (in the funeral games):

> vitamque reliquit in astris.
>
> and left her life amid the stars.

But again one feels that it is the felicity of the individual phrase rather than the contextual reference that is important. The allusions are fairly casual (included 'for the entertainment of the classical reader', to adopt a phrase of Fielding's) and lacking in the expansiveness of the earlier patriotic references, but they are significant as a continuing indication of the poem's generic relationships.

There is certainly nothing inappropriate in the introduction of hunting material. Virgil does not deal with hunting in the *Georgics*, but his post-classical successors adopted the structure of the *Georgics* in writing didactic poems on hunting and fishing, and mingled the characteristically Virgilian themes of nationalism and the praise of country life with their instructive and descriptive passages. Discussion of that aspect of the Georgic tradition must wait until Chapter V, but it can be said now that it was because of this historical development of the Georgic form that John Gay, writing at exactly the same time as Pope, felt that it was appropriate to include descriptions of hunting, fowling and fishing in *Rural Sports*, a poem specifically sub-titled 'A Georgic'. It is clear from the opening section of *Windsor Forest* that Pope was concerned to write a poem which would also be in some sort an English Georgic, and like Gay he was able to introduce hunting material into his work without violating the conventions of his kind. The generic appropriateness of the hunting section may be easily admitted then, but what of its function in the poem? In particular, how does it relate to the Norman hunting scene that precedes it? Much of the evidence in the two passages suggests that the relationship is one of contrast. The Norman hunt is inspired by passion and leads to the disintegration of order. The modern huntsman, in contrast, takes his place in a fruitful and prosperous scene. In Norman times the peasant was famished 'amidst his ripening fields', but in Pope's England the partridge is hunted in a field from which the harvest has already been gathered in. The Norman kings were 'furious and severe' in their application of the

Paysage Moralisé

forest laws, but Anne is likened to Diana in the protection she gives to 'the sylvan reign'. In the Norman age hunting was an extension of warlike blood-thirstiness, but in Augustan England it had become 'the image of war without its guilt'.

Obviously this contrast is important and Pope is praising his own age in comparison with the past. But the picture of contemporary hunting is not simply idealistic, as the details summarized in the previous paragraph would suggest, and it is important to notice that Pope's attitude changes as the section develops. In ll. 93-134 one's mind is constantly taken beyond the athletic vigour of the chase to wider and more morally equivocal considerations. This happens first in an elaborate comparison between the netting of partridges and the capture of a town (possibly the capture of Gibraltar in 1704) by British troops. There is an apparent naïveté in Pope's patriotism which many modern readers find disconcerting:

> Sudden they seize th'amaz'd defenceless Prize,
> And high in Air *Britannia's* Standard flies.
>
> (109-10)

But the complacency cannot last long because, once it has been made, the comparison between hunting and war is bound to affect one's reading of subsequent paragraphs, and they reflect back in their turn upon this one. This partridge may, like this town, be captured by a ruse and without bloodshed. But the pheasant is less fortunate:

> he feels the fiery Wound,
> Flutters in Blood, and panting beats the Ground . . .
>
> (113-14)

If, as it surely must do, this *memento mori* leads the reader to turn his mind again to the world of war ('if small things we may with great compare') then the implications will inevitably be disturbing, and the line

> Ah! what avail his glossie, varying Dyes
>
> (115)

will apply to the soldier as well as to the bird. The activities of the hunt and of war, and of different kinds of hunt and different kinds of war, are being compared and called in question. The point is perhaps not so much the superiority of Augustan over Norman England (although obviously Pope is on the side of order opposed to disorder) as the fact that all human activities are ambivalent, and potentially either good or bad.

This awareness of ambivalence is particularly marked in the lines on winter activities:

> To Plains with well-breath'd Beagles we repair,
> And trace the Mazes of the circling Hare.
> (Beasts, urg'd by us, their Fellow Beasts pursue,
> And learn of Man each other to undo.) (121–124)

To a reader who felt that the hunt had, up to this time, been presented in idealistic terms the result of this last couplet would be complete moral confusion. Suddenly, after eulogizing the hunter, Pope turns on him, and makes him, not only immoral, but a prime corrupter of the animal world. In the following line.

> With slaught'ring Guns th'unwearied Fowler roves

the huntsman is seen as tireless in his desire to kill, and the paragraph ends with the death of the lark, presented, as we saw, with a pathos and element of sentimentality which reflects damagingly upon the sportsman himself. But this conclusion should not be surprising: it is a natural development from the ambiguities of the earlier couplets.

At this point Pope has evoked a powerful sense of the nature of the passions that hunting is calling into play, and the precariousness of the line that divides the Stuart from the Norman hunt. The contemporary chase is idyllic only in a comparative sense, and one function of the description is to illustrate that human nature is always subject to the same forces. Humanity does not change: it is only that the degree of restraint varies at different times. And because Pope is primarily concerned in *Windsor Forest* with the value of the control which can be exercised through the country's social and political organization, he now turns to overt political reference, as he had done at the end of the first paragraph of the poem, both heightening and simplifying his tone as he does so.

Queen Anne is now to be seen as a patron who harmonizes all the discords that have previously been hinted at. But before she is introduced Pope paints as a setting for her a genuinely idealized picture of fishing and hunting. In these lines there is no sense of the cruelty and destructiveness that, as we have seen, is strongly marked in the preceding paragraphs. The brief fishing section draws heavily on heraldry to present a beautiful but intentionally static and 'unreal' picture:

> The bright-ey'd Perch with Fins of *Tyrian* Dye,
> The silver Eel, in shining Volumes roll'd,
> The yellow Carp, in Scales bedropp'd with Gold,
> Swift Trouts, diversify'd with Crimson Stains ...
> (142–5)

If there is any sense of evil it is now firmly located in the natural scene itself in the reference to

> ... Pykes, the Tyrants of the wat'ry Plains.
> (146)

The following lines on hunting, indebted to Statius and Virgil, and perhaps intended to recall also the royal hunt in *Cooper's Hill*, establish an heroic tone from the first line:

> Now *Cancer* glows with *Phoebus* fiery Car ...
> (147)

The horse becomes at this point almost a symbol of strength:

> Th'impatient Courser pants in ev'ry Vein,
> And, pawing, seems to beat the distant Plain:
> Hills, Vales, and Floods appear already crost ...
> (151–3)

and the sense that the whole earth is subject to his power is conveyed in a verbal metaphor which is simple, but vast in proportions:

> And Earth rolls back beneath the flying Steed ...
> (158)

In the following line the Queen herself is introduced as the equal of Diana, a huntress and a patron of the hunt, the figure who controls the energy and force that has been displayed in the preceding lines. The transition to Queen Anne is accomplished very smoothly:

> Let old *Arcadia* boast her ample Plain,
> Th'Immortal Huntress and her Virgin Train;
> Nor envy, *Windsor*! since thy Shades have seen
> As bright a Goddess, and as chaste a Queen.
>
> (159–62)

All the difficulties which contemplation of various kinds of hunt have produced are resolved with the appearance of the Queen. But this is not the arbitrary imposition of a magical formula. The political virtues of the Stuart reign have been established in the first paragraph of the poem, established in terms of prosperity, peace, harmony, order in variety. And, although the Queen is now introduced in a semi-mythological manner as the leader of the hunt, the emblematic significance of the scene is inescapable. The hunting episodes are seen to have a double purpose. First, to examine the implications of various social and political states of mind, in so far as they tend, for example, towards tyranny or freedom; prosperity or desolation; and, secondly, to exalt Queen Anne as the head of a stable and benevolent Government. But from the formal point of view, when one considers the organization of the poem, the important thing is that these interests are developed within an established framework of description and reflection deriving from Virgil and that this allows the political point to be expressed obliquely and to be given a more general validity than would otherwise be possible.

Having presented Queen Anne in mythological terms Pope now turns briefly to a fully mythological episode. He tells the story of Lodona, a nymph who strayed from the forest and was chased by Pan, but who escaped from him when she was metamorphosed into the Loddon, a tributary of the Thames. The passage is Ovidian in character, but the formal justification for including it here springs from Virgil's use of the Orpheus and Eurydice legend in the fourth *Georgic*.

Following this episode lines 220–34 commend the Thames and the ladies of the Court in terms which are modelled very closely on *Cooper's Hill* and the *Georgics*. The Thames is praised again because its banks nurture 'tow'ring oaks', the raw material of 'future navies', and because it is a great highway of trade:

> Not *Neptune*'s self from all her Streams receives
> A wealthier Tribute than to thine he gives ...
>
> (223–4)

Paysage Moralisé

This emphasis on practicality and the value of commerce is not, as is sometimes suggested, a novelty that Pope is artificially injecting into the tradition. As we have seen, Pope's pleasure in the wealth that the Thames brings had been foreshadowed by Denham, and this is true also of his panegyric on the Court. Denham had written in praise of Charles and Henrietta Maria that

> Mars with Venus dwells,
> Beauty with strength . . .   (39-40)

and Pope extends the eulogy to the whole Court:

> Not all his (Eridanus') Stars above a Lustre show,
> Like the bright Beauties of thy Banks below,
> Where *Jove*, subdued by mortal Passion still,
> Might change *Olympus* for a nobler Hill.
>
> (231-4)

From this point Pope modulates to a passage in praise of retirement (ll, 235-58). It has been claimed that Pope modifies the characteristic Virgilian-Horatian attitude in his opening couplet by violating the traditional assertion that only a man who retires from the world of affairs can be truly content:

> Happy the Man whom this bright Court approves,
> His Sov'reign favours, and his Country loves . . .

But while it is true that Virgil condemns the pomp of fashionable life, he also loses no opportunity of praising Augustus as the leader of Rome. Pope's praise of the Court is surely to be thought of as parallel to Virgil's many passages of political eulogy, and the deliberate formalization of the imagery in the previous lines supports this reading.

The rest of the passage is a conflation of *motifs* from *Georgics* II and IV. The man who retires to the shades of Windsor Forest is thought of first as following the same kind of life as Virgil's Corycian swain:

> He gathers Health from Herbs the Forest yields,
> And of their fragrant Physic spoils the Fields,
> With Chymic Art exalts the Min'ral Powers,
> And draws the Aromatic Souls of Flow'rs.
>
> (241-4)

It is an ideal enriched also by memories of the life recommended by Horace in the *Second Epode* which Pope had rendered into English in one of his earliest works, the *Ode to Solitude*:

> Happy the man whose wish and care
> A few paternal acres bound,
> Content to breathe his native air,
> In his own ground.

But in addition Pope's retired man has the scientific enthusiasm which Virgil had praised in lines which made a profound appeal to a period whose imagination was stirred by the achievements of Newton:

> Felix, qui potuit rerum cognoscere causas ...
>
> (II, 490)

> Blessed is he who has been able to win knowledge of the causes of things ...

To 'win knowledge of the causes of things' Pope's ideal figure becomes an amateur astronomer who 'marks the Course of rolling Orbs on high'. Retirement is thought of as providing the opportunity for study ('Of ancient writ unlocks the learned store') and moral contemplation:

> T'observe a Mean, be to himself a Friend,
> To follow Nature, and regard his End.
>
> (251–2)

The introduction of such a strongly Virgilian passage at this stage (a paragraph which inevitably has something of the quality of a set-piece) provides a focal point for the many Georgic echoes that are found earlier in the poem. Virgilian attitudes that had been presented in an unsystematic form now begin to take their place in a consistent and coherent scheme. It gives the poem an even more decidedly formal and generic character than it had had before.

From this point to the end *Windsor Forest* is consistently Virgilian in its themes. With the concluding line of the retirement section (l. 258) Pope moves to a panegyric of famous men:

> Such was the life great *Scipio* once admired: –
> Thus *Atticus*, and *Trumbal* thus retir'd.
>
> (257–8)

Paysage Moralisé

and immediately an invocation to the Muses, reinforces the Georgic 'atmosphere' by recalling a Virgilian apostrophe (*Georgics*, II, 486–9) which, in Dryden's translation, reads:

> Ye sacred Muses, with whose Beauty fir'd,
> My soul is ravish'd, and my brain inspir'd.
>
> (II, 673–4)

Pope writes

> Ye sacred Nine! that all my Soul possess,
> Whose Raptures fire me, and whose Visions bless . . .
>
> (259–60)

Amongst poets Pope praises Denham, Cowley, Granville and Surrey, and then he turns to a roll-call of famous monarchs, Edward III, Henry VI, Charles I and Anne. The passage calls to mind similar heroic lists in Virgil and also Denham's praise of Edward III, and Pope's rather more extended treatment has an obvious appropriateness in a poem occasioned by the victorious conclusion of a war.

In two places this passage restates themes that were important at the opening of the poem and that are fundamental to its meaning. Writing about the immortality that his verse will give to these heroes, Pope says:

> Oh wou'dst thou sing what Heroes *Windsor* bore . . .
> Then, from her Roofs when *Verrio*'s Colours fall,
> And leave inanimate the naked Wall;
> Still in thy Song shou'd vanquish'd *France* appear . . .
>
> (299–309)

Here the vision of the transitoriness of Windsor Castle seems to echo

> The hollow Winds thro' naked Temples roar.
>
> (68)

Later some lines on the Civil War recall once more the picture of Norman desolation, and emphasize the recurrent nature of historical crises:

> She saw her Sons with purple Deaths expire,
> Her sacred Domes involv'd in rolling Fire,
> A dreadful Series of Intestine Wars,
> Inglorious Triumphs and dishonest Scars . . .
>
> (323–6)

The English Georgic

Civilization, balance, order – these are states that are constantly assailed, and that must be constantly defended if they are to be maintained. The Peace of Utrecht, referred to directly in ll. 327–8, is to be welcomed, even rapturously:

> At length great ANNA said – Let Discord cease!
> She said, the World obey'd, and all was *Peace*!

But the Peace is placed in an historical context that makes facile optimism inappropriate.

This qualification becomes particularly important as one approaches the end of the poem with its masque-like appearance of Father Thames and his prophecy of the triumphs that will attend the coming of peace. The tone is enthusiastic and confident, but not complacent. Like the retirement section, this passage exemplifies the way in which Georgic *motifs* were modified and incorporated in an eighteenth-century interpretation of experience. The final picture of a recreated Golden Age is the most markedly Virgilian element, deriving in spirit partly from the fourth *Eclogue* and partly from the first *Georgic*:

> O stretch thy rein, fair *Peace* from Shore to Shore.
>
> (407)

But there are other Virgilian references earlier on. The exaltation of the Thames above other and more exotic rivers, for example, derives again from Virgil's praise of Italy:

> Tho' *Tiber*'s streams immortal *Rome* behold,
> Tho' foaming Hermus swells with Tides of Gold . . .
> These now no more shall be the Muse's Themes . . .
>
> (357–61)

Considering these emphatic references it seems likely that in the following description of London Pope is aware of Virgil's enthusiasm for 'all the noble cities, the achievement of man's toil, all the towns his handiwork has piled high on steepy crags, and the streams that glide beneath those ancient walls . . .' He links this neatly and naturally with the patriotic *motif* and, one of his main themes, the praise of peace:

> Behold *Augusta*'s glitt'ring Spires increase,
> And Temples rise, the beauteous Works of Peace.

Paysage Moralisé

> I see, I see, where two fair Cities bend
> Their ample bow, a new White-Hall ascend
> There mighty Nations shall inquire their Doom,
> The World's great Oracle in Times to come;
> There Kings shall sue, and suppliant States be seen
> Once more to bend before a BRITISH QUEEN.
>
> (379–84)

Finally the conclusion of *Windsor Forest* is a variation on the closing lines of the *Georgics*. Virgil 'sang of the care of fields, of cattle and of trees, while great Caesar thundered in war by the banks of deep Euphrates', and Pope more incongruously contrasts his 'humble Muse' who

> in unambitious strains,
> Paints the green Forests and the flow'ry Plains
>
> (427–8)

with Granville's more aspiring poetic flights. The last line of *Windsor Forest* completes the structure of the imitation. The Twickenham editors note that, as 'Virgil closed his *Georgics* with the first line of his *Eclogues*, so Pope's final couplet echoes the opening line of *Spring*'.

This successful blending of varied *motifs* enables Pope to move once more in his conclusion, and with greater emphasis, to the theme that had already been introduced in a fairly muted way at ll. 220 ff., that of exploration and trade:

> Thy Trees, fair *Windsor*! now shall leave their Woods
> And half thy Forests rush into thy Floods . . .
>
> (385–6)

It has already been argued that there is nothing inherently incongruous in the appearance of this theme in a poem based predominantly on a Virgilian model and on *Cooper's Hill*. This is corroborated by the fact that it here fits entirely naturally into a markedly Georgic passage and leads with perfect ease to the vision of the new Golden Age. The modification of strictly Georgic attitudes is accomplished with no sense of strain or falsity: Virgil's poem is guiding Pope's response, but not in any way limiting it.

In the year that saw the publication of *Windsor Forest* Henry

Felton wrote *A Dissertation of Reading the Classics*. He defined the best kind of imitation by saying that it is,

> when we are possessed of the Expression, Way of Thinking, and the Genius of any Author, in such an abstracted Manner, as without writing out of him, or making use of him for particular Thoughts and Phrases, we can write in his Way and after his Manner ...

Windsor Forest does not fit this formula exactly: use is often made of Virgil for 'particular Thoughts and Phrases'. But Pope does not, as Felton expresses it, 'write out of' Virgil; unlike Phillips or Dyer, he does not write a poem whose structural development is guided in detail by the Virgilian model. He uses the Virgilian interpretation of experience and the Georgic pattern of contrast and digression in 'an abstracted manner' to formalize his response to the subject matter – topographical and political – of the poem, and he shows an extraordinary ease and flexibility of mind in the use that he makes of a powerful and very highly-esteemed tradition.

Notes

1. The first edition of *Cooper's Hill* in 1642 was unauthorized and incomplete. The first authentic text appeared in 1655, and the last version to appear in Denham's lifetime was in *Poems and Translations* (1688).
2. *Windsor Forest* was published in folio on 7 March, 1713, and was reprinted in the following month. It appeared in *Miscellaneous Poems and Translations* 1714, and, with many revisions, in Pope's *Works* of 1717. In a note to an edition in 1736 Pope claimed that the poem had been 'written at two different times: the first part of it which relates to the country in the year 1704, at the same time with the *Pastorals*', and the later part just before publication. Although it seems clear that an earlier version of some sort certainly existed, the exact history of the poem's composition is obscure. For a discussion of the issues involved see the Introduction to *Windsor Forest* in Vol. I of the 'Twickenham Edition' of the *Poems of Alexander Pope*, edited by E. Audra and Aubrey Williams.
3. *The Poems and Letters of Andrew Marvell*, edited by H. M. Margoliouth (1952), Vol. I: *Poems*, pp. 56–7.
4. Samuel Johnson *Lives of the English Poets*, edited by George Birkbeck Hill (1905), Vol. I, p. 77.
5. *To Penshurst* was written by 1612 and published in 1616. See *Ben Jonson*, edited by C. H. Herford and Percy and Evelyn Simpson, Vol. VIII, pp. 93–6.

Paysage Moralisé

6. For a discussion of the concept of imitation see Chapter Two, pp. 34–7.
7. *London* was published in *Songs of Experience* (1794). See *The Complete Writings of William Blake*, edited by Geoffrey Keynes (1957), p. 214.
8. Maren-Sofie Røstvig *The Happy Man, Vol. II: Studies in the Metamorphoses of a Classical Ideal* 1700–1760 (1958), p. 222.
9. See the Introduction to *Windsor Forest* in *Pastoral Poetry and an Essay on Criticism*, edited by E. Audra and Aubrey Williams ['The Twickenham Edition of the Poems of Alexander Pope', Volume One] (1961) and R. A. Brower, *Pope and the Poetry of Allusion* (1959, Chapter II).
10. For a discussion of Gay's poem see Chapter V.
11. Wakefield's suggestion of this source dates from the 1790s. See the 'Twickenham' edition (cited above), p. 148.
12. Earl R. Wasserman, Jr. *The Subtler Language* (1959), pp. 101–13.

Four

Thomson's 'Seasons'

Thirteen years after the publication of *Windsor Forest* Thomson brought out *Winter* and by 1730 *The Seasons* in its first version was complete.[1] It was a poem which achieved and long retained an extraordinary popularity.[2] There were often more than eight editions a year until the mid-nineteenth century, and there was a total of considerably more than three hundred separate editions in the hundred years from 1750–1850. It was frequently illustrated, and the illustrations range from grand designs by William Kent to humble woodcuts by obscure artists. After nearly a century Hazlitt wrote that Thomson was, perhaps, the most popular of English poets because,

> he gives most of the poetry of natural description ... treating a subject that all can understand, and in a way that is interesting to all alike, to the ignorant or the refined, because he gives back the impression which the things themselves make upon us in nature.[3]

Yet what strikes the modern reader is not so much Thomson's faithful reflection of 'impressions' as the variety and complexity of the responses that nature evokes in the poet. Because of this variety *The Seasons* is one of the most difficult of works to characterize at all briefly, or to represent adequately by a passage in an anthology. Asked to choose some typical lines, one might, for example, select from *Spring* a picture of domestic fowl which is detailed, sharply etched, almost heraldic in its vividness, and which characteristically owes something to Milton's picture of the cock in *L'Allegro*:

> The careful Hen
> Calls all her chirping Family around,
> Fed and defended by the fearless Cock
> Whose Breast with Ardour flames, as on he walks
> Graceful, and crows Defiance. In the Pond

> The finely-checker'd Duck before her Train,
> Rows garrulous . . .   (*Spring*, 1728, 714–20)

But it might be thought that sublimity is a commoner Thomsonian mood, the spacious sweep of emotion and style that is found so often in *Winter* and that produces great elevation:

> Thro' the black Night that sits immense around,
> Lash'd into Foam, the fierce-conflicting Brine
> Seems o'er a thousand raging Waves to burn.
> Meantime the Mountain-Billows, to the Clouds
> In dreadful tumult swell'd, Surge above Surge,
> Burst into Chaos with tremendous Roar,
> And anchor'd Navies from their Stations drive,
> Wild as the Winds, across the howling Waste
> Of mighty Waters . . .   (*Winter*, 1746, 158–66)

Here again there is a strong Miltonic note, this time recalling *Paradise Lost*, which is heard in the syntax, the handling of the blank verse, and especially in the repetition of the phrase 'Surge above Surge'. The sense here of man's insignificance in the face of natural forces is common enough in *The Seasons*: it occurs dramatically, for example, in the episode of Celadon and Amelia in *Summer* where Thomson tells the story of an innocent girl who was struck by lightning. On the other hand some readers might argue that the most common and characteristic note in *The Seasons* is that of winning pastoral softness and lush sensuous description. This is perhaps the dominant tone in *Spring*, as, for example, in Thomson's description of the flowers of the season which owes something to 'I know a bank whereon the wild tyme blows':

> Then seek the Bank where flowering Elders crowd,
> Where scatter'd wild the Lily of the Vale
> Its balmy Essence breathes, where Cowslips hang
> The dewy Head, where purple Violets lurk,
> With all the lowly Children of the Shade . . .
>   (*Spring*, 1746, 446–50)

These are three very different moods, each of which might be thought of as typical, and obviously the list could be made much longer without any danger of overlapping. Most importantly there is no example so far of the feature of Thomson's verse which seems most clearly to point forwards to Wordsworth, the moralizing passages in which man is transformed by the power of nature,

> And all the Tumult of a guilty World,
> Tossed by ungenerous Passions sinks away.
>
> (*Spring*, 1744, 936–7)

This variety of styles points to one of the crucial questions that has to be faced in any attempt to give a critical account of *The Seasons*. What sort of poem is it that can contain such stylistic diversity, and is the diversity 'contained' in the sense that it is kept under control, or is it just contained in that everything is piled into an expandable suitcase of a poem?

A second question is raised by an apparent flabbiness in the structure of the work. Dr. Johnson said that 'the great defect of *The Seasons* is want of method'. Like *Tristram Shandy*, Thomson's poem is 'progressive and digressive too' and it sometimes seems that the digressive element is so strong as to inhibit progression altogether. The reader easily gets lost (or at least loses his sense of direction), and when he reaches the end he may have difficulty in ordering his memories of the ground that has been covered: the various episodes of the poem are not linked by an easily perceived structural thread. There is also some difficulty in deciding what the basic mode of the poem is. Is it fundamentally descriptive, reflective or didactic? Is there, in other words, a modal organization which in any way takes the place of a structural one?

Finally, *The Seasons* sometimes appears inconsistent in its enthusiasms. The most frequently criticized example is Thomson's apparently conflicting praise of pastoral innocence on the one hand and commercial progress on the other, and this conflict recurs in a way that cannot be ignored.

These are some of the critical problems put at their baldest, and they point to real qualities in the work itself, indeed to central elements in its make-up. In this chapter these problems will be examined in the light of *The Seasons*' relationship to the Virgilian tradition, and it may be suggested in anticipation that, although Thomson's poem lacks the formal Virgilian structure that is so prominent in *Cyder* or *The Fleece*, it is at once the most thoroughgoing, the most complex, and the most sensitively serious eighteenth-century imitation of the *Georgics*.

2

Writing in *The Background to Thomson's Seasons* A. D. McKillop remarked that

> we often overlook the unspectacular competence of the eighteenth century in adapting or even creating literary genres for its own needs. The L'Allegro/Il Penseroso model, the more expository parts of *Paradise Lost* and the *Georgics* gave Thomson his scheme.[4]

More recently, Maren-Sofie Røstvig accepted the main lines of this account of *The Seasons*' origins, but introduced some modifications:

> Thomson's true originality consisted in creating a new poetic form for already well-known poetic themes. While Sir John Denham had hit upon a new loco-descriptive genre (following the example of Casimire Sarbiewski) by expanding the limits of the Horatian philosophic lyric, James Thomson went even further by merging the Horatian ode (in the form established by Milton's companion poems as well as in the expanded form popularized by Denham and Pope) with the classical Georgic and with the new type of philosophical poem on the Creation which grew so popular in the eighteenth century.[5]

Although both critics acknowledge the Virgilian influence (as indeed Durling had previously done) they do not attempt to show, because their preoccupations are otherwise, how widely pervasive the Georgic influence is or how it affects the form and feeling of the poem. I propose first to trace the influence of the *Georgics* in order to show more clearly how Thomson's 'unspectacular competence' works, in other words to consider more fully the form of the poem.

As early as the Preface to the second edition of *Winter* (June, 1726) Thomson specifically acknowledged his use of the *Georgics* as a model:

> I know no Subject more elevating, more amusing; more ready to awake the poetical Enthusiasm, the philosophical Reflection, and the moral Sentiment, than the Works of Nature ... It was this Devotion to the Works

of Nature that, in his Georgicks, inspired the rural Virgil to write so inimitably ...

Here Thomson is thinking primarily of subject matter, but the question arises of the formal relationship between the *Georgics* and Thomson's poem.[6]

To make a list of the passages in *The Seasons* which were written under direct Georgic influence is a reasonably straightforward exercise. In *Spring*, for example, a list would include:

1. The description of the onset of Spring (1728, 32–43).
2. The exaltation of agriculture (1728, 65–75).
3. Some of the practical advice, for example that on destroying insects (1728, 112–35).
4. The account of the signs of the weather (1728, 169–210).
5. The account of the Golden Age and the contrast with 'these Iron Times' (1728, 259–379).
6. The fishing section (1744, 377–440).
7. The account of the 'Passion of the Groves' and the loves of the beasts (1728, 534–776).
8. The sections in praise of rural retirement (1744, 901–59 and 1158–62).

These are the most important passages and there are others that have a decided although less pronounced Georgic colouring. However, even taken on their own these passages form a very substantial section of the poem: 402 lines are directly modelled on the *Georgics* themselves and a further sixty-two (those on fishing) on material which belongs directly to the Georgic tradition. That is to say that in a poem of 1,170 lines 464 are recognizably Georgic in kind and the character of the poem that Thomson is writing is thus overwhelmingly established. It is also significant that some of the characteristically Georgic materials (that on fishing and a passage on the pleasures of retirement near the end of the poem) were added only in 1744. In other words the poet continued, even when revising the work, to emphasize its Georgic origins. This was not a phase that Thomson grew out of, nor was it a decorative impulse that came to him late in the poem's development. The Georgic influence is important from beginning to end of *Spring*'s composition.

In *Summer, Autumn* and *Winter* the Georgic influence does not dominate the poems so completely but it remains very considerable. In *Summer* five extended passages show direct Virgilian influence: the haymaking and sheep-shearing episodes (1744, 352–422); the account of the plague (1744, 1044–94); the signs of the weather (1744, 1108–35); the formal praise of England (1744, 1430–1593), and, finally, the contrast of the Golden and Iron Ages (1727, 1104–24). In addition the influence of the *rerum cognoscere causas* notion, and consequent enthusiam for scientific speculation, from the second *Georgic* is clear at two points (1727, 21–30 and 1125–46). The retirement passage (1744, 1371–1429) also derives ultimately from Georgics II (although certainly with a good deal of modification by Thomson) and it leads, in lines already cited above, into a section in praise of England which is in places a paraphrase of Virgil's praise of Italy:

> Rich is thy Soil, and merciful thy Clime;
> Thy Streams unfailing in the Summer's Drought;
> Unmatch'd thy Guardian-Oaks; thy Valleys float
> With golden Waves ... (1744, 1438–41)

Finally the exotic digressions in ll. 663/1040 probably have their structural justification with reference to Virgil. One remembers, for example, that Somerville later introduced the exotic digressions of *The Chace* with an appeal to Virgilian precedent. In *Summer*, then, it is true to say that the *Georgics* are continuously brought to the reader's mind and that remembrance of Virgil's poem is an important factor in determining his response to Thomson's work.

In *Autumn* there occurs (1730, 1131/1269) the most extended piece of Virgilian paraphrase in the whole of *The Seasons* – the version, almost a translation, of the passage *O fortunatos agricolas* (O happy husbandmen) from *Georgics II*. This is a positive and detailed statement of Thomson's attitude to country life, and the fact that he bases himself so closely on Virgil (and that the section is placed at a most emphatic point, at the end of *Autumn*) shows how seriously he looked upon his relationship to his major source. The treatment of retirement here is reinforced by further passages at lines 641–70 (on Dodington's estate) and lines 902ff:

> *Thus* solitary, and in pensive guise,
> Oft let me wander o'er the russet mead,
> *And* thro' the *sadden'd* grove ...

The English Georgic

Elsewhere in *Autumn* there are several examples of Georgic influence although naturally none so clear-cut as the *O fortunatos* passages. In two places (1744, 775–837 and 1730, 1029–33) there are lines written under the influence of the *rerum cognoscere causas* conception. And in lines 43–155 (1730) we find another expression of the Golden/Iron Age antithesis which had appeared previously in *Spring* and *Summer*.

In terms of the number of examples *Winter* is less obviously influenced by the *Georgics* than other sections of the *Seasons*, but even so the debt is clear. First, lines 118–194 (1726) deal with signs of the weather; more extensively lines 794–949 (1744) give, often with close approximation to Virgil, an account of the Scythian Winter; and, more generally, there is the long retirement passage beginning at line 424 (1744). And, in discussing *Winter*, of course, one also has the supporting evidence of Thomson's Preface which has already been quoted.

This extensive use of derivative thematic material is supported by direct references to Virgil's example, and by occasional echoing of individual lines. In lines which form part of the original 1728 version of *Spring* Thomson defends the agricultural aspect of his work by reference to Virgil:

> Nor, Ye who live
> In Luxury and Ease, in Pomp and Pride,
> Think these lost Themes unworthy of your Ear.
> 'Twas such as these the Rural Maro sung
> To the full Roman Court, in all it's height
> Of Elegance and Taste. The sacred Plow
> Employ'd the Kings and Fathers of Mankind,
> In antient Times.   (1728, 52–9)

Very early in the final form of *The Seasons*, therefore, the Virgilian reference is made explicit. In effect the reader is told to be aware of this influence as he reads. And in the final version of *Spring*, in the passage on fishing which Thomson added in 1744, this explicit acknowledgement is supported by a further reference:

> Then seek the Bank where flowering Elders croud,
> Where scatter'd wild the Lilly of the Vale
> It's balmy Essence breathes ...
> There let the Classic Page thy Fancy lead

> Thro' rural Scenes; such as the Mantuan Swain
> Paints in immortal Verse and matchless Song . . .
>
> (1744, 444–55)

By his revision Thomson makes it even more difficult to ignore Virgil. The lines are also interesting because they look back very clearly to *Rural Sports* and, taken in conjunction with a reference to Phillips' *Cyder* in *Autumn*, they show Thomson as aware that he is writing not only with Virgil in mind, but also in a tradition of English Georgic verse.[7]

Echoes of individual lines occur frequently: many have been noted by Zippel and it is sufficient to give one or two examples. Compare, for example,

> Forth fly the tepid Aires; and unconfin'd,
> Unbinding Earth, the moving Softness strays . . .
>
> (*Spring*, 1728, 32–3)

with

> parturit almus ager Zephyrique tepentibus auris
> laxant arva sinus;   (II, 330–1)

The bountiful land brings forth, and beneath the West's warm breezes the fields loosen their bosoms.

or

> his lusty Steers
> Drives from their Stalls, to where the well-us'd Plow
> Lies in the Furrow, loosen'd from the Frost.
>
> (*Spring*, 1728, 35–7)

with

> Vere novo, gelidus canis cum montibus umor
> liquitur et Zephyro putris se glaeba resolvit,
> depresso incipiat iam tum mihi taurus aratro
> ingemere, et sulco attritus splendescere vomer.
>
> (I, 43–6)

In the dawning Spring, when icy streams trickle from snowy mountains, and the crumbling clod breaks at the Zephyr's touch, even then would I have my bull groan over the deep driven plough, and the share glisten when rubbed by the furrow.

This sort of echoing would not be particularly significant were it not for the more extended and explicit Virgilian references elsewhere. But, taken in conjunction with the material that has already been cited, its importance (as an element in the total scheme of the poem) is clearly greater.

3

What has been said so far has established that the Georgic influence on *The Seasons*, calculated in terms of derivative thematic material, direct reference and echoing of details, is continuous, that the reader is constantly made aware of Virgil while he is reading the poem, and that he is invited to compare Virgil's treatment of the themes with Thomson's. The rest of this discussion will involve an attempt to estimate the importance of this influence and the way in which full recognition and acceptance of it may be expected to modify our critical attitude to the poem.

The main discussion will be divided into three sections dealing in turn with three themes which are central to Thomson's purpose. These are: the contrast between the Golden and Iron ages; the theme of patriotic exaltation; the theme of retirement. A consideration of these three leading ideas and their relation to the *Georgics* will be found to lead to a consistent interpretation of the poem as a whole.

But first it will be as well to formulate as explicitly as possible the kind of critical problem that this discussion can be expected to illuminate. The problem is met acutely in lines like these in praise of agriculture:

> Ye generous Britons, venerate the Plow!
> And o'er your Hills, and long withdrawing Vales,
> Let Autumn spread his Treasures to the Sun,
> Luxuriant and unbounded. As the Sea,
> Far thro' his azure, turbulent Domain,
> Your Empire owns, and from a thousand Shores
> Wafts all the Pomp of Life into your Ports,
> So with superior Boon may your rich Soil,
> Exuberant Nature's better Blessings pour
> O'er every Land; the naked Nations cloath,
> And be th'exhaustless Granary of the world!
>
> (*Spring*, 1744, 65–75)

The lines make an immediate impression by their complete assurance (a hostile critic might say by their bland complacency). This assurance is felt, in the first place, through the firm control that Thomson retains in handling the extended comparison: 'As the Sea, etc. ... So with superior Boon, etc.' The Miltonic expansiveness of syntax reflects the vastness of the idea itself, and, although this is a fairly obvious effect it is an obviousness that works, especially in the second half of the comparison where a rising rhythm is maintained, first by the adjectival form and placing in its line of *exuberant*

> may your rich Soil,
> Exuberant, Nature's better Blessings pour ...

and secondly the rhythmic effect of the syntactic catalogue ('Blessings pour/O'er every Land, the naked Nations cloath, etc.') which allows a sense of complete rhythmic resolution, a full close in the last line. Rhythmic emphasis is given by the frequent alliteration: 'Pomp ... Ports; superior ... Soil; better Blessings; naked Nations', and this emphasis is increased by the juxtaposition, in the last two cases, of the alliterating words. Finally a sense of the spontaneity of the prosperity that is described, of man as the passive recipient, is induced by the words themselves: the sea *wafts*; the soil *pours* and this sense of gratuitous vitality is increased by *boon, exuberant, exhaustless*.

The problem is that, taken by themselves, the lines seem to breathe a spirit of jingoistic patronage. Britain is the end towards which all Creation ministers and she must treat outsiders with benevolent compassion. There is difficulty in deciding whether this is the true or the only feeling in the lines, how they relate to the rest of the poem, and how far they are justified both intrinsically and in relation to the work as a whole. And the same sort of question is constantly arising: it occurs, for example, in *Summer*:

> Happy Britannia! where the Queen of Arts,
> Inspiring Vigour, Liberty, abroad,
> Walks thro' the Land of Heroes unconfin'd,
> And scatters Plenty with unsparing Hand.
> Rich is thy Soil, and merciful thy Skies ...
>
> (1727, 498–502)

Writing on this passage one of Thomson's most recent critics, Patricia Spacks, says:

> The fact that the digression was 'noble' and that it was undoubtedly agreeable to Thomson's contemporaries, in no way lessens its digressiveness or the sense of inappropriateness with which one plods through it. The scheme of values upon which the passage is based has virtually no relation to the scheme underlying the rest of the poem.[8]

This condemnation forms part of an extended discussion of an alleged inconsistency in Thomson in his attitude to Primitivism and Progress and Miss Spacks concludes that Thomson's centre of interest gradually changed from Nature to Man during the poem's various revisions and that this change 'was marked by the development of emotional and intellectual confusion'. This idea is a fundamental and common one, and I quote Miss Spacks here simply because she is its most recent and most cogent proponent. But it seems to me to show a failure to sympathize with Thomson's own attitudes and intentions and also seriously to underestimate the emotional content of passages like that in praise of Britain, just quoted.

These may be taken as typical of many intransigent passages in *The Seasons* and it is with their interpretation, with difficulties having to do with the consistency and coherence of the poem as a whole that this discussion is now concerned. The starting point will be Thomson's attitude to Primitivism and to the Golden Age.

4

The vision of the Golden Age that we get in the *Seasons* is essentially literary: it is a traditional imaginative experience which is necessarily conceived by Thomson in terms of Virgil, Ovid and Milton. The Miltonic frame of reference – largely that of *Paradise Lost*, Books IV, V and IX – is the most obvious, because it is reinforced by the Miltonic suggestions of Thomson's blank verse. Adam's sleep was 'from pure digestion bred,/And temperate vapours bland'; Thomson's primal men rise 'vigorous as the sun' when their light slumbers are 'gently fum'd away'. In Milton's

Eden all the beasts of the wood play together in happy amity; in Thomson's Golden Age

> The Herds and Flocks, commixing, play'd secure.
> (*Spring*, 1728, 287)

Just as in Paradise 'Blossoms and Fruits at once of golden hue/ Appeerd', so, Thomson says, Spring once

> Green'd all the Year; and Fruits and Blossoms blush'd
> In social Sweetness on the self-same Bough.
> (*Spring*, 1727, 366–7)

And the reader may be reminded at this point not only of Milton, but also of Spenser's Garden of Adonis:

> There is continuall spring and harvest there
> Continuall, both meeting at one time:
> For both the boughs do laughing blossoms bear ...
> And eke attonce the heavy trees they clime,
> Which seem to labour under their fruits load.
> (*Faerie Queene*, III, VI, xlii)

One constantly feels the pressure of analogues like these when reading Thomson's poem, and, because he works so much in terms of literary reference, it is important, if one is to define Thomson's attitude to the Golden Age, to establish what general attitudes to primitivism and progress he is drawing upon. What general ideas is Thomson referring to?

For the polar viewpoints one can most usefully take Lucretius and Ovid. In *De Rerum Natura* the balance is heavily weighted in favour of the Age of Iron: the notion of a progression from a state of nature to one of civilization is very clearly marked. It is true that the men of ancient days were strong and healthy and were pleased to eat nuts and berries that Nature provided in abundance: there was then no need of regular work. But the disadvantages were overwhelmingly greater. In his primitive state Man was unsociable, a solitary hunter, and his life was nasty, brutish and short. It was only in the course of time that communal feeling developed, but eventually men did begin to build huts and to use skins and fire, marriage was established and the human race began to mellow.

> tunc et amicitiem coeperunt iungere aventes
> finitimi inter se nec laedere nec violari ...
>
> (*De Rerum Natura*, V, 1019–20)[9]
>
> Then also neighbours began eagerly to join friendship amongst themselves to do no hurt and suffer no violence.

The line of development from native simplicity to a sophisticated social contract is straightforward and all that is valuable in life is thought of as springing from men's efforts. Sea-faring, laws, defence, the arts, all were acquired gradually:

> sic unumquicquid paulatim protrahit aetas
> in medium ratioque in luminis erigit oras.
> namque alid ex alio clarescere corde videbant
> artibus, ad summum donec venere cacumen.
>
> (*De Rerum Natura*, V, 1454–7)
>
> So by degrees time brings up before us every single thing, and reason lifts it into the precincts of light. For their intellect saw one thing after another grow famous amongst the arts, until they came to their highest point.

Sometimes, for example in *Autumn*, when he describes the rewards of industry, Thomson's thought seems to take on an almost entirely Lucretian cast. At first Man was 'naked, and helpless'

> ... the sad barbarian, roving, mix'd
> With beasts of prey; or for his acorn-meal
> Fought the fierce tusky boar: a shivering wretch!
> Aghast, and comfortless ...
>
> (*Autumn*, 1730, 57–60)

but as he developed the social virtues progress became possible until

> ... every form of cultivated life
> In order set, protected, and inspir'd,
> Into perfection wrought. Uniting all,
> Society grew numerous, high, polite,
> And happy.
>
> (*Autumn*, 1730, 110–14)

The progressive point of view could hardly be put more clearly.

For the opposite attitude one can turn to Ovid who, in the *Metamorphoses*, emphasizes the excellence, both material and moral, of primitive Man:

> Aurea prima sata est aetas, quae vindice nullo,
> sponte sua, sine lege fidem rectumque colebat.
> (*Metamorphoses*, 1, 89–90)[10]
>
> Golden was that first age, which, with no one to compel,
> without a law, of its own will, kept faith and did the right.

Then rivers flowed with milk and nectar and honey dripped from the green oak tree. When this ideal, harmonious, state was succeeded by the Age of Iron there was a complete moral disaster: modesty, truth and faith disappeared from the earth and in their place came tricks, plots, violence and greed. The Iron Age is certainly seen as one of tremendous energy. Only now did men begin to build ships and sail the seas, to farm and discover the use of minerals, but all this power led to evil because the moral harmony of the Golden Age had been completely shattered:

> victa iacet pietas, et virgo caede madentis
> ultima caelestum terras Astraea reliquit.
> (*Metamorphoses*, 1, 149–50)
>
> Piety lay vanquished, and the maiden Astraea, last of
> the immortals, abandoned the blood-soaked earth.

The contrast with Lucretius is complete, yet, just as one can find Lucretian passages in Thomson, so one can find sections which seem purely Ovidian. When, for example, Thomson turns in *Spring* from the Golden Age to 'these Iron Times,/These Dregs of Life!' and describes the psychology of fallen Man, the picture that he gives is a despairing one:

> ... the Human Mind
> Has lost that Harmony ineffable,
> Which forms the Soul of Happiness; and all
> Is off the Poise within; the Passions all
> Have burst their Bounds; and Reason half extinct,
> Or impotent, or else approving, sees
> The foul Disorder. Anger storms at large,
> Without an equal Cause ...
> (*Spring*, 1728: 327–34)

Obviously there is a conflict here, but it is not one which Thomson left unresolved, and he found the resolution in his major source, Virgil's *Georgics*. On the subject of the Golden and the Iron Ages we find in Virgil attitudes of greater complexity than in either Lucretius or Ovid. There is a vivid contrast presented in *Georgics* I between the two Ages, but it is not a straightforward shift from idyllic pleasure to unrewarding labour, or from brutality to social sophistication. Certainly the Golden Age was a time when the Earth 'yielded all, of herself', and when material prosperity was matched by moral harmony: it was unlawful even to divide the fields and men worked for the common good. But this idyllic harmony passed and then Jove made life hard and difficult:

> ille malum virus serpentibus addidit atris,
> praedarique lupos iussit pontumque moveri,
> mellaque decussit foliis, ignemque removit,
> et passim rivis currentia vina repressit ...
>
> *Georgics*, I, 129–32

> 'Twas he that in black serpents put their deadly venom,
> bade the wolves plunder and the ocean swell; shook
> honey from the leaves, hid fire from view, and stopped
> the wine that ran everywhere in streams ...

However, this change in Man's condition was not purposeless. Jove acted as he did for a reason, and it is a reason that rendered the movement from a Golden to an Iron Age ambivalent. Jove made Man's life difficult in order that all the arts of civilization might be developed:

> ut varias usus meditando extunderet artis
> paulatim et sulcis frumenti quaereret herbam,
> et silicis venis abstrusum excuderet ignem.
>
> (*Georgics*, I, 133–35)

> so that practice, by taking thought, might little by little
> hammer out divers arts, might seek the corn-blade in
> furrows, and strike forth from veins of flint the hidden
> fire.

Now men could learn how to make boats, to hunt, to fish and to build:

> labor omnia vicit
> improbus et duris urgens in rebus egestas.
>
> (*Georgics*, I, 145–46)

> Toil conquered the world, unrelenting toil, and want
> that pinches when life is hard.

In other words an age of naïve, effortless and therefore morally neutral happiness was succeeded by a time of moral triumph in which Man, by his own efforts, became the master of the world. Clearly there can be no simple attitude to the change of values described by Virgil because the ideas themselves are complex.

The fourth *Eclogue*, in its forecast of the passing of the Iron Age and the return to the Golden, has a similar ambiguity of attitude, and Virgil is clearly unwilling to give up or utterly condemn either Age. On the one hand the birth of the wonder-child which the poet celebrates will be heralded by a bounteous nature, and this excites Virgil's imagination. Everywhere there will be spontaneous abundance and a new natural harmony in which,

> ipsae lacte domum referent distenta capellae
> ubera, nec magnos metuent armenta leones;
> ipsa tibi blandos fundent cunabula flores.
>
> (*Eclogues*, IV, 21–3)
>
> Uncalled, the goats shall bring home their udders swollen
> with milk, and the herds shall not fear huge lions;
> unasked, thy cradle shall pour forth flowers for thy
> delight.

But despite the excitement which this forecast generates Virgil is not prepared to give up too easily his satisfaction in Man's Iron Age triumphs. For a time, he says, some few traces of sin will remain to urge men to sail the seas, to build walled cities and to cultivate the earth:

> alter erit tum Tiphys, et altera quae vehat Argo
> delectos heroas; erunt etiam altera bella
> atque iterum ad Troiam magnus mittetur Achilles.
>
> (*Eclogues*, IV, 34–6)
>
> A second Tiphys shall then arise, and a second Argo to
> carry chosen heroes; a second warfare, too, shall there be,
> and again shall a great Achilles be sent to Troy.

Finally, after these, the ultimate products of Man's state of sin, the Golden Age really will return in all its spontaneous magnificence. The very wool itself will no longer need to be dyed: the ram will change his colour at will from 'blushing purple' to

'saffron yellow', and
>sponte sua sandyx pascentis vestiet agnos.
>>(*Eclogues,* IV, 45)
>of its own will shall scarlet clothe the grazing lambs

Obviously there is a conflict of values in Virgil's mind, and there is no question, in the *Eclogue* or in the *Georgics*, of either the Golden or the Iron Ages being given automatic precedence. Nostalgia for an idyllic past (or future) is entirely blended with pride in a vigorous present. The benefits that work can bring are in some ways greater than those accessible in a prelapsarian state, but, of course, the cost too is high. Consequently a man is forced to entertain contradictory feelings; there is no simple solution.

When one turns again to Thomson one finds that, despite the Lucretian and Ovidian elements that have already been illustrated, his central position is a Virgilian one. He has intense nostalgia for the Golden Age (and therefore feels very acutely the occasional golden manifestations of external nature), but he is also very much aware of the potentialities of the Iron Age in which he lives. Man in the historical period is a worker and organizer capable of transforming his environment, and the comparative stability and prosperity of modern life is due to his efforts. In the past Britain was disunited and disrupted by internecine warfare, but now, because of organized labour and the will to prosperity,

> ... Wealth and Commerce lift their golden Head,
> And o'er our Labours Liberty and Law
> Illustrious watch, the Wonder of a World!
>>(*Spring,* 1728, 792–4)

The basis of social and political unity is economic success. This is made clear many times: for example, in Thomson's comment on the sheep-shearing scene in *Summer* (an episode added in 1744), that 'hence Britannia sees/Her solid Grandeur rise.' (423–4) It is important, critically, to accept that when Thomson writes in this way he is not gratuitously adulterating a descriptive genre. The combination of pastoralism and progressivism, and consideration of the relationship between them, was one that he found in his formal model, and it was because the combination was important to him that he introduced it into his poem. The motif of *labor omnia vicit* is fundamental to the interpretation of life presented in

Thomson's 'Seasons'

The Seasons, and in it Thomson, following Virgil, finds a resolution for many of the apparent contradictions of his subject matter.

In the description of the tropics we find the idea treated from an original point of view. The tropics are shown as luxuriating in a prelapsarian fertility, so rich indeed that it is 'beyond whate'er/ The Poets imag'd in the Golden Age' (Summer, 1744, 678–9). The picture is completely idyllic in its atmosphere of casual abundance:

> ... Gardens smile around, and cultur'd Fields;
> And Fountains gush; and careless Herds and Flocks
> Securely stray; a World within itself,
> Disdaining all Assault ...
> A Land of Wonders! which the Sun still eyes
> With Ray direct, as of the lovely Realm
> Inamour'd, and delighting there to dwell.
>
> (*Summer*, 1744, 762–75)

But the defects of this tropical paradise are seen just as clearly:

> But what avails this wondrous Waste of Wealth?
> ... the softening Arts of Peace,
> Whate'er the humanizing Muses teach;
> The Godlike Wisdom of the temper'd Breast;
> Progressive Truth, the patient Force of Thought;
> Investigation calm, whose silent Powers
> Command the World; the Light that leads to Heaven;
> Kind equal Rule, the Government of Laws,
> And all-protecting Freedom, which alone
> Sustains the Name and Dignity of Man:
> These are not theirs.
>
> (*Summer*, 1744, 852–76)

The easy (although, of course, inaccessible) delights of innocence are rejected for the hard-won pleasures of experience. But this does not preclude intense longing for what is being given up – the 'odorous Woods, and shining Ivory Stores'. Indeed it is a condition of the paradoxical subject-matter which Thomson is dealing with that neither choice can be made without regret.

It is the same paradox that underlies apparent contradictions of attitude in *Winter*. Two remote northern races are described.

First the Lapps who, after an idealized account of the northern summer, are described as a

> Thrice happy Race! by Poverty secur'd
> From legal Plunder and rapacious Power:
> In whom fell Interest never yet has sown
> The Seeds of Vice; whose spotless Swains ne'er knew
> Injurious Deed, nor, blasted by the Breath
> Of faithless Love, their blooming Daughters Woe.
>   (*Winter*, 1744, 881–6)

This race, uncorrupted by contact with more progressive peoples, continues to live in a state of perfect moral harmony. Thomson is frequently criticized for including also in *Winter* a very different account of a primitive northern race. The remote Russians, 'the last of men', are presented with an emphasis which is very far from idyllic:

> Here Human Nature wears it's rudest Form.
> Deep from the piercing Season sunk in Caves,
> Here by dull Fires, and with unjoyous Chear,
> They waste the tedious Gloom. Immers'd in Furs,
> Doze the gross Race. Nor sprightly Jest, nor Song,
> Nor Tenderness they know ...   (*Winter*, 1744, 940–54)

Here again the primary problem – for both Thomson and the reader – is the complexity of the subject itself. A life of remote and diligent labour cannot be given a single and immutable value. What Thomson does is to take the two extremes of near Arctic experience – the happiness of summer and the misery of dead winter – to express two possible but opposed values. The different significance of the two passages is clearly marked. The Lapps are thought of as living a frugal but adequate existence. Life is hard, but they are not destitute:

> They ask no more than simple Nature gives
>   (*Winter*, 1744, 845)

and this is sufficient. The Russians, on the other hand, live where 'Human Nature wears it's rudest Form' in a state of almost total privation. After contemplating this Thomson reacts against the harshness of Scythian life and returns, quite legitimately, to his staple theme:

> What cannot active Government perform,
> New-moulding Man?
>
> (*Winter*, 1744, 950–1)

and to praise of Peter the Great's government.

Had Thomson presented contrasting passages of this kind in a straightforwardly descriptive poem they would undoubtedly have been confusing. But he is not being merely descriptive, and the whole tendency of his concern with primitivism and progress has to be seen in relation to the literary kind that he is fashioning. Since he has established the Georgic intentions of his work so clearly he is able to use Virgil's own resolution of the Golden/Iron Age antithesis as the basis for an attitude which might be described as that of nostalgic progressivism.

5

Virgilian practice is also the inspiration behind a good deal of the overtly patriotic and political material. The most important source here is naturally Virgil's memorable passage in praise of Italy in *Georgics* II. In that passage Virgil finds four main reasons for the intensity of his patriotic feeling. First there is a rhapsodic appreciation of the natural beauty of the country, in which the Italian scene is interpreted in terms of Golden Age imagery. Italy is a country of eternal spring and summer: all is fruitful and nothing evil threatens the land, 'ravening tigers are far away, and the savage seed of lions.' Secondly, as might be expected, Virgil is proud of what Man has done to the country. Think too, he says, of all the noble cities that have been built by men. Thirdly, and springing from the first point, Virgil points to the country's abundant material wealth, her silver, copper and gold. Finally, he praises his countrymen and their martial triumphs and, greatest of all, Caesar himself who has been victorious in the farthest extremities of Asia. This last theme, praise of the present government of the country, is, as we have seen before, a recurrent one which is found, for example, in the opening invocation and also in the concluding lines.

In *Summer* Thomson has a fairly direct paraphrase of Virgil's patriotic section. The opening lines have already been quoted:

> Happy Britannia! where the Queen of Arts,
> Inspiring Vigour, Liberty, abroad,
> Walks thro' the Land of Heroes, unconfin'd,
> And scatters Plenty with unsparing Hand.
> Rich is thy Soil, and merciful thy Skies;
> Thy Streams unfailing in the Summer's Drought:
> Unmatch'd thy Guardian-Oaks: thy Vallies float
> With golden Waves; and on thy Mountains Flocks
> Bleat, numberless: while, roving round their Sides,
> Bellow the blackening Herds, in lusty Droves.
> Beneath, thy Meadows flame, and rise unquell'd,
> Against the Mower's Sythe. On every Hand,
> Thy Villas shine. Thy Country teems with Wealth;
> And Property assures it to the Swain,
> Pleas'd, and unweary'd, in his certain Toil.
>   Full are thy Cities with the Sons of Art;
> And Trade, and Joy, in every busy Street,
> Mingling, are heard: even Drudgery, Himself,
> As at the Car He sweats, or dusty, hews
> The Palace-Stone, looks gay. Thy crowded Ports,
> Where rising Masts an endless Prospect yield,
> With Labour burn, and echo to the Shouts
> Of hurry'd Sailor, as He, hearty, waves
> His last Adieu, and, loosening every Sheet,
> Resigns the spreading Vessel to the Wind.
>   Bold, firm, and graceful, are thy generous Youth,
> By Hardship sinew'd ...   (*Summer*, 1727, 498–524)

From this point Thomson gives an extended account of British heroes (and, more briefly, heroines), and ends with lines which owe something to Virgil and something to Shakespeare's John of Gaunt:[11]

> Island of Bliss! amid the Subject Seas,
> That thunder round thy rocky Coasts, set up,
> At once the Wonder, Terror and Delight
> Of distant Nations ...
>   (*Summer*, 1727, 585–8)

Again some difficulty may be felt in reconciling the notions of casual, Golden, abundance on the one hand and, on the other, riches won by hard labour; and there is no doubt that Thomson does sometimes attribute to external nature a prelapsarian quality. In *Spring*, for example, there is a long list of flowers which gives a strong sense of the idyllic bountifulness of nature – a sense which is reinforced by pastoral echoes from Browne, Milton and Shakespeare. (1728, 485–507) Hagley Park is described as the 'British Tempe'; Dodington's seat in *Autumn* is lavishly abundant:

> ... Autumn basks ...
> Presents the downy peach; the purple plumb,
> With a fine blueish mist of animals
> Clouded; the ruddy nectarine; and dark,
> Beneath his ample leaf, the luscious fig.
> The vine too here her curling tendrils shoots;
> Hangs out her clusters, swelling to the south;
> And scarcely wishes for a warmer sky.
>   (Autumn, 1730, 662–70)

But again this idealistic treatment of the natural scene has to be seen against the background of rhapsodic Virgilian patriotism. The hyperbole is not incompatible, when considered in terms of literary tradition, with pleasure in British institutions and in the political aspect of national expansion. When Thomson prays,

> So with superior Boon may your rich Soil,
> Exuberant, Nature's better Blessings pour
> O'er every Land; the naked Nations cloath,
> And be th'exhaustless Granary of the World.
>   (Spring, 1728, 73–5)

he may be being over-optimistic, but he is certainly not showing any literary indecorum. On the contrary the blend of idealized natural description and nationalistic enthusiasm that we find in *The Seasons* is entirely characteristic of the 'kind' that Thomson is imitating. One may reasonably infer that he chose the 'kind' partly at least because it encouraged the particular combination of attitudes that was most congenial to him. In other words this combination, far from being the result of 'emotional and intellectual confusion' is one of the most conscious, consistent and completely realized elements in the poem.

6

The third main Georgic theme in *The Seasons*, that of retirement, is also closely linked with the Golden/Iron Age antithesis. Since Thomson's modifications of Virgilian attitudes are in this case particularly important, it will be as well to recall fairly precisely what Virgil says on the subject in the second *Georgic*.

The husbandman is happy in the first place, Virgil says, because he avoids the evils of an active life. He is 'far from the clash of arms' and from the anxiety of superfluous luxury. He is not constantly agitated by a desire for fame:

> Him no honours the people give can move, no purple of kings, no strife rousing brother to break with brother, no Dacian swooping down from his leagued Danube, no power of Rome, no kingdoms doomed to fall ...
> (II, 495–8)

He gains 'an easy sustenance' and enjoys simple pleasures – 'repose without care ... the ease of broad domains, caverns and living lakes and cool vales, the lowing of the kine, and soft slumbers beneath the trees.' The unchanging cycle of the year makes for an ordered, stable life blest with domestic satisfactions:

> Meanwhile his dear children hang upon his kisses; his unstained home guards its purity. (II, 523)

The satisfactions of country life are typified in a little scene which shows the husbandman enjoying a holiday, 'stretched on the grass, with a fire in the midst'. Finally, this life is identified – and here we find the main Virgilian link with the previous section of this chapter – with prelapsarian perfection:

> Such a life the old Sabines once lived, such Remus and his brother ... nay ... such was the life golden Saturn lived on earth, while yet none had heard the clarion blare, none the sword-blades ring, as they were laid on the stubborn anvil. (II, 532–43)

With this hyperbolical praise of retirement as a re-creation of the Golden Age the Second Book of the *Georgics* ends.

But interwoven with this idealization of retirement there is, rather incongruously it seems at first sight, praise of scientific speculation:

> But as for me – first above all, may the sweet Muses ...
> take me to themselves and show me heaven's pathways ...
>
> (II, 475-7)

Understanding of the nature of the Universe is the highest good. If Virgil is unfit for this, then, he says, he will seek a life of retirement, and he repeats these priorities very memorably in lines 490-93:

> Felix qui potuit rerum cognoscere causas ...
> fortunatus et ille, deos qui novit agrestis.
>
> Blessed is he who has been able to win knowledge of the causes of things ... Happy too, is he who knows the woodland gods.

On the one hand there is pursuit of pure knowledge, and on the other a quiet life of useful labour.

How does this theme appear and what is its structural significance in *The Seasons*? That the theme itself was central to Thomson's conception of his poem is clear from the Preface to the second edition of *Winter*. Part of it has already been quoted. There is, says Thomson, 'no Subject more elevating, more amusing; more ready to awake the poetical Enthusiasm, the philosophical Reflection, and the moral Sentiment, than the Works of Nature.' The noblest poets of the past have relied upon this subject and,

> For this Reason the best, both Antient, and Modern, Poets have been passionately fond of Retirement and Solitude.

And Thomson gives as examples the *Book of Job* and the *Georgics*, providing his own translation of the first of the passages in which Virgil sets forth the nature of the two acceptable ways of life as he sees them:

> Me may the Muses, my supreme Delight!
> Whose Priest, I am, smit with immense Desire,
> Snatch to their Care ...

Thomson was to paraphrase the same passage again in the final lines of *Autumn* and the themes and imagery of these lines, and indeed of the whole of this section of the *Georgics*, recur constantly throughout *The Seasons*.

The English Georgic

In the first version of *Winter* the theme is comparatively undeveloped, but we find lines which involve a coalescence of the two Virgilian notions:

> Nature! great Parent! whose directing Hand
> Rolls round the Seasons of the changeful Year,
> How mighty! how majestick are thy Works!
> With what a pleasing Dread they swell the Soul,
> That sees, astonish'd! and, astonish'd sings!
> (1726, March, 143-7)

The significance of Nature here is that it provokes wonder and consequently leads to scientific questioning:

> You too, ye Winds! that now begin to blow,
> With boisterous Sweep, I raise my Voice to you...
> Where are your aerial Magazines reserv'd,
> Against the Day of Tempest perilous?
> (1726, March, 148-51)

The study of Nature leads insistently to Virgil's desire to 'know the causes of things' and, in view of the June Preface it can be assumed that the lines were written under the direct influence of the *Georgics*.

Another manifestation of the retirement theme, also in the first version of *Winter*, is found in the passage beginning at line 253. Here Thomson both coalesces the two strands of Virgilian idealism and introduces his own modifications. He wishes to retire to a life of literary and historical study, a life of cultured ease:

> Now, all amid the Rigours of the Year
> In the wild Depth of Winter, while without
> The ceaseless Winds blow keen, be my Retreat
> A rural, shelter'd, solitary, Scene;
> Where ruddy Fire, and beaming Tapers join
> To chase the chearless Gloom: there let me sit,
> And hold high Converse with the Mighty Dead,
> Sages of ancient Time, as Gods rever'd...
> (1726, March, 253-60)

This leads to praise of Socrates, Lycurgus, Cato, Homer, and Virgil as they pass in a visionary procession in front of Thomson's eyes. This emphasis upon retirement as the instigator of philosophical and scientific meditation is continued in the first version of *Summer*. Thomson gives an account of the influence of the Sun upon animate and even inanimate Nature:

> The very dead Creation, from thy Touch,
> Assumes a mimic life ... (1727, 145-6)

He leads from this to praise of God and follows with lines that echo Virgil clearly and yet with a difference:

> To Me be Nature's Volume, wide, display'd;
> And to peruse the broad, illumin'd Page;
> Or haply catching Inspiration thence,
> Some easy Passage, raptur'd, to translate,
> My Sole Delight; as thro' the falling Glooms,
> Pensive, I muse, or, with the rising Day,
> On Fancy's Eagle-Wing, excursive, soar.
> (1727, 176-82)

Perusal of Nature's 'broad, illumin'd Page' leads to 'knowledge of the causes of things'. Whereas Virgil had seen scientific understanding as an alternative to retirement, for Thomson the two are inextricably bound together, and they lead forward to poetic *rapture*.

The notion of retirement as a contemplative condition which harmonizes the passions and induces a psychological state favourable to mental and spiritual insight is soon carried further in *Summer*. After describing the oppressive effects of a heatwave Thomson produces an allegorical picture of a man who 'on the Sunless Side/Of a romantic Mountain'

> Sits cooly calm; while all the World without,
> Unsatisfy'd, and sick, tosses in Noon ...
> (1727, 350-1)

and this, Thomson suggests, is an instructive emblem

> of the virtuous Man,
> Who keeps his temper'd Mind serene and pure,
> And all his Passions aptly harmoniz'd,
> Amidst a jarring World with Vice inflam'd.
> (1727, 352-5)

But in effect it is not simply that the figure who 'sits cooly calm' is an image of 'the virtuous Man' whose passions are restrained and ordered. He *is* that man. Virtue springs from retirement and contemplation of the natural scene. It is this psychological benefit that Thomson particularly values and it is this value that he has in mind when he goes on to apostrophize the woods:

> Welcome, ye Shades! ye bowery Thickets hail!
> Ye lofty Pines! ye venerable Oaks!
> (1727, 356–7)

The shelter of the woods is 'delicious to the soul'; it cools the nerves; it is life-giving. After describing the effects of heat upon animals – particularly the ox and the horse – Thomson returns again to the psychological influence of the woods:

> These are the Haunts of Meditation, these
> The Scenes where antient Bards th'inspiring Breath,
> Extatic, felt . . . (1727, 409–11)

Here angelic voices are heard, or seem to be heard. They have attained to the harmony which Thomson still seeks, and they invite him to share their happiness:

> Oft, in these dim Recesses, undisturb'd
> By noisy Folly, and discordant Vice,
> Of Nature sing with Us, and Nature's God.
> (1727, 440–2)

This is, of course, a far more immediate and emotionalized, more Shaftesburyian, moral influence than anything suggested by Virgil. Virgil's husbandman led a better life, certainly, than the town-dweller, and there is some slight suggestion implicit that the country setting itself has a beneficent effect. But the main moral influences are first the absence of immoral temptations (to ambition, for example) and secondly the regular pattern of work which is imposed by the seasons. There is not the ecstatic moral influence that Thomson attributes to the natural scene, an influence which he points to again the next year in the first version of *Spring*, and most directly in these lines:

> Serenity apace
> Induces Thought, and Contemplation still.

> By small Degrees the Love of Nature works,
> And warms the Bosom; till at last arriv'd
> To Rapture, and enthusiastic Heat,
> We feel the present Deity, and taste
> The Joy of God, to see a happy World.
>
> (1728, 858–64)

The various stages in the psychological development which country retirement induces are here set out explicitly – serenity, thought, contemplation, rapture.

Various additions strengthened the retirement element in *Spring* in 1744, but it seems best for the moment to continue with a chronological account of Thomson's developing attitude and the additions to *Spring* will therefore be considered later.

Autumn, the last of *The Seasons* to be written, emphasizes the moral influence of the natural scene in its description of Dodington's Dorset seat:

> Oh lose me in the green, majestic walks
> Of, Dodington! thy seat, serene, and plain;
> Where simple Nature reigns . . .
>   Here oft alone,
> Fir'd by the thirst of thy applause, I court
> Th'inspiring breeze; and meditate the book
> Of Nature, ever-open; aiming thence,
> Heart-taught like thine, to learn the moral song.
>
> (1730, 643–60)

But apart from this *Autumn* also contains, in its concluding section, by far the most extensive formulation of the retirement theme.

> Oh knew he but his happiness, of men
> The happiest he! who far from public rage,
> Deep in the vale, with a choice few retir'd,
> Drinks the pure pleasures of the rural Life.
>
> (1730, 1131–4)

The passage of approximately 135 lines is very closely modelled on Virgil: indeed much of it is straightforward translation. Thomson lists first the evils which a country life *avoids* (importunate suitors, the obligatory show of useless wealth), and then touches upon some of the advantages of rural retirement:

> Rich in content, in Nature's bounty rich,
> In herbs, and fruits; whatever greens the Spring,
> When heaven descends in showers; or bends the bough,
> When Summer reddens, and when Autumn beams ...
> (1730, 1155–8)

Then again the rejection of ambition, military, political and legal, in favour of the patterned life of Nature is clearly set forth:

> The rage of nations, and the crush of states
> Move not the man, who, from the world escap'd,
> In still retreats, and flowery solitudes,
> To Nature's voice attends, from day to day,
> And month to month, thro' the revolving Year ...
> (1730, 1199–1203)

The life of retirement is identified, as in Virgil, with the Golden Age, with Paradisal experience when 'God himself, and Angels dwelt with men!', and finally, placed in a more emphatic position than in Virgil, there is a new version of the passage which Thomson had already translated in the Preface to *Winter*:

> Oh Nature! all-sufficient! over all!
> Enrich me with the knowledge of thy works!
> (1730, 1248–9)

Thomson wishes, with Virgil, to understand the rolling wonders of heaven's 'infinite extent', to understand the mystery of animal, mineral and vegetable life and the complexity of human psychology (and here he is going beyond the Virgilian original). But, despite the intensity of these desires, he prays that

> if the blood
> In sluggish streams about my heart, forbids
> That best ambition; under closing shades,
> Inglorious, lay me by the lowly brook,
> And whisper to my dreams.   (1730, 1263–7)

Thus, although praise of scientific speculation has certainly been given a very prominent position, the either/or formula of *Georgics* II is here maintained and *Autumn* ends with this tribute to the 'inglorious' but nonetheless valuable pleasures of a retired country existence.

The chief figure in the idyllic picture of a country life which Virgil paints is the husbandman. 'O fortunatos ... agricolas!' He is engaged in the normal country occupations and is leading a frugal existence. He is 'hardened to toil and innured to scanty fare.' 'No respite is there.' Each season brings its proper work and the holiday is a rare event, a justified rest from continual labour. The countryman certainly enjoys the pleasures of country life. This is hinted at in lines which refer to 'lakes and cool vales, the lowing of kine, and soft slumbers beneath the trees.' But also, and distinct from the picture of the husbandman, although the two tend to merge together, is the figure of Virgil himself, desiring scientific knowledge, yet prepared to opt for the delights of the country. Although the two figures are close together, and although Virgil seems at times to be identifying himself with the husbandman, they do not coalesce. The very fact that Virgil postulates scientific knowledge as one of the most desirable objectives in life sets him apart from the husbandman and implies that his attitude will be different from that of the husbandman even towards those simple country pleasures which they share. The poet saying: 'O for one to set me in the cool glens of Haemus, and shield me under the branches' mighty shade!' (II, 488–9) is different psychologically from the man who enjoys the pleasures of Nature unreflectively. That the husbandman *is* unreflective is shown in the opening line of the section 'Oh happy husbandmen! too happy, should they come to know their blessings' (II, 458–9). In Thomson's version of the section the husbandman is left almost entirely on one side. His presence is implied in references to farming activity:

> whatever greens the Spring,
> When heaven descends in showers; or bends the bough,
> When Summer reddens, and when Autumn beams ...
>   (1730, 1156–8)

but for the most part it is not farming that is stressed. Thomson's retirement is much more literary and philosophical than anything that Virgil hints at. He proposes to retire with a few *choice* friends and to lead a thoroughly cultivated life. Some of his expansions reveal this emphasis very clearly. Lines 1212–6, for example, begin in an entirely Virgilian manner. They are modelled on lines 496–7 of *Georgics* II:

> In Summer he, beneath the living shade,
> Such as from frigid Tempe wont to fall,
> Or Haemus cool . . .

But Thomson now adds his own gloss on this activity:

> In Summer he . . .
>   reads what the muse, of these
> Perhaps, has in immortal numbers sung;
> Or what she dictates writes . . .

Literary activity is an essential part of this retirement, an idea which is developed a little later on when Thomson is speaking of the way in which the evenings should be spent:

> A friend, a book, the stealing hours secure,
> And mark them down for wisdom. With swift wing,
> O'er land and sea, imagination roams;
> Or truth, divinely breaking on his mind,
> Elates his being, and unfolds his powers . . .
>
>   (1730, 1229–33)

The importance of the social aspect of retirement is already clear. Thomson withdraws from the world with a few choice friends and his search for wisdom is thought of as an essentially social activity. Thomson's social enthusiams appear very clearly in the scene where he draws nearest to the Virgilian husbandman, in the picture of domestic happiness with its natural appeal to sentiment:

> The touch of love, and kindred too he feels,
> The modest eye, whose beams on his alone
> Extatic shine; the little, strong embrace
> Of prattling children, twin'd around his neck,
> And emulous to please him, calling forth
> The fond parental soul. Nor purpose gay,
> Amusement, dance, or song, he sternly scorns;
> For happiness, and true philosophy
> Are of the social still, and smiling Kind.
>
>   (1744, 1235–43)

The last line was emended in 1744 from 'Still are, and have been of the smiling kind'. Once again Thomson begins with a very close imitation of Virgil and then provides an addition which is personal in its emphasis. The conclusion that happiness and true philosophy 'are of the social still, and smiling Kind' is unvirgilian, but entirely characteristic of Thomson's attitude to the pleasures of retirement.

The discussion so far has dealt with Thomson's use of the retirement theme up to the publication of the first collected edition of *The Seasons* in 1730. A clear idea of the changes which Thomson made in his treatment of the theme after the publication of the first collected edition can be gained from a study of *Spring*.

There is one substantial addition, namely the account of Hagley Park (Lyttleton's house), a fifty-nine line passage first included in 1744. The passage immediately follows lines which have already been quoted

>   Serenity apace
> Induces Thought and Contemplation still.
> By small Degrees the Love of Nature works,
> And warms the Bosom . . .   (1728, 858–61)

Lyttleton is an example of a man who is moved in this way:

> These are the Sacred Feelings of thy Heart . . .
>   (1744, 901)

His emotions are controlled by 'Reason's purest Ray' and he responds both intellectually and emotionally to Nature as he wanders 'Courting the Muse, thro' Hagley-Park'. Nature produces her effects in well-defined stages. Lyttleton is pictured first in a state of simple receptivity towards the sensuous pleasures of the scene. He listens pensively

>   to the various Voice
> Of rural Peace: the Herds, the Flocks, the Birds,
> The hollow-whispering Breeze, the Plaint of Rills . . .
>   (1744, 914–16)

But 'abstracted oft' from these he enters the world of philosophical speculation or historical study, study which is not purely theoretical but which enables him to plan,

> with warm Benevolence of Mind,
> And honest Zeal unwarp'd by Party-Rage,
> Britannia's Weal . . .   (1744, 925–7)

The English Georgic

Again, as in *Summer*, contemplation of Nature is a life-giving force, only now it produces not only psychological harmony, but action as well.

Finally, there is a very typical addition to the closing section of *Spring*. Thomson is speaking about the satisfactions of virtuous love. The vanities of the World – 'Its pomp, its pleasure, and its nonsense all' – become unimportant as the happily married pair enjoy

> The richest Bounty of indulgent Heaven.
> (1728, 1056)

Children provide the culminating satisfaction and often provoke tears of happiness in their parents. Thomson addresses the married pair directly:

> Oh speak the Joy! You, whom the sudden Tear
> Surprizes often, while you look around,
> And nothing strikes your Eye but sights of Bliss,
> All various Nature pressing on the Heart . . .
> (1728, 1069–72)

At this point, in 1744, Thomson interpolated four lines which go a long way towards summing up his attitude to retirement:

> All various Nature pressing on the Heart,
> An elegant Sufficiency, Content,
> Retirement, rural Quiet, Friendship, Books,
> Ease and alternate Labour, useful Life,
> Progressive Virtue, and approving Heaven.
> These are the matchless Joys of virtuous Love . . .
> (1744, 1058–63)

All the elements of retirement as envisaged by Thomson are here. For the cultivated existence that he visualizes more than a bare competence is necessary. 'I've often wish'd that I had clear/For life, six hundred pounds a year,/A handsome House to lodge a friend . . .' said Swift and Thomson's 'elegant sufficiency' echoes this without any hint of self-mockery. Peace, sociability, literature are all mentioned. The objective is clear:

> Progressive virtue, and approving Heaven.

Thomson's view of retirement is complex, far from simple frugality on the one hand, and wise passiveness on the other, and most of the elements of the complexity are included in these lines. They make a fitting epitome of the many passages in *The Seasons* which deal with similar subject-matter.

What needs to be stressed about this analysis of the retirement passages in *The Seasons* is the extent to which Thomson's modifications of the self-sufficient stoicism that is the dominant ideal of Virgil's *O fortunatos agricolas* section are made within a framework of ideas that is characteristic of the *Georgics* taken as a whole. Thomson's main developments as they have emerged during the preceding analysis are: first, the stress upon the social pleasures of retirement itself and even upon its recuperative value for a man who is still engaged in an active life in the world; secondly, the emphasis on the positive moral influence of the countryside in harmonizing the passions and therefore encouraging virtue. If one looks at Thomson's use of the retirement theme on its own (without reference to its place in the poem as a whole) then the first of these developments will seem a more revolutionary break with Virgil than it really is. The *Georgics* themselves, as we have seen before, are not without internal contradictions: condemnation of courts and praise of retirement are juxtaposed, for example, with eulogies on the greatness of Augustus. In discussing Thomson's attitude to primitivism and progress it has been suggested that a leading factor in both Thomson's and Virgil's view of life is the notion of a fall from the Golden Age which is at once a calamity and an opportunity. Through labour the evils of the fall can be overcome and a greater Golden Age achieved again. In this context it is not so surprising that Thomson's treatment of retirement should tend towards the social and that he should show himself aware of the virtues of the active life. What Thomson does is to bring together ideas which are present, but left in a sharper contrast, in Virgil, and to give his poem an easier harmony in consequence. In doing this Thomson is not, it would seem, being unmindful of Virgil. Rather he is interpreting Virgil quite legitimately in terms of the conditions of his own age. He is following Henry Felton's advice to write in his model's 'Way and after his Manner', but without following him in meticulous detail. The second of Thomson's developments of the retirement theme, the stress upon sentimental morality, is much more to be looked upon, especially in its degree of emphasis, as an innovation. But it is an innovation which gains some sanction from passages in *Georgics*

II and IV where Virgil writes of the aesthetic and sensory pleasure given by the country scene, and it can be accommodated without violating the nature of the genre. It is a sign of Thomson's sureness of touch, and of the contemporary vitality of the poem that he is using as a source, that he can modify and develop the ideas and motifs of his source in this way.

7

It is Thomson's handling of these twin themes that gives the poem its fundamentally Georgic character. However, there are also many passages which are less radical in their influence, but which are justified by the essentially Georgic character of the whole. In this category, for example, one must place the lines in *Spring* on the destruction of insect pests:

> And hence the skillful Farmer Chaff
> And blazing Straw before his Orchard burns,
> Till all involv'd in Smoak the latent Foe
> From every Cranny suffocated falls ...
>
> (1728, 128-31)

This is a passage which readers have frequently objected to on grounds of its irrelevance to the supposed purpose of the poem (assuming that to be description of nature and the inculcation of sentimental morality): but it takes its place perfectly well once the poem is accepted for what it is – a modified Georgic. The *labor omnia vicit* side of Thomson's concern with the Iron Age needs (in a poem which is basically concerned with the country) to be rooted in country occupations, and in its context the passage is not an unwarranted digression or a misguided piece of ornamentation. It is justified because it serves the intentions, both thematic and formal, of the poem as a whole. Thomson should be assumed to know what he is about: in the 1744 version he revised this section considerably, but presumably, since he retained it, felt no doubts as to its essential relevance.

Also very strongly Georgic is the passage on the loves of the beasts.[12] This is one of the most popular Georgic elements both in Virgil's poem and in post-classical developments of the Georgic form; in the eighteenth century itself one might instance Gay's *Rural Sports*, or, later than Thomson, Somerville's *The Chace*.

Thomson deals first with 'a Theme/Unknown to Fame, the Passion of the Groves', then with cruder passions in 'the rougher World/Of Brutes' and finally with Man (adopting in this detail the ascending scale of value which Addison perceived in the *Georgics* as a whole).[13] Thomson takes over many details, even of phrasing, from Virgil's account. Here also we find Thomson modifying Virgil for his own purpose. Speaking of human love Virgil included a reference to Leander swimming the Hellespont:

> What of the youth, in whose marrow fierce Love fans the mighty flame? Lo! in the turmoil of bursting storms, late in the black night, he swims the straits. Above him thunders Heaven's mighty portal, and the billows, dashing on the cliffs, echo the cry; yet neither his hapless parents can call him back, nor thought of the maid who in cruel fate must die withal.
>
> (III, 258–63)

Thomson's lover dreams of similar difficulties:

> ... he wanders waste,
> In Night and Tempest wrapt; or shrinks aghast,
> Back, from the bending Precipice; or wades
> The turbid Stream below, and strives to reach
> The farther Shore, where succourless, and sad,
> His Dearer Life extends her beckoning Arms ...
>
> (1728, 974–9)

By echoes of this sort Thomson makes his Virgilian debt clear. The utility of the theme for his purpose is that it enables him to point to the essential harmony (or the essential oneness) of all living creatures. Birds, beasts and men are all impelled by the same 'infusive force'; they are all subject to the same divine influence:

> 'Tis Harmony, that World-embracing Power
> By which all Beings are adjusted, each
> To all around, impelling and impell'd
> In endless Circulation, that inspires
> This universal Smile ...   (1728, 865–9)

Moreover this section on love enables Thomson to lead up to the praise of marriage which brings *Spring* to its conclusion:

> But happy They! the Happiest of their Kind!
> Whom gentler Stars unite, and in one Fate
> Their Hearts, their Fortunes, and their Beings blend.
> (1728, 1025–7)

In other words it is again true that Georgic *motifs*, which have an entirely adequate formal appropriateness to the kind of poem that Thomson is writing, are adopted by him and used in a way that serves his central purpose. The form and its conventions go hand in hand with what Thomson has to say, and there is no sense of clash between them.

Indeed, at every turn in the analysis of the poem one is impressed by the extent to which the poet's interpretation of his subject-matter depends upon the modification and development of Georgic patterns. For all its variety and apparently random development the poem does present a coherent interpretation of life. Thomson's three dominant elements – natural description, praise of the retired life and patriotic exaltation – are, as we have seen, closely linked. The fundamental fact in the presentation of his poetic attitude, and one which is given a dominant position in *The Seasons* as a whole, is that we live in the Age of Iron. This brings with it two premises about life. First, that nothing can be accomplished without labour but that out of the struggle comes all that we most value; and secondly, that Man lives in a state of psychological disharmony which is only partly remediable. He is subject to conflicting passions which can only with great difficulty be brought under the rule of Reason. It is from the starting-point of these premises that Thomson develops his patriotic ideas and his attitude to retirement. British successes in exploration and in trade are the clearest evidence of what can be accomplished by labour. Through retirement, through contemplation of the natural scene (which still retains, in part at least, its prelapsarian beauty) psychological harmony can be achieved. And in the later revisions to the poem the value of this is seen to lie in the strength it gives to enable one to engage once more in an active life. This, in the simplest possible form, is the argument which underlies *The Seasons*, and it is an argument which has been adapted, but without any fundamental changes, from Virgil.

8

Granted that these central preoccupations were encouraged by the Virgilian source it still needs to be asked why Thomson chose the seasons as his particular subject. He could have written on a locality as Denham and Pope had done, or, like Gay, about *Rural Sports*. He could have followed Milton in making a psychological approach to the countryside, or, obviously, he could, like Philips, have followed Virgil still more closely and taken farming as his theme. As we have seen, Thomson was in many ways a traditionalist, but in choosing a subject he avoided the most authoritative ways of proceeding and turned to the seasons instead. Not that this was entirely new: Pope's *Pastorals* are divided seasonally, and William Hinchliffe had published a short poem actually called *The Seasons* in 1718.[14] Hinchcliffe's poem has affinities with Thomson's work and seems to have given him the idea, but it still remains worth asking why this framework appeared to be a suitable one for his most ambitious poem.

No doubt the original choice of winter as a subject was due to the opportunities it offered for description accompanied by a lofty strain of meditation. Thomson makes much, in his Preface to the June 1726 edition of *Winter*, of the sublimity of his subject. We must, he says, choose

> ... great and serious Subjects, such as at once amuse the
> Fancy, enlighten the Head, and warm the Heart.

Subjects of this character are to be found above all in the works of nature; where we meet with 'all that enlarges and transports the soul'.

The mood expressed here is certainly the predominant one in this first version of the poem:

> SEE! Winter comes, to rule the varied Year,
> Sullen, and sad; with all his rising Train,
> Vapours, and Clouds, and Storms. Be these my Theme,
> These, that exalt the Soul to solemn Thought,
> And heavenly musing. . . .
> Oh! bear me then to high, embowering, Shades;
> To twilight Groves, and visionary Vales;
> To weeping Grottos, and to hoary Caves;

> Where Angel-Forms are seen, and Voices heard,
> Sigh'd in low Whispers, that abstract the Soul,
> From outward Sense, far into Worlds remote.
>
> (ll. 1–79)

This is a strain of self-intoxication which the modern reader finds a little indigestible, but it is the germ from which the whole poem developed, and we can be glad that, in choosing a subject which gave full reign to his yearning for sublimity of feeling and elevation of language, Thomson found a topic which was capable of varied and subtle extensions.

He was already, in the June 1726 Preface, apparently looking forward to writing on all the seasons:

> How gay looks the Spring! how glorious the Summer! how pleasing the Autumn! and how venerable the Winter! – But there is no thinking of these Things without breaking out into Poetry ...

and as he worked the subject was quickly seen to offer more than simply an excuse for sublime and picturesque description and for self-conscious 'philosophical reflection and moral sentiment'. In reflection of the kind that has just been quoted from *Winter*, the natural scene acts as a spur to meditation but in the poem as it developed the important thing is not so much the set pieces of meditation as the meaningful pattern of comparisons and contrasts that is found in the subject itself.

Thomson is inevitably impressed by the seasons in their cyclical aspect, as a recurrent pattern which contains within itself the great facts of birth and death, growth and decay. He is even more impressed by the notion of plenitude, that in the external scene there is to be found an interlinked chain of being, each segment of which forms a vital part of the whole. The sheer abundance of external nature is a frequent theme, that 'full nature swarms with life'. The species of flowers, Thomson says, are uncountable. They are

> profusely wild
> O'er all the deep-green Earth, beyond the Power
> Of Botanist to number up their Tribes ...
> With such a liberal Hand has Nature flung
> Their Seeds abroad ...   (*Spring*, 1728, 247–256)

Among other things *The Seasons* is a celebration of Nature's 'liberal hand', the richness of teeming animal and vegetable life, which is not quite the same thing as the celebration of the farmer's prosperity, although, as we have seen, that too is an important theme. Thomson, however, is fascinated not only with prosperity, the harnessing of natural forces to man's purpose, but also with the vast scope and interpenetration of existence, with how

> From stage to stage, the vital scale ascends . . .[15]

In his description of the 'vital scale' Thomson places great emphasis on the idea of harmony. His muse, he says, is most delighted

> when she social sees
> The whole mixed animal creation round
> Alive and happy.   (*Autumn*, 1744, 378–80)

The ideal landscape is one where 'Harmonious Nature looked smiling on', where 'the herds and flocks commixing played secure' and where 'music held the whole in perfect peace'. Thomson knows perfectly well that this idyllic harmony is not always to be found in external nature, but he does believe that there is an over-riding harmony which reconciles local disruptions and injustices. Addressing God, and calling him the 'Source of Being! Universal Soul . . . Essential Presence', Thomson says:

> to Thee my Thoughts
> Continual climb, who, with a Master-Hand
> Hast the great Whole into Perfection touched . . .
>   (*Spring*, 1728, 510–12)

Properly understood the whole of life is a perfect unity. This is one of the dominant themes of the *Hymn on the Seasons* where Thomson makes a more specifically Christian invocation to God as the 'Almighty Father':

> THESE, as they change, Almighty Father! these,
> Are but the varied God. The rolling Year
> Is full of thee. . . .
>
> Mysterious round! what skill, what force divine,
> Deep-felt in these appear! a simple train,

> Yet so delightful mix'd, with such kind Art,
> Such Beauty and Beneficence combined;
> Shade, unperceiv'd, so softening into shade,
> And all so forming an harmonious whole,
> That, as they still succeed, they ravish still.
>
> (1744, 1-27)

Man, 'with brute unconscious gaze' sometimes fails to understand this 'harmonious whole', and this is ironical because he has a special place in the harmonious scheme:

> Man superior walks
> Amid the glad Creation...
>
> (*Spring*, 1728, 195-6)

and as he walks he should be 'musing praise and looking lively gratitude', aware of the unity of the scene of which he forms a part.

It is because the seasons mirror this overriding harmony so perfectly that Thomson was attracted to them as a subject. In their perpetual cycle and recurring balance Thomson found reflected the ideal unity which sustained the universe. But 'overriding' is a key word. Although it is Thomson's firm belief that, however far he may travel, he cannot go 'Where universal love not smiles around', and though he believes that universal love

> From seeming evil still educes good,
> And better thence again, and better still,
> In infinite progression...
>
> (*Hymn*, 1730, 117-19)

although, in other words, he was a metaphysical optimist of the most steadfast kind, yet *The Seasons*, taken as a whole is by no means easily and complacently optimistic. Thomson knows that life is full of sudden shifts of fortune, disruptions and dislocations which are very difficult to explain in terms of universal order or justice. And here again the seasons are invaluable to him because they impose variety (at the very least climatic variety) while at the same time maintaining a sense of order and progression. On a larger scale the seasons have for Thomson the significance that the landscape of Windsor had for Pope:

> Not Chaos-like together crush'd and bruis'd,
> But as the World, harmoniously confus'd:

> Where Order in Variety we see,
> And where, tho' all things differ, all agree ...
>
> (*Windsor Forest*, 13–16)

They allow and indeed encourage important juxtapositions and contrasts of subject-matter, and hold them all in a state of tension.

On the largest scale there is a balance between the different books, in that *Spring* and *Autumn* are seen as predominantly fruitful and creative, whereas *Winter* and *Summer* are often powerfully destructive. There is built into the final form of the poem a clearly perceptible oscillation of mood.

The destructiveness of *Winter* arises naturally from the subject itself, and Thomson's prose *Argument* shows clearly where the emphasis will fall:

> First approach of Winter. According to the natural course of the season, various storms described. Rain. Wind. Snow. The driving of the snows: a man perishing among them; *whence reflections on the wants and miseries of human life.* The wolves descending from the Alps and Appenines.

The passage to which the italicized *reflections on the wants and miseries of human life* refers is a set piece of extreme despondency:

> Ah! little think the gay licentious proud,
> Whom pleasure, power and affluence surround;
> They, who their thoughtless hours in giddy mirth,
> And wanton, often cruel, riot waste;
> Ah little think they, while they dance along,
> How many feel, this very moment, death
> And all the sad variety of pain.
>
> (1730, 296–302)

This is the mood of *Winter:* man is at the mercy of elemental forces which he is unable to understand or control.

But *Summer* provides a central episode almost as bleak in its implications. The general tone is naturally less stark. There is a good deal of very attractive natural description; there are the hay-making and sheep-shearing scenes and, towards the end, a transition, as Thomson says, 'to the prospect of a rich, well-cultivated country' in order to introduce a 'panegyric on Great Britain.' Thomson explicitly attacks 'impious' scoffers who attack

> Creative Wisdom, as if aught was form'd
> In vain, or not for admirable Ends. (1744, 319-20)

Yet, the most memorable episode in *Summer* is the tale of Celadon and Amelia, two lovers caught in a thunder-storm in which Amelia is killed. The tale is introduced by a description of a storm which is both terrifying and destructive. Trees are uprooted and cattle killed and this is thought of as frightening to the guilty-minded:

> Guilt hears appall'd, with deeply troubled Thought ...

But there is an immediate modification because Thomson realizes that this is too easy a moral:

> Guilt hears appall'd, with deeply troubled Thought;
> And yet not always on the guilty Head
> Descends the fated Flash. (1744, 1161-3)

This introduces the episode of Celadon and Amelia who are built up by Thomson as a completely innocent couple. Not only are they innocent, but their relationship is idyllic:

> They lov'd. But such their guileless Passion was,
> As in the Dawn of Time inform'd the Heart
> Of Innocence, and undissembling Truth.
> (1744, 1069-71)

Their love is such as to make 'eternal Eden smile around'. When the storm begins and Amelia is frightened Celadon tries to calm her by an appeal to the divine order and justice which Thomson himself frequently evokes:

> 'Fear not, he said,
> Sweet Innocence! thou Stranger to Offence,
> And inward Storm! He, who yon Skies involves
> In Frowns of Darkness, ever smiles on thee,
> With kind regard. O'er thee ...
> that very Voice,
> Which thunders Terror thro' the guilty Heart,
> With Tongues of Seraphs whispers Peace to thine.
> 'Tis Safety to be near thee sure, and thus
> To clasp Perfection!' (1744, 1196-206)

However, Celadon's confidence, which could in another context be Thomson's, is soon shattered, because

> From his void Embrace,
> ... that moment, to the Ground,
> A blacken'd Corse, was struck the beauteous Maid.
>
> (1744, 1206–8)

From this sad story Thomson passes immediately, with no comment, to a description of how, once the storm is past, everything becomes gay and happy. The unjustifiable tragic event is left to make its own impact, but Thomson has done all he can, short of explicit comment, to make us feel that this story renders an easy acceptance of God's harmonious plan impossible. The sharpness of the contrast with scenes of peace and prosperity is too great for that.

The sense of nature as hostile or potentially hostile is strongest in *Winter* and *Summer*. In *Spring* an idyllic pastoral tone prevails and in *Autumn* it is naturally the harvest – with nature as the great benefactor – that is at the centre of the poem. The equivalent digression in *Autumn* to *Summer*'s Celadon and Amelia is the tale of Palamon and Lavinia, an optimistic story of how a poor gleaner of noble birth is restored to fortune by her benevolent master. There is no serious disruption of the harvest-home theme.

Looking at the poem as a whole, therefore, the four books might be labelled very crudely as 'Optimism', 'Doubt', 'Optimism', 'Doubt', each book playing off against the preceding one. And within the books one finds similar contrasts constantly being made by the juxtaposition of different kinds of material. For a sharp contrast on a localised scale one might consider a passage early in *Spring*. In the spring, Thomson says, it is pleasant to get out into the country and see

> far-diffus'd around
> One boundless Blush, one snow-empurpled Shower
> Of mingled Blossoms; where the raptur'd Eye
> Travels from Joy to Joy, and, hid beneath
> The fair Profusion, yellow Autumn spies.
>
> (1727, 107–11)

But then comes the contrast, the doubt and, surely, inevitably, the question about how far Nature's benevolence extends. The 'raptured eye' is justified in seeing yellow autumn hidden in the blossom of spring only

> If brush'd from Russian Wilds, a cutting Gale
> Rise not, and scatter from his humid Wings
> The clammy Mildew, or dry-blowing breathe
> Untimely Frost; before whose baleful Blast,
> The full-blown Spring thro' all her Foliage shrinks
> Joyless and dead, a wide-dejected Waste.
>
> (1744, 112–17)

By this sort of contrast – characteristic Georgic montage – Thomson gradually builds up a sense of the complex interplay of forces that underlies human activity. Even the bleak storms of *Winter* are interspersed with domestic scenes,

> Where ruddy fire and beaming tapers join,
> To chase the chearless gloom.
>
> (1730, 413–14)

And there is, of course, the celebrated robin who 'pays to trusted man/His annual visit' and makes himself at home in the family. The overall effect is like a pageant, and it is so above all in that there is no progression; it is the total picture that is important. Everything is held as it were in suspension. No single scene or passage is really significant; it is the accumulation of scenes and the way they play off one against another that matters.

9

This general point about the structure of *The Seasons* gains a good deal of support when one looks at its style or rather its styles. In contrast to the descriptive and reflective poems discussed in the previous chapter *The Seasons* is stylistically extremely varied, and it frequently happens that a major effect depends upon transpositions of mood which are reinforced by stylistic means. Thomson himself was certainly aware of these transpositions. He sometimes says explicitly: 'Let us leave this mood on one side now and turn to something different'. He does this very clearly in *Spring* after his account of the loves of the beasts:

> But this the Theme
> I sing, transported, to the British Fair,

> Forbids, and leads me to the Mountain-brow,
> Where sits the Shepherd on the grassy Turf,
> Inhaling, healthful, the descending Sun.
>
> (1728, 776-80)

And at another point when he turns to 'the fair sex' he makes clear the stylistic implications of the shift in direction:

> May my Song soften, as thy Daughters I,
> Britannia, hail! for Beauty is their own,
> The feeling Heart, Simplicity of Life,
> And Elegance, and Taste ...
>
> (*Summer*, 1744, 1572-5)

When Thomson *softens* his song and uses language appropriate to women, mellifluousness and fluency are emphasised and he avoids all harshness of diction and rhythm.

In reading *The Seasons* it soon becomes clear that the different styles complement each other and so provide a strong reinforcement for the central themes of the poem. Three may be distinguished here – the pastoral, the heroic and the mock-heroic.

A pattern of the pastoral style occurs in *Spring*, in the catalogue of flowers:

> Fair-handed Spring unbosoms every Grace;
> Throws out the Snow-Drop, and the Crocus first,
> The Daisy, Primrose, Violet darkly blue,
> The Polyanthus of unnumbered Dyes ...
> Anemonies, Auriculas ...
> And full Renunculus, of glowing red.
>
> (1744, 527-32)

In passages of this kind Thomson is deeply indebted to the tradition of pastoral writing and here we find echoes from Browne's *Britannia's Pastorals*, from *Lycidas* and from the pastoral section of *The Winter's Tale*. The emphasis is upon the piling up of visual images to give an impression of richness and spontaneity. Suggestions of worldliness and violence and indeed all associations incongruous with the idea of innocent abundance, are excluded.

At the opposite extreme is the heroic. In its purest form this is found, for example, in the storm scene or in the account of the plague. A few lines from *Winter*, describing the descent of wolves upon a village, provide a pattern:

> By wintry Famine rous'd, from all the Tract
> Of horrid Mountains which the shining Alps,
> And wavy Apennines, and Pyrenees
> Branch out stupendous into distant Lands,
> Cruel as Death, and hungry as the Grave!
> Burning for Blood, bony, and ghaunt, and grim!
> Assembling Wolves in raging Troops descend ...
>
> (1744, 389–95)

The lines could almost be pastiche, but they do indicate in an exaggerated form the characteristics of the heroic mood in Thomson. There is the strongly emotive effect of *horrid*, where the root meaning is dominant, and a similar effect with *stupendous*. There is the exoticism of the scene ('wavy Apennines and Pyrenees'), the horror of the subject itself ('Burning for Blood, bony, and ghaunt and grim'), and, perhaps above all, the sense of Man's helplessness in the face of disaster. 'The godlike Face of Man avails him naught' as the wolves descend upon the villagers.

Stylistically the poem oscillates between these two extremes of pastoralism and the heroic. But mediating between these two extremes there is a variety of more neutral styles which help to relate the extreme modes to ordinary life. One of the most important is mock-heroic.

There is only one sustained passage of mock-heroic, namely the account of the hunt, and particularly the hunt-supper, in *Autumn*. Thomson dislikes hunting. This is part of his humanitarianism, and springs from the feeling that killing animals (especially for pleasure) is a man-made discord, a deliberate disruption of natural harmony. And consequently the picture that he gives of the huntsmen's feast is satiric: he emphasizes its boorishness and drunkenness, and he uses a mock-heroic style which rises to a climax as, one by one, the drinkers sink into stupor beneath the table:

> Before their maudlin eyes,
> Seen dim, and blue, the double tapers dance,
> Like the sun wading thro' the misty sky.
> Then, sliding sweet, they drop. O'erturned above
> Lies the wet, broken scene; and stretch'd below,
> Is heap'd the social Slaughter ...
>
> (1744, 550–5)

Thomson's 'Seasons'

The third line has a particularly authentic mock-heroic ring. The last phrase (*social slaughter*) is an interesting one. The word *social* is a very important one for Thomson and it occurs with exceptional frequency in the poem. It connotes the integration of different elements, the unity in variety which, it is suggested, is one of the central themes of the work as a whole, and its use here consequently has a good deal of ironic force. The section ends with a description of the greatest hero of all, the man who survives the battle, and who looks back to an even more heroic period:

> Perhaps some Doctor of tremendous Paunch,
> Awful and deep, a black Abyss of Drink,
> Out-lives them all, and from his bury'd Flock
> Retiring, full of Rumination sad,
> Laments the Weakness of these latter Times.
>
> (1744, 559–63)

This, then, is a mock-heroic set-piece which shows how completely Thomson could produce the style when he wanted. But more interesting, I think, are passages in which mock-heroic is used, almost in passing, to modify a different style.

When, early in *Spring*, for example, Thomson wants to give some advice on cures for a plague of insects, he begins with some straightforward instruction:

> the skillful Farmer Chaff
> And blazing Straw before his Orchard burns . . .
> Or scatters o'er the Blooms the pungent Dust
> Of Pepper . . .
>
> (1744, 127–32)

This is simple enough advice: it gives information and puts it in the simplest terms consistent with verse. The vocabulary is mundane. But Thomson modifies this dry instruction with a distinct touch of mock-heroic by describing the insects in lofty terms: they are

> A feble Race! yet oft
> The scared Sons of Vengeance! on whose Course
> Corrosive Famine waits, and kills the Year . . .
>
> (1744, 124–6)

When smoke from the burning straw reaches them

> ... all involv'd in Smoak, the latent Foe
> From every Cranny suffocated falls. (1744, 129–30)

The effect of this is two-edged. On the one hand Thomson is no doubt mildly amused at himself for writing about insects, and the mock-heroic contains elements of self-irony. On the other hand the fight against insects is really the heroic aspect of the farmer's life, and the implications of his fight affect the whole of society. Looked at from this point of view (and the stylistic changes force some such viewpoint upon the reader) the lines question whether the normal distinction between heroic and non-heroic is a valid one. Is the soldier the only hero or is the farmer engaged in just as strenuous a battle?

Finally, for a very different example of mock-heroic, it is worth looking at the Damon and Musidora episode in *Summer*. Damon, having accidentally seen Musidora undressing for a bathe, is overcome by the sight, but manages to summon up enough will-power to leave. Before doing so he leaves a note for Musidora in which he says that he is going to guard her from the 'licentious eye' of any further visitors. When Musidora discovers the note she writes in reply:

> 'Dear Youth! sole Judge of what these Verses mean,
> By Fortune too much favour'd, but by Love,
> Alas! not favour'd less, be still as now
> Discreet: the Time may come you need not fly.'
>
> (1744, 1359–62)

The critical question is clearly whether this is anything more than the sentimental and rather silly episode which it is generally held to be. But this attitude is possible perhaps partly because not enough attention is paid to Thomson's stylistic variety. One should notice, for example, how Thomson describes Damon's state of mind when he catches sight of Musidora undressing:

> Ah! then! not Paris on the piny Top
> Of Ida panted stronger, when aside
> The Rival-Goddesses the Veil divine
> Cast, unconfin'd, and gave him all their Charms,
> Than, Damon, thou; as from the snowy Leg,
> And slender Foot th'inverted Silk she drew ...
>
> (1744, 1296–1301)

Thomson's 'Seasons'

The reader is caught in a moment of genuine mock-heroic ambiguity. However beautiful Musidora may be it is absurd to compare her with Hera, Aphrodite and Athene. On the other hand, by the conventions of love, she is goddess-like to Damon. By a deft use of mock-heroic at this point Thomson is both achieving a detached, mildly-ironical, view of his subject and pointing to its real importance by forcing epic ideas into a relationship with everyday life.

It is characteristic of Thomson that this sort of sceptical re-evaluation should arise from his work. This brief examination of the elaborate system of juxtapositions, comparisons and contrasts, and different stylistic levels that make up *The Seasons* is sufficient to show that Thomson was prepared to present and come to terms with the complexity of his subject matter, and that he was not a man for easy answers. It is an essential part of his view of life that experience should seem sometimes humdrum, sometimes heroic, sometimes comic, sometimes bathetic. To this extent *The Seasons* is a singularly 'realistic' work – it does not present a single, simplified view of reality, but a complex of different views in which first one and then another interpretation of experience seems to predominate. The choice of the seasons as a framework enables Thomson to give full expression to this modal complexity while still maintaining his belief in an underlying pattern, order and harmony.

Notes

1. The first edition of *Winter* appeared in March 1726, and the second, enlarged and revised, in the following June. *Summer* was published in 1727, *Spring* in 1728, and *Autumn* appeared in 1730 as part of the first edition of the collected *Seasons*. The final *Hymn* was first published with the collected edition. Passages from the poem are quoted from *Thomson's Seasons: Critical Edition*, being a reproduction of the original texts, with all the various readings of the later editions, historically arranged, edited by Otto Zippel (1908)—Palaestra LXVI.
2. For a bibliography of *The Seasons* see 'A Check List of Editions of *The Seasons*' in Ralph Cohen *The Art of Discrimination* (1964), pp. 472–507.
3. William Hazlitt *Lectures on the English Poets* ('On Thomson and Cowper') (1818).
4. A. D. McKillop *The Background to Thomson's Seasons* (1942), p. 13.
5. Maren-Sofie Røstvig *The Happy Man, Vol. II: Studies in the Metamorphoses of a*

Classical Ideal 1700–1760 (1958), p. 285. Chapter Five of this work, 'The Smiling God' is devoted to Thomson.

6. The debt to Virgil has long been recognized, but it seems to me to have been inadequately taken into account in critical evaluations of the poem. However, see D. L. Durling's important discussion in *The Georgic Tradition in English Poetry* (1935).
7. For a discussion of *Rural Sports*, see Chapter V, pp. 141–63.
8. Patricia Meyer Spacks *The Varied God: A Critical Study of Thomson's 'Seasons'* (1959), p. 169.
9. Lucretius *De Rerum Natura*, with an English translation by W. H. D. Rouse (1937).
10. Ovid *Metamorphoses*, with an English translation by Frank Justus Miller, Two Volumes (1929).
11. *Richard II*, II, i, 61–3.
12. See Chapter V, pp. 156–163.
13. See the Argument prefixed to Book IV of Dryden's translation: 'Virgil has taken care to raise the subject of each Georgic'.
14. Ralph Cohen, *op. cit.*, p. 17.
15. For a full discussion of the idea of plenitude see A. O. Lovejoy *The Great Chain of Being* (1936).

Five

John Gay: 'Rural Sports' and 'Trivia'

The debt to Virgil that has been analysed in the previous chapter was at root an ideological one. The *Georgics* dealt with political and personal issues that were important also in the English Augustan world; suggested, without being in the least dogmatic, an overall interpretation of experience that gave a pattern to many aspects of life; and held out an ideal that seemed accessible in terms of the eighteenth-century English world. For Denham or Pope recognition of the relevance of Virgil's ideas was primary, and adaptation of the Georgic form secondary. A study of the development of *The Seasons* demonstrates that even Thomson showed only a gradual understanding of the way in which the ordered variety, the juxtaposition and balance, of Virgil's poem embodies the poet's sceptical yet firm view of life. And as it develops, this understanding springs from the high seriousness with which Thomson responds to Virgilian ideas.

With John Gay's *Rural Sports*, a poem that is sub-titled 'A Georgic' in its final version, the Virgilian influence is, at least in the first instance, more purely literary, perhaps more complex in its intermingling with other elements, certainly more elusive, but of great interest in showing how flexible the concept of 'kinds' was.

Rural Sports has its origin, like *Windsor Forest*, in the conclusion of the War of the Spanish Succession, and is, in its first form, a celebration of approaching peace.[1] The long negotiations which preceded the signing of the Treaty of Utrecht gave poets an opportunity to prepare work for the occasion, and the party differences which the prospect of peace aroused (the Whigs jealous in case the glorious victories of Marlborough should be forgotten; the Tories anxious to emphasize the futility of prolonging the struggle) gave every encouragement to write partisanly. Gay's work, however, although a product of this period and written fundamentally from a Tory point of view, is only very obliquely controversial. The topical situation only once becomes explicit when, after describing how remote England is from 'War's Alarms' Gay praises Queen Anne as the author of peace:[2]

> *Anna* who binds the Tyrant War in Chains,
> And Peace diffuses o'er the chearful Plains;
> In whom again the bright *Astrea* Reigns.
>
> (1713: 373-5)

The 'occasion' of the poem is never more obtrusive than this, and the theme of returning peace, and the political considerations that spring from it, are of much less importance here than in *Windsor Forest*. The poem is an account of Gay's retirement from the town, a description of the country, and especially the sports of fishing and hunting, and a celebration of rural life.

It is a less straightforward work to interpret than this definition would suggest, but one of the fortunate facts about *Rural Sports* is that it exists in two versions (published in 1713 and 1720), and that Gay's changes suggest how he wished the poem to be read. In the first version the structure of the work was determined by a double time scheme, the cycle of the seasons and the passage of a day from sunrise to sunset. It is Spring when the poet retires to the country at the beginning of the poem, and he progresses in his imagination to late Autumn introducing appropriate subjects as he goes. Similarly it is early morning when he makes his way into the fields near the beginning and at the end night 'in silent state begins to rise'. Gay's themes are varied, but this double temporal framework unobtrusively controls the sequences of the 1713 *Rural Sports* and successfully imposes a pattern on material as diverse as the techniques of fishing and Queen Anne's statesmanship. In the 1720 version the material, although in itself substantially unaltered, was rearranged and in the process some violence was done to the articulation of the original work. The changes were announced by the division of the poem into two books and the addition of the sub-title 'A Georgic'.

But this was the development of a generic relationship that had already been latent in the first form of the poem where the reader was constantly invited to regard the countryside from a Virgilian point of view. At the very beginning of the poem, for example, Gay addresses Pope as one of those who 'the sweets of Rural Life have known', attacks town life and says that he intends to follow his friend's example and retire to the country. His picture of metropolitan corruptions is similar to Virgil's in the *O fortunatos agricolas* passage:

> Faction embroils the World; and ev'ry Tongue
> Is fraught with Malice and with Scandal hung ...
> Each Rival *Machiavel* with Envy burns,
> And Honesty forsakes them All by turns;
> Whilst Culmny upon each Party's thrown,
> Which Both abhor, and Both alike disown.
> Thus have I 'midst the Brawls of factious Strife,
> Long undergone the Drudgery of Life ...
> (1713, 17–26)

Apart from Virgilian echoes there are probably references here also to Horace's Second Epode and to Juvenal's Third Satire, but Gay makes the predominantly Virgilian debt clear in the last lines of his introduction:

> My Muse shall rove through flow'ry Meads and
>   Plains ...
>
> And the same Road ambitiously pursue,
> Frequented by the Mantuan Swain, and You.
> (1713, 37–40)

Later the retirement theme is introduced again with a passage which draws on Virgil's general attitude. Gay describes the happiness of the 'Rural Maid' and contrasts it with the fever and fret experienced by a 'Courtly Dame'. The country girl is content to spend her time in 'chearful labour'; she enjoys natural health and beauty and, in lines which seem to be a direct echo of Virgil, Gay writes of her domestic happiness:[3]

> With secret Joy she sees her little Race
> Hang on her Breast, and her small Cottage grace.
> (1713, 265–6)

By contrast the town-bred lady puts all her pleasure in the ostentation of a 'glowing equipage' and 'midnight masquerades', and as a result suffers from spleen, jealousy, fading beauty and loss of health. At this point Gay makes direct and extended acknowledgement to Virgil. In the full heat of summer, he says, he retires to the shade of woods and settles down near a stream to read in peace:

> Here on the Mossy Couch my Limbs I lay,
> And taste an Ev'ning at the Noon of Day.
>
> (1713, 279-80)

He reads the *Georgics*, and over the next twenty-five lines he gives in miniature a complete survey of the four books of Virgil's poem. It is characteristic of Gay that his contact with the countryside should provoke a literary reaction. And when he turns from the literary experience back to the countryside itself he is in a Virgilian mood, prepared to reflect upon the causes of things. The heat of the day has passed; Gay sets the evening scene, and in so doing he prepares himself and the reader for meditation:

> Engag'd in Thought, to *Neptune*'s bounds I stray
> To take my Farewell of the parting Day; ...
>
> Here Pensive I behold the fading Light,
> And in the distant Billows lose my Sight.
>
> (1713, 327-34)

The speculation is of a kind associated with Virgil – of 'heaven's pathways, the stars, the sun's many lapses, the moon's many labours' – and it leads to a sense of religious exaltation:

> Millions of Worlds hang in the spacious Air,
> Which round their Suns their Annual Circles steer.
> Sweet Contemplation elevates my Sense
> While I survey the Works of Providence.
>
> (1713, 339-42)

In 1713 it was already clear then that Gay's response to the countryside was guided by the Virgilian model. What happens in the 1720 version of the poem is that the Virgilian elements are given a more co-ordinated significance by being placed in a framework which has a closer structural relationship than the earlier version to the *Georgics*.

The change has been analysed in detail by John M. Aden who demonstrates how thoroughgoing the revision was.[4] In the 1713 version, for example, the description of haymaking in the middle of the poem serves to introduce reflections on the happiness of the 'rural maid'. In 1720 these reflections were held back in order to follow the section in praise of country life which was itself moved to the end of the poem, and these alterations helped to make for a much more emphatically Georgic conclusion to the work. At the same time the opening sections gave a new emphasis to Virgilian features, and the division into books, together with the introduction of a motto from Nemesianus, made the genre unmistakable. The reader cannot help wondering why Gay chose to make this substantial alteration in a poem which already possessed its own unity, that of the temporal framework. The reasons can be discovered, perhaps, by concentrating attention on the characteristic excellence of *Rural Sports* and considering how far Gay might have felt that the Virgilian model provided the most appropriate vehicle for this particular kind of achievement. For, despite the changes, the most striking feature of *Rural Sports* remained the same, namely a personal note in the style, an exceptional easiness of tone. Just as one may locate the critical problem of *The Seasons* in passages on commercial expansion, so the central interest of *Rural Sports* is to be found in the individuality of its style.

As Gay addresses Pope in the opening lines he might be venturing on a familiar epistle:

> You, who the sweets of rural life have known,
> Despise th'ungrateful hurry of the Town ...
>
> (1720, 1–2)

and as he contrasts Pope's happy and retired country life with his own town-bound existence, Gay's inflection becomes individual and correspondingly hard to characterize. The following passage is from the 1720 version:

> But I, who ne'er was bless'd by Fortune's hand,
> Nor brighten'd plough-shares in paternal land,
> Long in the noisie town, have been immur'd,
> Respired its smoak, and all its cares endur'd,
> Where news and politicks divide mankind ...
> Fatigu'd at last, a calm retreat I chose,
> And sooth'd my harrass'd mind with sweet repose,
> Where fields and shades, and the refreshing clime,
> Inspire the sylvan song, and prompt my rhime.
> My muse shall rove through flow'ry meads and plains,
> And deck with Rural Sports her native strains,

> And the same road ambitiously pursue,
> Frequented by the *Mantuan* swain, and you.
>
> (1720, 9–30)

The tone eludes adequate definition, but it is obviously important, perhaps the most important thing about the lines. In other words the relationship between the poet and his subject-matter is felt to be more significant than the subject-matter itself. When Gay says, for example, that he has never 'brightened plough-shares in paternal land' the actual 'statement' is not very serious. We learn that Gay has never been a ploughboy, but it is more important that the expression introduces a hint of comical surprise: the alliteration and the artificial brilliance of the image combine to suggest that he is regarding rather mockingly his decision to write a country poem, and trying to establish a viable relationship with his topic. And this sense is reinforced by the self-conscious latinisms of the diction, particularly in a couplet which was considerably revised for the 1720 edition. In 1713 Gay wrote:

> Have long been in the noisie Town immur'd,
> Respir'd it's Smoak, and all it's Toils endur'd ...
>
> (1713, 11–12)

Already the weight of attention is on the words themselves and this modifies in a curious way the criticism of urban life that is ostensibly being offered. 'Immur'd' and 'respir'd' strike a note of affectionate comedy (the languidness of a theatre star faced by an 'appalling' crowd of autograph hunters) modifying rather than reinforcing the apparent sense. The 1720 version introduces a parallel rhythmic effect, an assured, somewhat lazy rhythm counteracting the actual complaint and thus softening it:

> Long in the noisie town have been immur'd. . . .
>
> (1720, 11)

The style and the subject are counterpointed. And when Gay reaches the countryside and adopts an attitude of rococo pastoralism we have the same sense that relationships are being explored and attitudes tested:

> My muse shall rove through flow'ry meads and plains,
> And deck with Rural Sports her native strains.
>
> (1720, 27–8)

John Gay

At every turn the distinctiveness of Gay's treatment is felt, even in passages which are very largely conventional like, for example, the description of evening:.

> Or when the ploughman leaves the task of day,
> And trudging homeward whistles on the way;
> When the big-udder'd cows with patience stand,
> Waiting the stroakings of the damsel's hand;
> No warbling chears the woods; the feather'd choir
> To court kind slumbers to their sprays retire;
> When no rude gale disturbs the sleeping trees,
> Nor aspen leaves confess the gentlest breeze;
> Engag'd in thought, to *Neptune*'s bounds I stray,
> To take my farewel of the parting day . . .
>
> (1720, 91–100)

In a sense this is a paradigm of what we expect to find in eighteenth-century country poetry. The poet is led by the atmosphere of evening to meditate, and when it comes the meditation is guided by wonder at the harmony of the universe:

> Sweet contemplation elevates my sense,
> While I survey the works of providence.
>
> (1720, 113–14)

There is a characteristic Miltonic echo in the description of the ploughman (in 1713 Gay had written 'the Lab'rer') which is presumably intended to recall *L'Allegro*:

> While the Plowman neer at hand,
> Whistles ore the Furrow'd Land . . .   (63–4)

The passage contains pattern examples of poetic diction – the 'feather'd choir', the 'rude gale'. Yet working against all this there are the 'big-udder'd cows', a piece of direct description which stands in contrast to the pastoralism of the surrounding couplets and which calls attention, deliberately and purposively, to the artificiality of its context. There is nothing so violent as a deflation, but Gay does make the reader aware that different possible attitudes are being held in balance and that he is himself carefully adjusting his approach.

These passages from *Rural Sports* suggest that from the beginning Gay was establishing a relationship by such stylistic means be-

The English Georgic

tween his own personality and aspects of the external world. In a passage on fishing we find repeated some of the characteristics that have already been observed, but set now in a more complex framework. The passage forms ll. 159–190, of the 1720 version of the poem:

> You must not ev'ry worm promiscuous use,
> Judgement will tell thee proper bait to chuse;
> The worm that draws a long immod'rate size
> The trout abhors, and the rank morsel flies;
> And if too small, the naked fraud's in sight,
> And fear forbids, while hunger does invite.
> Those baits will best reward the fisher's pains,
> Whose polish'd tails a shining yellow stains:
> Cleanse them from filth, to give a tempting gloss,
> Cherish the sully'd reptile race with moss;
> Amid the verdant bed they twine, they toil,
> And from their bodies wipe their native soil.
> But when the sun displays his glorious beams,
> And shallow rivers flow with silver streams,
> Then the deceit the scaly breed survey,
> Bask in the sun, and look into the day.
> You now a more delusive art must try,
> And tempt their hunger with the curious fly.
> To frame the little animal, provide
> All the gay hues that wait on female pride,
> Let nature guide thee; sometimes golden wire
> The shining bellies of the fly require;
> The peacock's plumes thy tackle must not fail,
> Nor the dear purchase of the sable's tail.
> Each gaudy bird some slender tribute brings,
> And lends the growing insect proper wings:
> Silks of all colours must their aid impart,
> And ev'ry fur promote the fisher's art.
> So the gay lady, with expensive care,
> Borrows the pride of land, of sea, and air;
> Furs, pearls, and plumes, the glittering thing displays,
> Dazzles our eyes, and easy hearts betrays.

The effect of these lines is many-sided. To some extent Gay is simply versifying useful information, and a study of seventeenth-century fishing manuals shows both how closely his advice followed accepted practice, and also how far his delight in the picturesque details of his subject echoes a common tradition. Gay's affectionate account of bait (not, *prima facie*, one of the most promising subjects for affectionate treatment) is something that is often found in seventeenth-century fishing manuals. An almost heraldic vividness is communicated, for example, by Walton's exact description of the flies' colouring:[5]

> First a black palmer ribbed with silver. Secondly a black palmer ribbed with an orange-tawny body. Thirdly, a black-palmer made all of black. Fourthly a red palmer ribbed with gold. Fifthly a red palmer mixed with an orange tawny body . . .[6]

Advice to scour bait with moss is also common. It is found in Walton again, for example, and also, as early as 1613, in John Dennys's *Secrets of Angling*, a poem that we shall return to in more detail shortly:

> The Pearch, the Tench, and Eele, doe rather bite
> At great red worms, in Field or garden bred,
> That have been scoured in moss and Fennel rough,
> To rid their filth and make them hard and tough . . .
>
> (II, 332–6)

But sound though the advice is, the permanent appeal of the lines obviously does not lie in their practicality. Gay gains his particular effect by adapting a traditional body of fishing lore, and giving it a comic dimension through the use of epic vocabulary and syntax, and through a specific Miltonic reference.

> The worm that draws a long immod'rate size
> The trout abhors . . .

is good advice, but on the literary level the language is more appropriate to serpents than to worms, and the line

> Cherish the sully'd reptile race with moss

is presumably intended to suggest particularly Milton's serpent who was also made more attractive in order to be the more tempting:

> not with indented wave,
> Prone on the ground, as since, but on his rear,

> Circular base of rising folds ... his head
> Crested aloft, and carbuncle his eyes;
> With burnished neck of verdant gold ...
> ... Pleasing was his shape
> And lovely.   (*Paradise Lost*, IX, 496–504)

The disproportion between the arch-corrupter of the world and bait for fishing is comic, but not inappropriately so. Gay's theme at this point is temptation, and the trappings of temptation are the same for the trout as they were for Eve. The comedy implies a single vision of life, is ultimately unifying rather than disruptive, comprehensive rather than exclusive. And because of this unifying tendency the apparent enormities of the language and imagery at this point are acceptable. The moral attitude which could comprehend an artificial fly and female beauty in a single unit is paralleled by a sort of theologico-literary unity which comprehends what are at first sight the widest possible ranges of experience. And the pleasure lies in perceiving unity emerge (within a framework of comedy) from apparent diversity.

It is perhaps this sense of unity that provokes an interest, akin to pathetic fallacy, in the character and response of the fish itself, a quality which appears in the couplet:

> He greedily sucks in the twining bait,
> And tugs and nibbles the fallacious meat.
>   (1720, I, 153-4)

Gay momentarily puts himself in the place of the fish – first voracious and soon deceived – and again the effect is to achieve a more comprehensive vision of the subject than might at first be looked for. But, more important, it is this sympathetic view of the natural world (and the assumption that it is guided by human motives) that enables Gay to exploit the moral and satirical implications of his subject.

Instructions on how to make artificial flies lead, for example, to a moral application which in its context seems entirely unforced:

> Silks of all colours must their aid impart,
> And every fur promote the fisher's art

and this leads directly to the moral point, the comment on female dress:

> So the gay lady, with expensive care
> Borrows the pride of land, of sea and air,
> Furs, pearls and plumes, the glittering thing displays,
> Dazzles our eyes, and lazy hearts betrays.

Again Gay is well within the tradition in his interpretation of his material. In the seventeenth century Walton had found it natural to use fishes to point a moral and adorn a tale:

> I pray hearken to what Du Bartas sings, for the hearing of such conjugal faithfulness will be musick to all chaste ears, and therefore I pray hearken to what Du Bartas sings of the mullet.[7]

One of the important things about the mullet indeed is that it provides an improving and illuminating analogue to human conduct. *The Compleat Angler* has a similar (although more incidental) passage on the spots of the salmon. The spots of the salmon give them

> such an addition to natural beauty as, I think, was never given to any women by the artificial paints and patches in which they so much pride themselves in this age . . .[8]

a direct piece of social criticism not unworthy of the *Spectator*. 'Go to the ant, thou sluggard, consider her ways and be wise' was, until comparatively recently, a Biblical injunction that was taken more directly and on a more literal level than is now easily understandable. And the use of animal analogies to serve moral points is obviously very common. It is the basis of the fable, it was a constant resource of Euphuistic prose, and it formed an essential complement to natural history. Heresbachius' *Four Books of Husbandry* (translated by Barnabe Googe in 1577) for example, has the following comment on the bee, admittedly one of the more easily and commonly moralized of insects:[9]

> It seemeth the almighty and most excellent majesty, hath of all other specially created this little poor creature, for the benefit and commodity of man; by whom, beside the commodity of the honey and wax that they both make, we might both take example to spend our lives in virtuous and commendable exercises.

It is not simply that the bee can be *used* to illustrate a moral point. Heresbachius goes much further: the bee has been created *in order* to provide man with an example of 'virtuous and commendable exercises'. In consequence there is nothing far-fetched about pointing the moral: one is simply making apparent an inherent quality of the object itself, a quality as essential to the nature of the object as fieriness is to the sun or whiteness to ivory.

It is this kind of moral parallel and exhortation that lies behind Gay's mildly satirical passage on women in the section of *Rural Sports* which deals with the artificial fly. Parallelism between the animal and human kingdoms was a customary part of natural history: indeed it was one of the functions of natural history to provide a repository of moral exampla. Consequently Gay may reasonably be expected to make such parallelism a part of his work. What is impressive is not the moral itself, but the ease and lightness, and the ambiguity, with which it is introduced:

> Each gaudy bird some slender tribute brings,
> And lends the growing insect proper wings:
> Silks of all colours must their aid impart,
> And ev'ry fur promote the fisher's art.
> So the gay lady, with expensive care,
> Borrows the pride of land, of sea and air;
> Furs, pearls and plumes, the glittering thing displays,
> Dazzles our eyes, and easy hearts betrays.

The lady's qualities are not wholly bad: one of the things that she ought to do is to 'dazzle our eyes' and insensibly to betray 'easy hearts' into falling in love with her. But the incongruity of the parallel and the key-word *pride*

> Burrows the *pride* of land, of sea, and air

and perhaps also some ambiguity in the phrase 'the *glittering* thing displays' introduces a satirical level which measures the lady's 'right' conduct against a severer standard by which it appears futile and meretricious. It is a characteristically mock-heroic effect, which includes a typical ambiguity of sympathy. And there is an additional comic level of incongruity introduced by Gay's refusal to keep within the traditional framework of moral reference which has just been outlined. When Walton says, 'I pray hearken to what Du Bartas sings of the mullet . . .' he is being straightforwardly serious and the elevation of language is intended simply to establish the seriousness. But with Gay the attitude is more complex and the response evoked from the reader is a mixture of conflicting emotions, sympathies and antipathies.

It is when one comes to consider the development of this more complex attitude that Gay's characterization of his poem as a *Georgic* becomes particularly interesting. At first sight the generic claim seems a loose one. Gay's poem has little to do with farming and the passages on agriculture that do occur are descriptive rather than didactic. But the statement that the poem is 'A Georgic' is very specifically made, and I think its meaning was a precise one for Gay.

The sources considered so far have shown attitudes similar to Gay's (and there seems little doubt that he was acquainted with Walton and other writers of fishing manuals) but these books obviously have no generic significance. A much more important work from this point of view and one that has already been mentioned is John Dennys' *Secrets of Angling*, published exactly a century before *Rural Sports*. Dennys' work begins with a clear statement of his didactic intentions:[10]

> Of Angling and the Art thereof I sing...

and an invocation to the water-nymphs to lend 'aid and power' to his verses, and much of the poem contains versified advice of a practical kind. It offers pedestrian information on such topics as the best hair to use for making lines, and the verse is sometimes extremely dull:

> Neither of mare nor gelding let it be;
> Nor of the hireling jade that bears the pack;
> But of some lusty horse or courser free,
> Whose bushy tail upon the ground doth track...
>
> (I, 66–9)

If there were nothing more vital than this the poem might be left to languish, but Dennys is not only concerned with practicalities. He has widened the scope of his poem by including many Georgic motifs which show that he has a sophisticated literary purpose as well as a practical interest in sport. He includes, for example, a fairly long passage on the origins of angling which is clearly parallel to Virgil's passage on the beginnings of husbandry.

Dennys gives an Ovidian account of Deucalion and Pyrrha, and then tells how Deucalion was faced by a world food problem when the population had been replenished after the flood. He invented the art of angling as a practical utilization of existing resources. At first the art was in a state of simplicity appropriate to the age of gold:

>   The fish as yet had felt but little smart
>   And were to bite more eager, apt and bold...
> (I, 429–30)

But gradually the fish began to fear man: more and more guile was needed for successful fishing, until in the end:

>   the Iron Age drew near,
>   Of all the rest the hardest and most scant:
>   Then lines were made of silk and subtle hair;
>   And rods of lightest cane and hazel plant;
>   And hooks of hardest steel invented were,
>   That neither skill nor workmanship did want;
>   And so this Art did in the end attain
>   Unto that state where now it doth remain.
> (I, 449–56)

Starting, in other words, from a surprising piece of mythology (since the Deucalion flood is a significantly post-lapsarian event), Dennys superimposes on it a thoroughly Georgic interpretation of the rise of an art.

There are also sections on such characteristic Georgic themes as the 'best times and seasons to angle' which are close in intention to Virgil's advice in Book I on days for planting, ploughing and so on, but it is the appearance of a fully developed *rerum cognoscere causas* passage that is the most unexpected and therefore the most prominent Georgic motif at this early date. Opening in the appropriate manner with lines in praise of retirement, Dennys begins by turning his back satirically on the life of the town:

>   Indeed it is a life of lesser pain
>   To sit at play from noon till it be night;
>   And then from night till it be noon again;
>   With damned oaths, pronounced in despite,
>   For little cause and every trifling vein:

John Gay

> To curse, to brawl, to quarrel and to fight;
>   To pack the cards, and with some coz'ning trick,
>   His fellow's purse of all his coin to pick.
>   (I, 265–72)

His own wish is for a more innocent life:

> O let me rather on the pleasant brink
> Of Tyne and Trent possess some dwelling-place;
> Where I may see my quill and cork down sink
> With eager bite of barbel, bleek or dace ...
>   (I, 281–4)

Up to this point the mood arises naturally from the subject (given a moment for reflection), but the next line is less automatic

> And on the world and his Creator think,   (285)

while the stanza which occurs after twenty-four lines of description of the countryside is a complete anticipation of the physico-theological attitudes which were to be so extremely popular a century later:

> All these and many more of His creation
> That made the heavens, the Angler oft doth see;
> And takes therein no little delectation
> To think how strange and wonderful they be;
> Framing thereof an inward contemplation
> To set his thoughts from other fancies free.
>   And whiles he looks on these with joyful eye,
>   His mind is rapt above the starry sky.
>   (I, 321–8)

The combination of practical instruction, moral reflection and philosophical speculation in a passage which is completely Virgilian in inspiration – is very close, despite the early date, to the mood of *Rural Sports*, and it seems extremely probable that Gay had Dennys in mind when he came to write. Certainly, in the original version of *Rural Sports*, the juxtapositions are the same. Description of rural happiness leads to rejection of the ostentation and bustle of the town and later to contemplation of the stars and to the hope that

> My soul should overflow in Songs of Praise,
> And my Creator's Name inspire my Lays.
>
> (1713, 347–8)

And certainly, in Dennys we find, for the first time in English, the adaptation of important elements of the Georgic form to country activities other than farming.

Gay could have used *Secrets of Angling* as a generic model, (whether he did or not it remains as a remarkably forward-looking poem to come from such a minor writer), but he must have been even more aware of the authority of various post-classical precedents for similar developments of the Georgic form.

In the second century, for example. Oppian had written his *Halieutica*, a work dealing both with the natural history of fishes and the ways of catching them, and we know from the translation of this work produced by William Diaper and John Jones, published in 1722, that it was interpreted by some eighteenth-century readers in a way that would have made it very relevant to Gay when he was writing his account of fishing. In an introduction to the translation Jones discusses the moral advantages that can be drawn from natural history, and he says:

> Those Faculties in the Souls of Brutes, which bear an Analogy to the Will and the Passions, and enable them to act with a resemblance of the Virtues and Vices of Mankind, furnish the poet with frequent occasions of insinuating the Precepts of Morality after the most easy and persuasive manner.[11]

The use of analogy in this way for a serious moral purpose is frequent in Oppian himself, as, for example, in lines where he discusses the instinctive nature of parental affection:

> Not men alone their lonely Offspring prize
> Sweet as their lives and dearer than their Eyes;
> Unreasoning Souls the same propensions move,
> Man can claim no prerogative from love
> One instinct runs through all.
>
> (Diaper's translation, I, 1181–5)

And Mrs. Broughton has shown, in her edition of Diaper's *Works*, how enthusiastically the translator used these opportunities.[12]

She points out, for example, that Oppian's statement that the Pilchard and the Shad 'run to the long shores, ever changing to a strange path like wanderers' is added to by Diaper:[13]

> They soon grow weary when they once enjoy,
> And Pleasures will, as soon as tasted, cloy.
>
> (I, 392–3)

Diaper's interpretation of Oppian is parallel to Dryden's interpretation of the *Georgics* in its interest in the moral and spiritual aspects of animal behaviour. For Gay the *Halieutica* would have been a valuable example of a poem which derived from the *Georgics*, extended Virgil's subject-matter in a useful direction, and gave a sanction to the kind of stylistic experiments that were to underlie the most vital sections of *Rural Sports*.

It was when he turned to post-classical hunting poetry, however, that Gay found his most fully developed generic sources. His own hunting section is little more than 100 lines long but in it he deals briefly with coursing, snaring, shooting, hawking and hunting with hounds. As far as it goes his advice is precise and practical. He writes about the best time and place for shooting, for example, and warns against rainy, misty weather. But despite the practical appearance of the writing Gay is not mainly concerned to instruct. He uses the hunting theme to develop several other interests, some of them involving implicit criticism of the sport. The huntsman, for example, should be careful not to 'render all the ploughman's labour vain' by spoiling the harvest. There is a strong humanitarian note in a description of the death of a hare, and Gay's ironical comment involves a temporary critical detachment (analogous to that of Pope in the fowling section of *Windsor Forest*):

> She flies, he stretches, now with nimble bound
> Eager he presses on, but overshoots his ground;
> She turns, he winds, and soon regains the way,
> Then tears with goary mouth the screaming prey.
> What various sport does rural life afford!
> What unbought dainties heap the wholesome board!
>
> (1720, 295–300)

This identification with the victim is common. The 'ill-fated' partridge leaves the '*friendly* shelter' of the undergrowth. The death of the woodcock is pathetically described with an emphatic syntactic repetition which gives a perhaps exaggerated sense of pathos:

> The wood resounds: he wheels, he drops, he dies ...
> (1720, 350)

The lark, attracted from the sky by a flashing mirror, is a similarly sad and sympathetic figure. Finally, Gay returns to the death of a hare, hunted now with a full pack, where the emotional demand is for a sympathetic response to the plight of an attractive animal, rather than for any exaltation at the success of the huntsman.

We have seen that in his fishing section Gay was extremely eclectic in his use of sources, mingling the literary and the vernacular to produce a very individual tone. The use of an epigraph from Nemesianus in the 1720 version gives a clear indication of the kind of tradition that he was following in the hunting section. In dealing with hunting Gay could have looked back to a number of poems in which similar material had been treated within the formal framework of a Georgic. Indeed the modification of the *Georgics* in this direction is a natural one. The third book of the *Georgics* deals with the breeding of animals, and the techniques that Virgil uses there can be made appropriate to some of the material of hunting – for example, the breeding and training of dogs, or a digressive account of the loves of wild beasts. Developing these hints late Latin literature had already gone a long way towards using hunting themes in a Virgilian manner.

Grattius, a contemporary of Ovid, has in *Cynegeticon* several passages which closely parallel sections of Virgil's poem.[14] The poet begins by saying that he proposes to sing the gifts of the gods. At one time men lived in a rough, uncivilized state. They were without training or skill – 'erat error in omni' – but afterwards Reason came to their aid, and they were able to avoid violence and work skilfully:

> From Reason came all their help in life: the true order of things shone forth: men learned out of arts to produce kindred arts: from Reason came the undoing of mad violence.
> (7–9)

This Lucretian-Virgilian attitude to progress parallels the account in *Georgics* I of the rise of agriculture and the useful arts. Later there is a section on the choice and care of hounds, and in particular some lines (II. 263 ff) on the mating of dogs, which owe a good deal to *Georgics* III. The signs of well-matched mates, the way to distinguish the most promising puppy in a litter, and even the tone in which the love of animals is treated

> primi complexus, dulcissima prima voluptas:
> hunc veneri dedit impatiens natura furorem (283-4)
>
> The first unions, the first pleasure is sweetest: such frenzy has uncontrolled nature given to love

all recall the Georgic treatment of a similar subject. Later (II. 497 ff) there is a passage on the characteristics of a good horse which is similarly reminiscent, and finally (II. 366 ff) some lines dealing with a plague amongst dogs:

> It is a serious plague, too deep for the treatments mentioned, when hidden causes have spread the malady through all the bodies of the pack, and the damage is only discovered in its final consummation. Then has pestilence been let loose, and by contagion deaths have come upon the pack at large, and the great host alike perishes beneath an infection that falls on all. (366-72)

Here again there seems to be a reference back both to *Georgics* III and beyond that to *De Rerum Natura*.

These passages serve in themselves to make the *Cynegeticon* more than a manual on hunting and to place the work in a particular literary setting. One of the characteristic features of the *Georgics* as we have seen is the breadth of its implications, and it is the function of the Georgic elements in *Cynegeticon* to widen the implications of the hunting theme.

Some two hundred and fifty years later Nemesianus achieved a similar broadening in his *Cynegetica*. He deals with many aspects of hunting (the breeding of dogs; the training of puppies; the illnesses of dogs and their remedies; the care of horses; the management of nets, etc.), but he also has sections which are less immediately practical, and which link his work again with the Virgilian treatment of country themes.

He begins by emphasizing the newness of his subject matter (although he was not in fact, of course, being entirely original), and deploring the choice of conventional subject matter:

> For ere now who has not sung of Niobe saddened by
> death upon death of her children?   (15–16)

The story of Niobe and of other legends has been treated to excess by the poets. In contrast

> ... we search the glades, the green tracts, the open
> plains, swiftly coursing here and there o'er all the fields,
> eager to catch varied quarries with docile hound...
>   (48–50)

Like Virgil, Nemesianus is excited to think that he is treating a comparatively unworn theme. It is, in fact, characteristic of the Georgic writer to assert that he is escaping from conventional subject matter.

Nemesianus links his hunting subject matter with two other themes in a typically Virgilian manner. One is that of political panegyric:

> Hereafter I will gird myself with fitter lyre to record
> your triumphs, you gallant sons of deified Carus, and will
> sing of our sea-board beneath the twin boundaries of our
> world, and of the subjugation, by the brothers' divine
> power, of nations that drink from Rhine or Tigris or from
> the distant source of the Arar or look upon the wells of
> the Nile at their birth...
> The golden standards gleam radiant afar with their
> purple drapery, and a light breeze waves the folds of the
> ferocious dragons.   (63–85)

This praise of leading political figures mingled with patriotic pleasure in the achievements of Roman arms is a conventional imitation of Virgil's attitude to Augustus and his victories.

Secondly, Nemesianus appropriately enough introduces a section in praise of country life

> Come hither then with me whosoever, smitten with
> the love of the chase dost condemn lawsuits and panic-
> stricken turmoil, and dost shun the din in cities, and
> the clash of war, or pursuest no spoils on the greedy surge
> of the deep.   (99–102)

The link with Virgil's *O fortunatos* passage is clear: country occupations are given a pronounced moral value and contrasted with the immorality of town-life. The passage is a brief one in Nemesianus perhaps because of the weight of the tradition that is being called in support of the idea. It is an attitude which can be referred to but which does not need to be established entirely from the beginning. But, as with the political passage referred to above, it serves to widen very considerably the implications of the poem as a whole, to set the hunting theme in a much wider context, and above all to relate the poem to a specific genre.

Writing at about the same time as Nemesianus, Oppian, probably, it is now thought, an imitator of the author of *Halieutica*, produced a *Cynegetica* which is much more elaborate than anything that had gone before.[15] It is in four books and contains a good deal of natural history as well as advice on the practical side of hunting. Like Nemesianus Oppian, though with even less justification, claims primacy for his work as he makes Artemis bid him to

> tread a rugged path, which never yet hath
> any mortal trodden with his song.   (20–1)

He renounces warlike themes – 'I will not sing of wars, not of Ares' works most evil', and he accepts instead Artemis' bidding to 'sing the battles of wild beasts and hunting men'. But having undertaken this theme Oppian uses every opportunity to enlarge it and to digress beyond the strictly practical limits of his subject matter. He digresses, for example, on the chastity of horses in Book I, and in Book II there is a section on the origins of hunting followed by a lyrical passage on the pleasures of the chase:

> How sweet the sleep upon the flowers in springtime;
> how sweet in summer the low couch in some cave; what
> delight for hunters to break their fast amid the rocks and
> what joy attends them when they cull for themselves the
> flower of honied fruit.   (II, 30–4)

Book III digresses on the loves of the beasts, mainly giving expression to a marvellous view of natural history and including such wonders as the idea that Hyenas are subject to changes of sex:

> This marvel also I have heard about the spotted Hyenas,
> to wit that the male and female change year by year, and
> one is now a weak-eyed bridegroom all eager to mate

and anon appears as a lady bride, a bearer of children
and a godly mother. (III, 288–92)

At the beginning of Book IV Oppian ostensibly turns single-mindedly to his central theme:

So many are the species of wild beasts, so many in the shady wood their nuptial loves and companionships, their hates and deadly feuds, their couches in the wild. Now let us sing the great business of the toilsome hunters. (IV,1–4)

There is a fine description of a lion-hunt, but this immediately leads to a long and involved digression on the mythological origin of tigers. The tendency all the time is to expand by using the implications of the subject-matter to the full.

It is clear from this brief account that classical poems on hunting were by no means merely practical handbooks. The various opportunities which the subject offered for expansion were eagerly used and the digressive sections of these poems are as important as the apparently more central didactic parts. In the case of Gratius and Nemesianus the direction of the expansion seems to have been directly influenced by the *Georgics*.

Gay's interest in Nemesianus at least, is explicit because he takes the epigraph for the 1720 edition of *Rural Sports* from *Cynegeticon*:

– securi proelia ruris,
Pandimus.

We sing the carefree battles of the country.

It is true that there is an important difference between Gay and the writers we have just been discussing: whereas Gratius and his successors were writing hunting poetry which is influenced by formal and thematic features of the *Georgics* Gay is writing a poem about rural sports and about country life in general with a hunting section.

Nevertheless it seems clear that when Gay called *Rural Sports* 'a Georgic' he had in mind not only Virgil, but the post-classical tradition of hunting poetry that had already freely adapted the Virgilian model to its own purposes. At least he felt free to think generically in Georgic terms because of the post-classical tradition. And the value of this tradition for Gay was not merely that it dealt with the country material that he proposed as a subject, but that within the tradition he could find precedents for the particular combination of interests that he had. From the beginning *Rural Sports* was a poem which expressed, as we have seen, complex attitudes towards its subject-matter. The countryside was at once described and idealized, treated speculatively and practically, regarded as the source of moral exempla and also of mock-heroic. In the 1713 version Gay expressed these diverse interests and attitudes through a structure which, successful though it was in many ways, could not, because of its individuality, give any clear indication of what character the work might be expected to have. The great advantage of the 1720 version was that it established a right relationship with the reader from the start. That is to say that the changes were dictated by an idea of decorum which involved having respect for the expectations of the audience.

In the other poem which is to be discussed in this chapter, *Trivia* (1716) there was no need for a revised version. The generic relationship is made clear from the beginning, but, as with *Rural Sports*, the significance of the genre is that it allows the fullest expression to Gay's preoccupations, and at the same time establishes a right relationship with the reader.

Gay's *Trivia, or the Art of Walking the Streets of London* is one of the very few poems in English to express sensuous pleasure in town life, and indeed it is hard to think of any writer who has shown a greater responsiveness to urban details. The sensitivity of Gay's experience of the town appears constantly. It can be felt in a single line which describes the Mall in autumn:

> When all the *Mall* in leafy ruin lies   (I, 27)

where the root meaning of ruin (*ruina:* a tumbling or falling down, a fall) combines with the derived sense to give a finely condensed impression of the mixed beauty and desolation of the autumn scene. More obviously there is the description of the fish-stalls in the second book where, in a very brilliant and almost heraldic way, the visual qualities of the display are caught:

> When fishy stalls with double store are laid;
> The golden-belly'd carp, the broad-finn'd maid,

> Red-speckeld trouts, the salmon's silver joul,
> The joynted lobster, and unscaly soale . . .
>
> (II, 413–16)

And this sensuous response is evoked not only, as it obviously very easily may be, by the melancholy of autumn avenues or the brilliant colours of a market, but also by quite ordinary town sights. Early in the first book we find Gay affecting to despise the degeneration of modern life with its increase in carriages and the decline of walking. He writes of Venice, praising the complete absence of traffic, and goes on to say that at one time London was in the same happy state. Luxury was unknown, coaches were not to be found, and then:

> the proud lady trip'd along the town,
> And tuck'd up petticoats secur'd her gown,
> Her rosie cheek with distant visits glow'd,
> And exercise unartful charms bestow'd;
> But since in braided gold her foot is bound,
> And a long trailing manteau sweeps the ground,
> Her shoe disdains the street; the lazy fair
> With narrow step affects a limping air.
> Now gaudy pride corrupts the lavish age,
> And the streets flame with glaring equipage;
> The tricking gamester insolently rides,
> With *Loves* and *Graces* on his chariot's sides;
> In sawcy state the griping broker sits,
> And laughs at honesty, and trudging wits . . .
>
> (I, 105–18)

But one is immediately aware of a contrast between the surface sense and the actual impression that the lines make. Gay says that there was once a Golden Age, before the days of vehicular transport, when people were kept healthy because they had to walk everywhere, but that nowadays they are corrupted and demoralized by the luxury and pride of which carriages and sedan chairs are symptoms. But while this is the sense of the lines it is certainly not all that they convey. Gay himself clearly finds the artful charms of the modern lady pleasing, and the braided gold of her shoe and the long trailing manteau form an attractive image. There is surely a very sympathetic admiration in the beautifully halting rhythm which is used to describe her walk:

> Her shoe disdains the street; the lazy fair
> With narrow step affects a limping air.

At the least there is careful observation, and a very subtle presentation, especially here in rhythmic terms, of what has been observed. Even in the following lines Gay's attitude is not simply condemnatory. He almost certainly dislikes the 'tricking gamester' and the 'griping broker', but he is responsive emotionally to the glaring equipage which flames along the street, and to the 'Loves and Graces' on the side of the chariot, and he takes pleasure in watching the 'sawcy state' of the broker even though that pleasure does not lead to approval. We find a similar pull between the moral and emotional response in a couplet describing the torches of the footmen outside the elegant houses of Pall Mall:

> Yet who the footman's arrogance can quell,
> Whose flambeau gilds the sashes of *Pell-mell* . . .
> (III, 157–8)

The splendid pictorial vividness of the image again modifies the explicit judgement, and the reader experiences a complex interplay between the two 'interpretations' of the scene, the criticism contrasting with a broad commitment to what is being described.

The extent of the commitment can be clearly seen if one compares the tone of *Trivia* with that of a poem which Gay certainly had in the forefront of his mind during the composition, that is Juvenal's *Third Satire*.[16] Juvenal is writing in praise of retirement and his poem is a sustained attack upon life in the capital. His attitude to the town is the traditional one: Rome is corrupt, a place to escape from, an impossibly uncongenial setting for ordinary life. He makes a contrast at one point, for example, between the way in which the rich move about the city, carried quickly and securely in litters, and the pushing and bustling that hinders the man who has to walk. Dryden's version of the lines reads:[17]

> And yet the wealthy will not brook delay,
> But sweep above our heads and make their way;
> In lofty litters borne, and read and write,
> Or sleep at ease: the shutters make it night.

> Yet still he reaches, first the public place:
> The press before him stops the client's pace:
> The crowd that follows crush his panting sides,
> And trip his heels; he walks not, but he rides.
> One elbows him, one justles in the shoal:
> A rafter breaks his head, or chairman's pole;
> Stockinged with loads of fat town-dirt he goes;
> And some rogue-soldier, with his hob-nailed shoes,
> Indents his legs behind in bloody rows.   (387–99)

Echoes of this passage are to be found several times in *Trivia*, but particularly in Book One. Here Gay has the same contrast between the rich man and the pedestrian, but his modifications of Juvenal are much more important than the direct borrowings. He is full of assumed contempt for those who are carried about the city, and boldly asserts the advantages of walking:

> In gilded chariots while they loll at ease,
> And lazily insure a life's disease;
> While softer chairs the tawdry load convey
> To Court, to *White's*, Assemblies, or the Play;
> Rosy-complexioned health thy steps attends,
> And exercise thy lasting youth defends.   (I, 69–74)

What has happened is that the insolent riders – a source of such aggravation to Juvenal, have become a spectacle to Gay. He enjoys the irony of watching them 'lazily insure a life's disease', whereas Juvenal's one desire is to retire with his friend to a villa at Cumae. Similarly, while Juvenal speaks of falling tiles, fires and all the dangers of the town with an intense bitterness which makes him wish only to escape 'while something yet remains for Lachesis to spin, and I can bear myself on my own legs', Gay, dealing with the same topics, is amused and tolerant. Dangerous incidents lose their unpleasantness as they develop something of the unreality of a ballet:

>   and from on high,
> Where masons mount the ladder, fragments fly;
> Mortar, and cumbled lime in show'rs descend,
> And o'er thy head destructive tiles impend.
>   (II, 267–70)

John Gay

As so often with Gay the latinate *impend* has a framing effect and produces a slightly ironical overtone at precisely the right moment. The reader is put at a distance where, with Gay, he enjoys in security what now appears as the delicate absurdity of the scene, and although Juvenal is clearly the 'source' of the lines, the mood has entirely changed.

The contrast between Gay and Juvenal is particularly clear in their respective treatments of the bully who assaults the innocent wayfarer. Juvenal's bully is a giant, vast and powerfully terrifying in the insulting questions that he throws out:

> Where did you whet your knife to-night, he cries,
> And shred the leeks that in your stomach rise?
> Whose windy beans have stuft your guts . .
> With what companion-cobbler have you fed,
> On old ox-cheeks or he-goats tougher head?
> What, are you dumb? Quick with your answer, quick,
> Before my foot salutes you with a kick . . .
> Answer, or answer not, 'tis all the same:
> He lays me on, and makes me bear the blame.
>
> (459–70)

This is the incarnation of all the terrors and unpleasantnesses that afflict Juvenal in Rome. No resistance is possible, and there is no escape from his attacks. Gay's bully is, on the contrary, all wind and swagger, but with very little real menace. He is soon cowed by the intrepid walker:

> But when the bully, with assuming pace,
> Cocks his broad hat, edg'd round with tarnish'd lace,
> Yield not the way; defie his strutting pride,
> And thrust him to the muddy kennel's side;
> He never turns again, nor dares oppose,
> But mutters coward curses as he goes.   (II, 59–64)

Gay dramatizes himself as assured, fully in command of any situation that may arise. Moving about London is an elaborate game requiring special skills which the poet commands, and so far as he uses Juvenal it is to point by contrast to his own acceptance of the enjoyments of London life.

Gay's tone can be characterized more exactly by comparing *Trivia* with Swift's fragmentary Georgic, *A City Shower*. Swift calls his poem a Georgic because it imitates the section on the signs of the weather in Book I of Virgil's poem, but his style is distinctly Juvenalian.[18] He opens with a latinism which reminds one of Gay, and with an attractive feline image, but this is a typically Swiftian piece of deceptiveness which emphasizes the more offensive 'sign' of rain in the next couplet:

> While rain depends, the pensive cat gives o'er
> Her frolicks, and pursues her tail no more;
> Returning home at night, you'll find the sink
> Strike your offended sense with double stink.
> (2–6)

There may be some jocularity in *stink*, but not enough to qualify the note of disgust. Later the grotesque comparisons are unpleasant and deliberately bathetic:

> Meanwhile the South, rising with dabbled wings,
> A sable cloud athwart the welkin flings,
> That swill'd more liquor than in could contain,
> And, like a drunkard, gives it up again. (13–16)

The only alleviation of this disgust comes when Swift looks sardonically at the effect of the rain on passers-by. Everyone takes cover, and even bitter political opponents find themselves under the same awning, absurdly united in preserving their threatened dignity:

> Forget their feuds, and join to save their wigs. (42)

But this is as close as Swift comes to comedy. Nausea predominates in the final lines which describe the appearance of gutters awash after heavy rain:

> Sweepings from butchers' stalls, dung, guts, and blood,
> Drown'd puppies, stinking sprats, all drench'd in mud,
> Dead cats, and turnip-tops come tumbling down the flood.
> (61–3)

The spectacle becomes a nightmare, a satiric caricature emblematic of moral degradation. The more Swift looks at the scene, the more emphatically repulsive it becomes.

The comparable passage in *Trivia* refers to the nastiness of wet weather in the city. Gay mentions the 'ungrateful odours' of the sewers and the muddy torrents which fill the gutters, but he also includes images which are attractive and even sensuous in their appeal. The oarsmen on the Thames 'to tempt a fare, cloath all their tilts in blue'. There is a characteristic note of verbal comedy in one of the 'signs':

> On hosiers poles depending stockings ty'd,
> Flag with the slacken'd gale, from side to side . . .
>
> (I, 165–6)

and it is clear that the scene is being valued for qualities other than its moral significance. The word *depending*, like *depends* at the beginning of *A City Shower*, is a sign of authorial control, but whereas Swift uses that control to provoke revulsion in the reader, Gay is concerned, as in *Rural Sports*, with the relationship itself. When the rain does come it is described in a sensuously attractive line which is a good pointer to the technique of *Trivia* as a whole: 'the tiles rattle with the smoking shower'. The words reinforce the imitative quality of the passage by recalling a couplet from Dryden's translation of the signs of the weather section of the *Georgics*:

> When ridgy roofs and tiles can scarce avail
> To bar the ruin of the rattling hail.
>
> (I, 599–600)

And the effect of the imitation is not, as it is in Swift, to establish a contrast between the literary model and real life (the values of the *Georgics* seem to be negated by the atmosphere of *A City Shower*), but rather to suggest an exceptional kind of interplay between the literary and the actual.

This is a quality which has been seen already in *Rural Sports*. The passage on bait in that poem is precisely detailed and in one sense 'realistic', yet at the same time the material is transformed by a complex of literary echoes ranging from *Paradise Lost* to fishing manuals. Gay creates his effect by experiencing the actual in terms of his literary knowledge, constantly using literature as a means of apprehension and evaluation. The problem of keeping his eye on the object scarcely arises; the object as it appears in the poem is a creation, a perfect fusion of direct experience and a modification by means of literary reminiscence, of that experience. The fusion in 'the tiles rattle with the smoaking shower', is precisely similar. Virgil's lines provide a mechanism which enables Gay to experience the London scene in a particular way.

An example of this kind of imitation occurs in a passage, presumably based upon Gay's experience of the exceptionally hard winter of 1710, which describes the frozen Thames. In his account of the north European winter Virgil had spoken with amazement about rivers freezing so hard that they can be used as roads:

> Swift rivers are with sudden ice constrained
> And studded wheels are on its back sustained;
> A hostry now for waggons, which before
> Tall ships of burden on its bosom bore . . .
>
> (III, 554–7)

The comparable passage of *Trivia* combines literary recollection with precisely observed detail:

> When hoary *Thames*, with frosted oziers crown'd
> Was three long moons in icy fetters bound.
> The waterman, forlorn along the shore,
> Pensive reclines upon his useless oar,
> Sees harness'd steeds desert the stony town,
> And wander roads unstable, not their own:
> Wheels o'er the harden'd waters smoothly glide,
> And rase with whiten'd tracks the slipp'ry tide.
>
> (II, 359–66)

It is a question of perceiving the London scene as a development of literary experience so that the actual images are seen with a shock both of recognition and new understanding. Something of Virgil's amazement appears in Gay's 'wandering roads unstable', but the observation that the wheels 'rase with whiten'd tracks the slipp'ry tide' is local and specific. The general expectation which is aroused by Virgil is fulfilled in the line 'hoary Thames with frosted oziers crown'd', or in the figure of the melancholy oarsman, so that constantly there is a situation in which the actual scene is given perspective by the literary reference, and the distant Virgilian description is substantiated in images from Gay's London. The passage ends with a more conventional kind of reference. Gay remembers that an ox was roasted on the Thames during the Great Frost, and that hucksters' stalls appeared:

John Gay

> Booths sudden hide the *Thames*, long streets appear,
> And num'rous games proclaim the crouded fair...
> (II, 369-70)

and then he interprets this in terms of a conventional epic simile:

> So when a gen'ral bids the martial train
> Spread their encampment o'er the spacious plain;
> Thick-rising tents a canvas city build,
> And the loud dice resound thro' all the field.
> (II, 371-4)

To a large extent it is Gay's remarkable ability to fuse literary experience with day-to-day actualities that gives *Trivia* its particular tone.

The imitative element in the description of the frost functions mainly as what I called a 'mechanism of apprehension'; it gives a particular order to the scene, and convinces the spectator that his perceptions are valid by relating what he sees to an accepted tradition. Imitation of a rather different kind also occurs in the section on signs of the weather. Virgil had said, while discussing prognostics of fair weather, that a calm and balmy day makes all nature happy:

> From hence proceeds the birds' harmonious voice;
> From hence the cows exult, and frisking lambs rejoice.
> (I, 569-70)

Gay, in the parallel passage, gives an imitation obviously modelled on Dryden's translation:

> The seasons operate on ev'ry breast;
> 'Tis hence that fawns are brisk, and ladies drest.
> (I, 151-2)

It is impossible here to make any simple statement about Gay's intentions. On one level the identification of the ladies with the fawns is satirical. Since women are rational creatures should they not be superior to the instincts which move mere animals? On the other hand the sympathetic tone of the passage makes it clear that any satire is, as it were, theoretical. The readers sees, intellectually, that a satirical attack might be made along these lines, but emotionally he is on the side of the ladies. And on another level the passage is philosophical and implies something about nature: all created things are subject to the influence of spring, and Gay is making an extension of Virgil's sense. The reader's reaction is first one of slightly shocked surprise at the identification of the ladies and the fawns; secondly, one of satisfaction at the realization that the identification is justified in various ways.

The delicate adjustment of tone which characterizes this passage is one which finds a perfect vehicle in the mock Georgic form of the poem as a whole. Of all the Georgic imitations of the period it is indeed in *Trivia* that the qualities which Dryden's translation emphasized are most fully realized. *Trivia* is often called a mock-epic, but there is little reason for this designation: it has no fable, no machinery, none of the formal qualities of the epic and mock-epic kinds. It is a didactic and descriptive poem, divided into books and varied with narrative digressions, and its generic relationships are made clear from the opening lines, which follow the *Georgics* as closely as the opening of *The Rape of the Lock* follows the *Aeneid*:

> Through winter streets to steer your course aright,
> How to walk clean by day, and safe by night,
> How jostling crouds, with prudence to decline,
> When to assert the wall, and when resign,
> I sing ... (I, 1–5)

A similar parallelism is found at the beginning of each book. Virgil's second Book begins with a recapitulation and a forecast:

> Thus far of tillage and of heavenly signs:
> Now sing my muse, the growth of generous vines ...
> (II, 1–2)

and *Trivia* repeats this pattern precisely:

> Thus far the Muse has trac'd in useful lays,
> The proper implements for wintry ways ...
> Now venture, Muse, from home to range the town,
> And for the publick safety risque thy own. (II, 1–4)

In his final book Gay seems deliberately to heed Addison's comment on the increasing seriousness of each book of Virgil's work, and to look forward to exploring a higher subject:

> O TRIVIA, Goddess, leave these low abodes,
> And traverse o'er the wide ethereal roads.
>
> (III, 1-2)

The book does in fact include episodes such as the funeral or the fire of a far more than usually solemn kind.

Finally, the end of *Trivia* plays a variation upon the general structural parallel. Virgil's contrast between his own peaceful life at Naples where he 'sang of the care of fields, of cattle, and of trees' while Caesar 'thundered in war by deep Euphrates' is clearly alluded to by Gay, but developed individually and in part satirically. After ingeniously working a reference to Naples into his account of a fire (as a town doomed to eventual destruction by Vesuvius and therefore the type of human mutability) Gay announces the conclusion of his own work:

> And now compleat my gen'rous labours lye,
> Finish'd, and ripe for immortality ...
>
> (III, 407-8)

And he also at this point contrasts himself with well-known public figures but, inverting Virgil's modesty, he chooses the notorious rather than the famous for comparison and makes claims for the lasting quality of his poem. Ward and Gildon, literary hacks will disappear, but *Trivia* will continue to be eagerly read:

> Death shall entomb in dust this mould'ring frame,
> But never reach th'eternal part, my fame.
> When W* and G**, mighty names, are dead;
> Or but at *Chelsea* under custards read;
> When Criticks crazy bandboxes repair,
> And Tragedies, turn'd rockets, bounce in air;
> High-raised on *Fleet-Street* posts, consigned to fame,
> This work shall shine, and walkers bless my name.
>
> (III, 409-16)

Thus, avoiding the conventional self-deprecatory stance of the poet, Gay asserts both his own claims and the mock nature of his work. No straightforward imitation could conclude in this way.

To insist, as Gay does, that this is a mock imitation is not, of course, to deny its essential seriousness. Rather, the point is that the seriousness of the work depends upon its many-sidedness, and upon its kaleidoscopic ability to shift from one mode of apprehension to another. Martin Price writes, in *The Palace of Wisdom*, about this kind of versatility:

> The use of a single pattern with different effects is inevitable in a literature that sees man as the 'glory, jest, and riddle of the world'. The first two terms converge on the third; man is a riddle because he is simultaneously glory and jest. The Augustans maintain the iridescence of the image of man; they deliberately create perspectives that shimmer into each other and apart again. The mock form is perhaps the finest means of achieving these double perspectives...[19]

It is a passage which, especially in the phrase 'perspectives that shimmer into each other and apart again', applies very precisely to the effect of *Trivia*.

Some of these perspectives have already been examined – the multivalent view, for example, of the proud lady, or the occupants of the elegant coaches. More violent contrasts and a much more obvious tension between the formal model and the imitation are found in the burlesque episodes where Gay draws on the account of the Aristaeus legend in Virgil's fourth book. The story of Aristaeus, a shepherd from whose attentions, in Virgil's account, Eurydice was fleeing when she was fatally bitten by a snake, is related to the main theme of the book – beekeeping – because Aristaeus was punished by the gods with the loss of his bees for having caused Eurydice's death. Virgil tells how Aristaeus discovered the reason for his punishment and gained a second swarm. Distraught at the loss, he complains to his mother, Cyrene, about the hardships he has to endure. Cyrene, in her bower below the river Peneus, hears his complaint, invites him to her Court, and advises him to consult Proteus about his troubles After much difficulty Aristaeus succeeds in capturing Proteus who tells him the reason for his calamity: 'Orpheus dying prayers at length are heard'. Aristaeus is now able to offer appropriate sacrifices to the gods, and nine days later 'behold a prodigy'. From the 'broken bowels and bloated skin' of a sacrificed bull a new swarm of bees emerges,

> Like a large cluster of black grapes that shew,
> And make a large dependence from the bough.
>
> (IV, 809–10)

Gay's story is on one level simply a burlesque of the Virgilian digression. Encouraged by Jove's habit of taking mortal lovers Cloacina

> Goddess of the tide
> Whose sable streams beneath the city glide...
>
> (II, 115–16)

descends to earth and takes as her lover 'a mortal scavenger'. A boy is conceived whom she eventually bears and leaves 'beneath a bulk'; the child grows up in hardship, a mere 'beggar's brat', and Cloacina, distressed at his condition, prays the gods to provide him with some useful trade. They agree to set the boy up as a shoe-black, all contribute to supply the necessary equipment, and the child is made happy.

The point that links Gay's story to Virgil's is the complaint which the relationship between mother and son provokes. One of the most memorable passages in Virgil's version of the legend is Aristaeus' complaint to Cyrene, which is itself reminiscent of Achilles' complaint to Thetis in the *Iliad* when she visits him after the death of Patroclus. The complaint of Aristaeus is repeated to his mother by one of her nymphs:

> 'Tis Aristaeus, 'tis thy darling son,
> Who to his careless mother makes his moan.
> Near his paternal stream he sadly stands,
> With downcast eyes, wet cheeks, and folded hands,
> Upbraiding heaven from whence his lineage came,
> And cruel calls the gods, and cruel thee, by name.
>
> (IV, 507–12)

Cloacina's son is unaware of his parentage, but he also makes his complaint. And as Aristaeus stands weeping by the banks of the Peneus so the beggar boy leans over the rails which guard Fleet ditch, viewing 'below the black canal of mud', weeping pensively and deploring his fate:

> Where common-shores a lulling murmur keep,
> Whose torrents rush from *Holborn's* fatal steep:
> Pensive through idleness, tears flow'd apace,

> Which eas'd his loaded heart, and wash'd his face;
> At length he sighing cry'd; That boy was blest,
> Whose infant lips have drain'd a mother's breast;
> But happier far are those (if such be known)
> Whom both a father and a mother own:
> But I, alas! hard fortune's utmost scorn,
> Who ne'er knew parent, was an orphan born!
>   (II, 173-82)

And as with Aristaeus his sad prayer is answered. Gay describes the response to the prayer in elaborate detail:

> While thus he fervent prays, the heaving tide
> In widen'd circles beats on either side;
> The Goddess rose amid the inmost round,
> With wither'd turnip tops her temples crown'd;
> Low reach'd her dripping tresses, lank, and black,
> As the smooth jet, or glossy raven's back;
> Around her waste a circling eel was twin'd,
> Which bound her robe that hung in rags behind.
>   (II, 193-200)

The primary effect is broadly comic, depending on the contrast between the elegance of the classical story and the vividly low details of Gray's description. But it is worth noticing that although some images, the 'withered turnip tops', for example, are simply farcical, others, like the goddess's hair, 'black as the smooth jet or glossy raven's back', have a potentially serious sensuous appeal. The potentiality is not realized, of course, because the description moves so quickly to the purely comic functional eel who holds the goddess's rags and tatters together, but it hints, like the mock element in the form, at dimensions beyond the one that is immediately dominant, so that perspectives are opened up even with the burlesque.

Even the trivial comic episode of Doll, whose story echoes Virgil's treatment of the Orpheus and Eurydice legend, shows a surprising variety of tone. It was Doll's fate to walk on the frozen Thames at a time when the ice was beginning to thaw, and to slip in:

> The cracking crystal yields, she sinks, she dyes,
> Her head, chopt off, from her lost shoulders flies;

> Pippins she cry'd, but death her voice confounds,
> And pip-pip-pip along the ice resounds.
>
> (II, 389–92)

This climax carries comic echoes of one of the most haunting passages in the *Georgics*:

> Eurydicen vox ipsa et frigida lingua,
> a miseram Eurydicen! anima fugiente vocabat,
> Eurydicen toto referebant flumine ripae.   (IV, 525–7)
>
> With his last voice, 'Eurydice', he cried,
> 'Eurydice', the rocks and river-banks replied.
>
> (Dryden, IV, 767–8)

But it is introduced by a moral of impeccable soundness:

> Ah *Doll*! all mortals must resign their breath,
> And industry itself submit to death!   (II, 387–8)

and is followed by a passage which reinforces the Orphean comparison with references to the Thracian furies, the bleeding trunk and the severed head. Again there is a sense that the passage points in many directions. The moral is certainly somewhat pompous in its context; on the other hand, it is unexceptionable in itself, and, since Doll's death is imminent, not inappropriate either. The disproportion between Doll and Orpheus introduces comic exaggeration, but it also brings to mind images whose effect can never be simply comic. The reader's reaction is one of laughter modified by the realization that the comic episode embodies in debased form elements of permanent seriousness.

The overall pattern of imitation in *Trivia* also has two more general effects than those discussed so far. In the first place the reader is aware of a continuous irony in Gay's presentation of the walker, the 'speaker' in the poem. He is full both of practical good sense and also of moral earnestness, convinced of the utility of his work to all 'honest men', and with a strong feeling of superiority to those who 'laugh at honesty and trudging wits'. He feels, in fact, that he embodies the kind of active virtue which is Virgil's ideal in the *Georgics* – simple, rugged, hard-working. But the reader also knows that this idealized view is a little spurious. The walker's constant activity conceals a real idleness in which, as we have seen, all the genuine activities of the town become the object of his contemplation and take on the quality of a ballet or a pageant. The choice of form and the imitation of episodes which constantly recall the values of Virgil's poem establish that the walker is not quite so virtuous as he claims, and successfully undercut his occasional pomposities.

The imitation is also important in establishing the essentially celebratory character of the poem. Armens claimed, in *John Gay, Social Critic*, that Gay saw the town as evil, diseased and barren, standing in sharp contrast to the country which is vital and fertile. Certainly, Gay knows what is bad in London life. There is dirt everywhere, crime and immorality are prevalent and ill-health is common. But to stress this at the expense of the pleasure that Gay shows in the animation and variety of the London scene is to distort the poem. A Georgic is, among many other things, always a patriotic poem, and the homeland, in *Trivia*, is London. Gay very clearly takes over the feeling of Virgil's passage in praise of Italy, and applies it to his own subject:

> Happy *Augusta*! law-defended town!
> Here no dark lanthorns shade the villain's frown;
> No *Spanish* jealousies thy lanes infest,
> Nor *Roman* vengeance stabs th' unwary breast;
> Here tyranny n'er lifts her purple hand,
> But liberty and justice guard the land;
> No bravos here profess the bloody trade,
> Nor is the church the murd'rer's refuge made.
>
> (III, 145-52)

The effect of this piece of formal imitation is to give a focus to the responsiveness to the varied sights and sounds of London which was analysed earlier. Themes which would otherwise remain isolated and independent achieve unity through Gay's choice of the appropriate form.

Like *Rural Sports*, *Trivia* leaves one with a sense of Gay's extraordinary sensitivity in the adaptation of a formal model to a particular purpose. The structure, the themes and the attitudes of Virgil's poem all contribute essential elements to the success of *Trivia* yet it establishes a complete and unmistakable individuality of tone.

John Gay

Notes

1. For a discussion of the poem's topical significance and much valuable analysis see Adina Forsgren *John Gay: 'Poet of a Lower Order'* (1964).
2. Quotations are from *The Poetical Works of John Gay*, edited by G. C. Faber (1926).
3. cf. *Georgics*, II, 523.
4. See John M. Aden 'The 1720 Version of *Rural Sports*', *Modern Language Quarterly* (1959).
5. Izaak Walton's *The Compleat Angler, or the Contemplative Man's Recreation* was published in 1653, and, 'much enlarged', in 1655. Charles Cotton's continuation was first published in 1678.
6. *The Complete Angler*, Chapter V.
7. *ibid.* Chapter I.
8. *ibid.* Chapter VII.
9. Googe, Barnaby *Foure Bookes of Husbandry, collected by M. Conradus Heresbachius. Conteyning the whole arte and trade of husbandry, with the antiquitie and commendation thereof. Newly Englished and increased by B. Googe* (1577).
10. *The Secrets of Angling: Teaching the Choicest Tools, Baits and Seasons, for the taking of any Fish in Pond or River: practised and familiarly opened in three Books* By I. D. Esquire (1613). There is a reprint in *An English Garner: Ingatherings from our History and Literature*, by Edward Arber, Volume I (1895).
11. See *The Complete Works of William Diaper*, edited with an Introduction by Dorothy Broughton (1951), p. lx.
12. *ibid.* p. lxii.
13. See *Oppian, Colluthus, Tryphiodorus*, with an English translation by A. W. Mair. Loeb Library (1928).
14. For texts and translations of Grattius and Nemesianus see the Loeb volume *Minor Latin Poets*, edited with an Introduction and English translations by J. Wright Duff and Arnold M. Duff (1954). Nothing is known of the life of Grattius. He is referred to by Ovid in a poem written in 8 A.D. and this, together with the fact that he imitates Virgil, gives the approximate date of his work. M. Aurelius Olympius Nemesianus, a native of Carthage, wrote eclogues as well as the *Cynegetica*. Internal evidence makes it possible to date the latter poem in 283-4 A.D. Both poets would have been available to Gay in *Grattii Falisci Cynegetica (cum poematio Nemesiani)*. London (1699).
15. For a discussion of this question see Mair's edition cited above in note 13.
16. See W. H. Irving *John Gay: Favorite of the Wits* (1940).
17. *The Satires of Decimus Junius Juvenalis, Translated into English Verse by Mr. Dryden, and Several Other Eminent Hands* was published in 1693.
18. *A Description of a City Shower* was first published in *The Tatler* in 1710. See *The Poems of Jonathan Swift*, edited by Harold Williams, Three Volumes (1958), Volume I, p. 136.
19. Martin Price *The Palace of Wisdom* (1964), p. 249.

Six

'The Mob of Gentlemen...'

In a passage of characteristic candour Dr. Johnson wrote of William Somerville that he....

> has tried many modes of poetry; and though perhaps he has not in any reached such excellence as to raise much envy, it may commonly be said at least, that *he writes very well for a gentleman.*
>
> *Life of Somerville*

The phrase is, if looked at from a rigorous point of view, damning enough, but it directs attention to one of the important facts of the period – that many 'gentlemen' could write, if not always with what Pope or Johnson would have recognized as professional competence, at least 'very well' for amateurs. That the amateur could write so well seems to have depended largely upon the existence of such concepts of form and its development as have been illustrated in previous chapters. The present chapter is concerned with the influence of these concepts upon the work of two 'amateurs': Somerville himself and Richard Jago. The interest is in seeing how their response to experience and their expression of it is guided by the tradition which they very self-consciously inherit in their two chief poems, *The Chase* (1735), and *Edge-Hill* (1767).

Somerville's Preface to *The Chase* gives a very unassuming account of the origins of the poem. Having grown old, he says (he was sixty when *The Chase* was published), he likes to run over 'in his elbow chair' some of those chases which 'were once the delight of a more vigorous age'. In order to gratify his taste for this 'entertaining and very innocent' amusement, he has composed a poem on hunting. It is partly preceptive, but the preceptive sections are intermixed 'with so many descriptions and digressions, in the Georgic manner, that I hope they will not be tedious'.

He then gives a brief history of hunting poetry, mentioning Xenophon, Oppian, Grattius and Nemesianus, and deploring

'*The mob of gentlemen . . .*'

Virgil's neglect of the subject both in the *Georgics* and the *Aeneid*. But England, although famous for her dogs and horses and for producing 'persons best skilled in the art of hunting' has no such literature:

> It is therefore strange that none of our poets have yet thought it worth their while to treat of this subject; which is without doubt very noble in itself, and very well adapted to receive the most beautiful turns of poetry. Perhaps our poets have no great genius for hunting. Yet, I hope my brethren of the couples, by encouraging this first but imperfect essay, will show the world they have at least some taste for poetry.

Evidently Somerville either did not know *Rural Sports* and *Windsor Forest* or chose to ignore them. Perhaps he thought they did not count since they do not deal exclusively with hunting. But the significant thing about the Preface is that Somerville, despite his modesty, is a very self-conscious writer, and he says enough to make it clear that his account of the origins of his poem is a little disingenuous. He has carefully scanned the literary authorities and deliberately adopts the 'Georgic manner' as being the most suitable for his purpose.

The impress of the *Georgics* is felt throughout *The Chase* both in passages of direct imitation, and as a general influence on style and method. Following a very brief statement of theme

> The Chase, I sing, hounds, and their various breed,
> And no less various use . . .   (I, 1-2)

the poem opens with a mixture of politics and patriotism. In this case it is patriotism with a difference: an address to Frederick, Prince of Wales, by this time the social leader of a powerful opposition to the policies of Walpole and the King. It embodies the idealized commercial jingoism, the blend of expansionist enthusiasm and moral fervour which was so soon (in 1739) to lead to war with Spain. The Prince is assured that

> . . . if, in future times, some envious prince,
> Careless of right and guileful, should invade
> Thy Britain's commerce, or should strive in vain
> To wrest the balance from thy equal hand;

The English Georgic

> Thy hunter train, in cheerful green array'd
> (A band undaunted and innur'd to toils)
> Shall compass thee around, die at thy feet,
> Or hew thy passage through th' embattled foe,
> And clear thy way to fame.   (I, 21–9)

This emphasis upon freedom of trade and the maintenance of Britain's commercial rights blends rather unexpectedly with nostalgic recreation of the past – Whig principles and Tory sentiment. The picture of the 'hunter-train, in cheerful green array'd', fighting boldly for Prince and country in hand-to-hand battle, provides a touch of romantic mediaevalism which colours Somerville's whole treatment of the chase, and which recurs strongly, as will be seen, in the description of a stag-hunt.

Somerville then writes on the rise of hunting from a primitive state. As in Virgil the development of the passage depends on a contrast between the Golden Age and present experience. The Golden Age was a time when the animals acknowledged man as their lord,

> But mild and gentle, and by whom as yet
> Secure they grazed.   (I, 49–50)

This happy state was followed by a period of indiscriminate killing:

> Death stretches o'er the plain
> Wide-wasting, and grim slaughter red with blood.
>   (I, 50–1)

But 'chance or industry in after-time some few improvements made' until eventually, following the Norman Conquest, huntsmen were

> taught to speak
> The proper dialect, with horn and voice...
> To cheer the busy hound...
> In bloody social leagues.   (I, 76–81)

The Georgic parallel is clear, but Somerville may also have Grattius in mind. Grattius apostrophizes the originator of hunting ('Fortunate the man whose industry made him first inventor of arts so great!'), and Oppian's second book opens with a similar account. It is one of the most natural expansions of the immediate

'The mob of gentlemen...'

subject, involving a measure of self-congratulation and leading very naturally in Somerville to a patriotic apostrophe:

> Hail, happy Britain! highly favour'd isle,
> And Heaven's peculiar care... (I, 84-5)

— a passage in which (as in Dyer's *Fleece*) even the damps and fogs of the British climate are called into service as so much apparatus for the huntsman's moral gymnasium:

> In vain malignant steams and winter fogs
> Load the dull air, and hover round our coasts,
> The huntsman ever gay, robust and bold,
> Defies the noxious vapour, and confides
> In this delightful exercise, to raise
> His drooping head, and cheer his heart with joy.
> (I, 97-102)

In the first book there is also a good deal of straight-forwardly didactic material — detailed instructions about the siting and construction of kennels and about the choice of hounds, a topic where Somerville is probably again indebted to Grattius. Finally, Somerville blends praise of retirement with exaltation of British liberty. When the weather is bad for hunting he advises the sportsman to employ his 'precious hours' in discussing scientific questions with an 'improving friend', or alternatively to read history, which will lead him to greater enthusiasm for British achievements:

> Converse familiar with th'illustrious dead;
> With great examples of old Greece or Rome,
> Enlarge thy free-born heart, and bless kind Heaven,
> That Britain yet enjoys dear liberty,
> That balm of life, that sweetest blessing cheap
> Though purchas'd with our blood. (I, 408-13)

It can be seen that Somerville's claim that he intends to imitate 'the Georgic manner' is substantiated in the most specific way; that the blend of didactic with more expansive themes is characteristic of the kind; and that the choice of themes — address to a patron, patriotic apostrophe and praise of scholarly retirement — is traditional. On the other hand Somerville's manipulation of the themes is not entirely conventional. The choice of the Prince of

Wales as a patron, and the inevitable anti-Government emphasis which follows, leads to a kind of romantic idealization which is new and which produces a break in the moral rigour which the form in its Virgilian state demands. The treatment of the retirement theme is significantly different also. In the *Georgics* the simple life of the husbandman is presented as an alternative to a life of scholarly investigation – they are disciplines each with its own firm demands and its own rewards. In Somerville scholarly interests are not a way of life in themselves: they are the relaxation not even of the hard-working husbandman, but of the jovial yet frustrated huntsman.

But despite this weakening and sentimentalizing of Virgilian ideas, the value of the Georgic framework to Somerville is beyond doubt. Its value is not so much that it provides him with a literary structure – although it helps to do that also – but that it helps him to apprehend the implications of his subject and to place it in a context. For Somerville hunting means a good deal more than an opportunity for healthy outdoor exercise, as it obviously did to many people in the period. When Nicholas Cox, for example, wrote in *The Gentleman's Recreation* that

> No musick can be more ravishingly delightful than a Pack of Hounds in full Cry, to such a Man whose Heart and Ears are so happy to be set to the tune of such charming Instruments...

he was suggesting that the pleasure to be gained from hunting is more significant and profound than might commonly be thought. For him and for Somerville the sport is related to the deepest emotions that they can experience. The value of the *Georgics* is that it enables Somerville to realize and to express this relationship.

In particular he is able to make explicit the link which he feels between hunting and patriotism, and between patriotism and enthusiasm for the Prince of Wales' party. But the framework also helps him to express the social value which he puts on the chase. The highest stage in the development of hunting is when men learn to join 'in bloody social leagues', and although, to the twentieth century observer, there is an unexpectedly transparent revelation about the fierce explicitness of *bloody*, it is the social aspect that is clearly of greatest importance for Somerville.

'*The mob of gentlemen . . .*'

And it is this that is emphasized when he turns to the question of relaxation:

> th' improving friend
> With open arms embrace, and from his lips
> Glean science. (I, 401–3)

The complex of Somerville's ideas can be expressed the more easily because he finds in Virgil's poem a model, a set of formulae, which help him to explain his own experience. The juxtapositions that are made in the *Georgics* establish a pattern which he finds meaningful, and which he sets out to transmit, with appropriate modifications, to a contemporary audience.

In the following Books specifically Georgic themes continue to occur, but not so concentratedly as in Book I. In Books II and III Somerville takes the opportunity, which he had justified in the Preface by reference to Virgil, of large-scale exotic digressions:

> I have intermixed the preceptive parts with so many descriptions and digressions, in the Georgic manner, that I hope they will not be tedious.

Book II contains nearly two hundred and fifty lines on 'the Asiatic way of hunting, particularly the magnificent manner of the Great Mogul, and other Tartarian princes', and Book III is largely filled with such exotic digressions as: 'Description of the pit-fall for the lion; and another for the elephant. The ancient way of hunting the tiger with a mirror. The Arabian manner of hunting the wild boar.' These episodes are intended to evoke wonder and are unashamedly sensational in style:

> Prostrate on the ground
> The grinning monsters lie, and their foul gore
> Defiles the verdant plain . . .
> The battle bleeds, grim slaughter strides along,
> Glutting her greedy jaws, grins o'er her prey.
> (II, 487–98)

The idea of describing such exotic hunting scenes presumably came from Oppian whose third Book deals among other things with lions, lynxes, bears, wolves, tigers and boars, and whose fourth gives an account of a lion-hunt and of boar-hunting with dogs and nets, and Somerville evidently thought of them as being parallel to, for example, the account of the Scythian winter in the third *Georgic*. But whatever the exact model for Somerville's descriptions, the impulse behind them is a straightforward pleasure in the marvellous.

The account of the stag-hunt in Book III is much more interesting. In places it is based quite closely on Denham's treatment of the same subject in *Cooper's Hill*. Denham writes, for example, that the driven stag

> Then tries his friends among the baser herd,
> Where he so lately was obey'd and fear'd,
> His safety seeks; the herd, unkindly wise.
> Or chases him from thence, or from him flies.
> (269–72)

and Somerville:

> There mingle with the herd, where once he reign'd...
> But the base herd have learn'd the ways of men,
> Averse they fly, or with rebellious aim
> Chase him from thence.
> (III, 477–83)

But Somerville's account also has a distinct and rather strange quality of its own, a quality which is most strongly marked in the opening lines of the section:

> The morning sun, that gilds with trembling rays
> Windsor's high towers, beholds the courtly train
> Mount for the chase, nor views in all his course
> A scene so gay: heroic, noble youths,
> In arts and arms renown'd, and lovely nymphs
> The fairest of this isle, where beauty dwells
> Delighted, and deserts her Paphian grove
> For our more favour'd shades...
> (III, 351–8)

The lines are analagous in tone to those on the Prince of Wales and his 'hunter-train, in cheerful green array'd' in the introductory section of the poem. Again there is a slight sense of romantic mediaevalism, but in a curious way the mediaevalism is inevitably modified by the reader's knowledge of mock-heroic:

> Not with more glories in th'etherial plain,
> The sun first rises o'er the purpled main,

> Then issuing forth, the rival of his beams
> Launch'd on the bosom of the silver Thames.
> *The Rape of the Lock*, (II, 1–4)

In other words the effect of Somerville's lines is not straightforwardly heroic: it is rather an inversion of mock-heroic, or heroic which bears the mock-heroic in mind. A similar effect is produced in lines on the Prince of Wales:

> But who is he
> Fresh as a rose-bud newly blown and fair
> As opening lilies; on whom every eye
> With joy and admiration dwells? See, see,
> He reigns his docile barb with manly grace.
> Is it Adonis for the chase array'd?
> Or Britain's second hope?
>   (III, 382–8)

It is not, as one might well suspect, that the passage is ironical. On the contrary Somerville's praise of Frederick is entirely genuine, but in Hanoverian England royal panegyric clearly gives rise to problems. Heroic adulation, following the pattern of, for example, Van Dyck's portraits or Spenser's praise of Queen Elizabeth, is scarcely possible any longer. Politically the age for that kind of idealization is past. What Somerville does is to translate the emotion that he feels to the level of high romantic fiction and, as it were, to challenge the mock-heroic face to face:

> Fresh as a rose-bud newly blown and fair
> As opening lilies . . .

is in the manner of

> Not with more glories in th'etherial plain
> The sun first rises o'er the purpled main . . .

but the intention is different. In effect Somerville's lines suggest that he has already taken the mock-heroic response into account and it is as though he transcends one critical attitude by including it in his poem. The stylistic manipulation is on a more sophisticated level than one expects from Somerville, but its success is assured.

There is a similar ambiguity of attitude in a later passage on the virtue of the 'British fair'. Somerville prays for fine weather so that the pleasures of the hunt will not be spoiled:

> O! grant, indulgent Heaven, no rising storm
> May darken with black wings this glorious scene!
> Should some malignant power thus damp our joys,
> Vain were the gloomy cave, such as of old
> Betray'd to lawless love the Tyrian queen.
> For Britain's virtuous nymphs are chaste as fair,
> Spotless, unblam'd, with equal triumph reign
> In the dun gloom, as in the blaze of day.
>
> (III, 453-60)

It seems impossible that a writer as self-conscious as Somerville could, in 1735, write

> For Britain's virtuous nymphs are chaste as fair

without bearing in mind the attitude expressed in

> This day, black Omens threat the brightest Fair,
> That e'er deserv'd a watchful spirit's care;
>
> Some dire disaster, or by force or slight;
> But what, or where, the fates have wrapped in night.
> Whether some nymph shall break Diana's law,
> Or some frail China jar receive a flaw.
>
> *The Rape of the Lock*, (II, 101-6)

Again there is a 'suppressed irony', an irony perceived but not exploited, which both Somerville and the reader are aware of, and which serves to make the quite serious statements of the passage acceptable. Without this awareness there would be a sense of exaggeration and fulsomeness which is not, in fact, present when the poem is read.

The degree of Somerville's stylistic awareness is made very clear if one compares *The Chase* with his burlesque poem of country life, *Hobbinol*. Like *The Chase*, *Hobbinol* has a Preface in which Somerville discusses his intentions. He addresses the poem to Hogarth, 'the greatest master in the burlesque way'. But Hogarth's province is the town and Somerville pleads that he may be left with 'a small outride in the country' where he, like Hogarth, can make vice and folly the object of his ridicule. His motto is the passage in the third *Georgic* where Virgil says that he well knows how hard it is to 'crown with glory a lowly theme'. But Somerville comforts himself with another Virgilian quotation:

'The mob of gentlemen . . .'

> In tenui labor, at tenuis non gloria . . .
> *Georgics* (**IV**, 9)
> Slight is the field of toil, but not slight the glory.

The great problem that he has to face is that of style: how high or low ought the style to be in a poem of this character? He takes as a starting point Addison's distinction (in *Spectator*, 249) between two types of burlesque:

> Burlesque is of two kinds. The first represents mean persons in the accoutrements of heroes; the other great persons acting or speaking like the basest among the people. Don Quixote is an instance of the first, and Lucian's gods of the second. It is a dispute among the critics whether burlesque run best in heroic, like the *Dispensary*; or in doggerel, like that of *Hudibras*. I think where the low character is to be raised, the heroic is the proper measure; but when an hero is to be pulled down and degraded, it is best done in doggerel.

Following this authority Somerville decides that the Miltonic style is appropriate to his own subject 'because it raises the low character more than is possible to be done under the restraint of rhyme'. As a further authority he refers to Edmund Smith's attack on rhyme in *A Poem on the Death of Mr. John Philips*. Edmund Smith, although he himself wrote in couplets, claimed that rhyme was intrinsically *meaner* than blank verse, and ranged his objections under four heads. First, rhyme has an equalising effect: all styles tend to merge together under the influence of the recurrent rhyming pattern:

> Tyrannick rhyme! that cramps to equal chime
> The gay, the soft, the florid and sublime.

A proper distinction of styles is rarely to be found in rhymed couplets. Moreover, the necessity for rhyming is apt to dictate the sense: 'confines the fancy and the judgement guides', or, at the very least, to have a constricting effect on the poet:

> I'm sure in needless bonds it poets ties,
> Procrustes like the axe or wheels applies
> To lop the mangled sense or stretch it into size.

His point presumably is that there is less syntactic freedom in the use of couplets than there is in blank verse. Sentences have to be manipulated so that the sense will, normally, close with the rhyme. Finally he suggests, apparently rather inconsistently with what has gone before, that rhyme is helpful to weak poets, but a hindrance to good ones:

> At best a crutch that lifts the weak along.
> Supports the feeble but retards the strong.

Edmund Smith's praise of Philips is essentially that he is great when dealing with humble subjects. In this respect it is even claimed that Philips is a more 'complete' poet than Milton or Dryden:

> Great Milton's wing on lower themes subsides
> And Dryden oft in rhyme his weakness hides...

but, and he addresses Philips directly at this point:

> You ne'er with gingling words deceive the ear.
> And yet on humble subjects great appear.

But although Edmund Smith provides a strong defence of blank verse as such he does not distinguish at all between burlesque and serious uses of the medium. He compares Philips with Butler ('Milton and Butler in thy Muse combine', and says that Philips is superior to Butler in 'manly beauty': his 'grave lines extort a juster smile'.

> In her best light the Comick Muse appears
> When she with borrow'd pride the buskin wears.

However, there is no distinction made between the style of *The Splendid Shilling* and that of the more straightforward parts of *Cyder*. To find a specific defence of the burlesque use of epic style (and to counteract Horace's dictum that the poet must not use a tragic style to treat comic matter) Somerville turns to Boileau's essay on La Fontaine:

> Que comme il n'y a rien de plus froid, que de conter une chose grande en stile bas, aussi n'y a-t-il de plus ridicule, que de raconter under histoire comique et absurde en termes graves et serieux...

And he quotes Dacier: 'Car rien ne contribue tant au *ridicule* que le *grand*'. This gives Somerville the critical backing that he needs:

> Nothing can improve a merry tale so much as its being delivered with a grave and serious air. Our imaginations are agreeably surprized, and fond of a pleasure so little expected.

But there is one difficulty that remains to be overcome, in many ways a more intractable one than all the others:

> ... the writer in this kind of burlesque must not only keep up the pomp and dignity of the style, but an artful sneer should appear through the whole work; and every man will judge that it is no easy matter to blend together the hero and the harlequin.

Unfortunately Somerville gives no indication of how this 'artful sneer' is to be made apparent. The reader has to deduce his methods from the work itself, and this is by no means easy. How, for example, is one to distinguish between the following passages?

> From the full cistern lead the ductile streams,
> To wash thy court well pav'd nor spare thy pains
> For much to health will cleanliness avail ...
>   Banish far off
> Each noisome stench, let no offensive smell
> Invade thy wide enclosure, but admit
> The nitrous air and purifying breeze.
>   *The Chase* (I, 156–65)

>   the bloated churl
> Listens in state, each arm reclin'd is prop'd
> With yielding pillows of the softest down.
> In mind composed, from short coeval tube
> He sucks the vapours bland, thick curling clouds
> Of smoke around his reeking temples play;
> Joyous he sits, and impotent of thought
> Puffs away care and sorrow from his heart.
> How vain the pomp of kings! look down, ye great,
> And view with envious eye the downy nest.
>   *Hobbinol* (I, 43–52)

The obvious Miltonisms are present in both – *ductile, noisome, invade, nitrous* in the passage from *The Chase*; *coeval, impotent of thought*, and the inversion of *vapours bland* in the lines from *Hobbinol*. Yet the intention seems to be clearly different. The first passage contains serious advice, in an elevated style, on the need to keep kennels clean. But the Miltonic language is not intended to reduce the subject itself to mockery. Its function is to make the subject susceptible to poetic treatment, to give literary pleasure by recognition of the element of incompatibility involved, and probably to introduce a touch of ironic self-depreciation for the poet himself. The element of play is very important. In the second passage, on the other hand, the style is being used to attack the self-satisfied complacency of the 'hero'. The heroic language mocks at Hobbinol by pointing to the disparity between his slothful existence and the heroic life, and the conclusion:

How vain the pomp of kings!

is clearly ironical. The 'artful sneer' is imparted by a directly ironical use of some of the Miltonisms. The most prominent is *impotent of thought*, but the inversion of *vapours bland* also calls attention to the ironical usage – Hobbinol's fug is acrid rather than balmy. A good deal of work is done by the forceful word *bloated* in preparing the reader for these ironical suggestions. In the first extract there is no such suggestion: there the streams really are *ductile* and the smell *noisome*.

But what is made entirely clear by Hobbinol and its Preface is the degree of Somerville's literary self-consciousness, and his interest in exploiting levels of style in order to achieve particular effects. It lends countenance to the view that the tone of the passages on the Prince of Wales or 'the British fair' in *The Chase* is likely to be over-complex rather than over-simple.

Book IV of *The Chase* is specifically Georgic in its account of the breeding of hounds, a section for which Somerville was able to find models not only in the third *Georgic*, with its rules 'for the breeding and management of horses, oxen, goats and dogs', but also in Grattius, Nemesianus and Oppian. Somerville's advice is traditional and has to do with the best season for mating, the psychology of dogs and bitches at mating time, and the characteristics of a good hound. The eclectic use of sources is particularly clear in this section. Dryden's Virgil is suggested, for example, by some of the details. Dryden has

> Watch the quick motions of the frisking tail
> Then serve their fury with the rushing male ...
>
> (III, 105–6)

and Somerville:

> Mark well the wanton females of thy pack
> That curl their taper tails.
>
> (III, 37–8)

And Virgil's advice to starve mares before mating is applied by Somerville to bitches. Elsewhere he seems to echo Nemesianus who had said that the gestation period for puppies is 'when Phoebe has completed the round of two full moons'. Somerville writes that puppies are born

> When now the third revolving moon appears
> With sharpened horns above th'horizon's brink.
>
> (IV, 84–5)

Somerville here makes full use of his sources not only for the general outlines of his advice but also for details, and his comments on the training of hounds are similarly derivative.

This very practical advice is immediately followed by a section on rabies which, in its context, is clearly a localized version of the account of the plague in the *Georgics*. Somerville paints the horror of the scene with a broad sweeping brush:

> Hence to the kennel, muse, return, and view
> With heavy heart that hospital of woe;
> Where horror stalks at large! insatiate death
> Sits growling o'er his prey: each hour presents
> A different scene of ruin and distress.
> How busy art thou, fate! and how severe
> Thy pointed wrath!
>
> (IV, 168–74)

The function of the plague in the *Georgics* is to present the range of experience that is furthest removed from the idyllic, prelapsarian pastoral mood which occurs in the account of the farmers' festival or in the praise of Italy. At one pole of experience

> Perpetual spring our happy climate sees:
> Twice breed the cattle, and twice bear the trees;
> And summer suns recede by slow degrees. . . .
>
> (II, 204–6)

At the other

> Tisiphone, let loose from under ground,
> Majestically pale, now treads the round.
>
> (III, 820–1)

The contrast between the beauty and fruitfulness of the one and the horror and desolation of the other measures the span of experience that the *Georgics* cover. It would be absurd to suggest that Somerville covers this range of experience in the way that Virgil does. What does happen is that, by the very fact that he adopts the *Georgics* as a model, he is brought to consider the range of experience and to interpret it in his own terms: in the contrast between the idyllic picture of the Prince of Wales and the misery of the attack of rabies.

It can reasonably be claimed that without the *Georgics*, and without the literary techniques that the notion of imitation gave him, Somerville would have produced a much more limited poem, and one of much less general value than he in fact achieved. In a sense *The Chase* cannot be adequately discussed in purely literary terms at all. Its justification is partly in sociological terms, in its value for a particular social group in raising a shared experience to a new level of meaning. This is a justification that Dr. Johnson seems to be hinting at when he writes:

> (He) must be allowed to have set a good example to men of his own class, by devoting part of his time to elegant knowledge . . . and has shown, by the subject which his poetry has adorned, that it is practicable to be at once a skilful sportsman and a man of letters.
>
> *Life of Somerville*

But the matter surely goes a little deeper than Johnson's phrase 'elegant knowledge' seems to suggest. Georgic treatment of a subject like hunting involves inevitably a measure of embellishment and pure decoration. But its value for its readers (and it was, after all, a widely popular poem until well into the nineteenth century) was that it helped them (to adopt a phrase of Richardson's) 'to think and feel justly upon the various occasions of life'. Hunting was put into a context which included a wide range of profound experiences. In details as well as in the general design the *Georgics* was useful to Somerville above all in enabling him to realize more completely ideas which would otherwise have remained latent.

Richard Jago's *Edge-Hill, or the rural prospect delineated and moralized* (1767) has a very similar, primarily social, value. The title suggests Jago's approach to his subject. The poem is a description (in four books divided according to the time of day – Morning, Noon, Afternoon, Evening) of the countryside around Edge Hill in Warwickshire. Description is combined with historical and moral reflection and with narrative digression, but there is no explicit practical purpose.

Jago makes it quite clear, however, that he is writing in the Virgilian tradition. One of his epigraphs is taken from the praise of Italy, and immediately suggests *Edge-Hill*'s patriotic purpose. Apart from this Jago has seven footnotes in which he calls attention to his imitation of passages in the *Georgics*, and two references which help to place his poem in the English tradition of Georgic imitation. In one of these he acknowledges John Philips by saying that, if *Edge-Hill* were only worthy of the countryside it describes then

> the cyder-land
> In Georgic strains, by her own Philips sung.
> Should boast no brighter fame ...
> (I, 332–4)

and he also refers in passing (I, 369) to his friendship with Somerville.

The significance of the footnote references varies considerably. In some cases Jago seems to be doing little more than bow gracefully to Virgil's direction. This happens, for example, when he comes to describe a summer storm:

> And oft the sudden show'r, or sweeping storm
> O'erflows the meads ...
> (IV, 278–9)

The lines from *Georgics* I are recalled:

> Often, too, there appears in the sky a mighty column
> of waters ...
> (I, 322–6)

but the imitation is not very detailed and Jago's main intention seems to be to stress a community of interest between himself and Virgil. It is the oneness of the experience that is important, combined with the pleasure of the literary reference itself.

Sometimes the pleasure seems to spring from a purely fortuitous literary recollection. In a section on British industry Jago has occasion, rather unexpectedly, to write on buttons, and he asks how he can possibly give an impression of their variety:

> What art
> Can, in the scanty bounds of measured verse,
> Display the treasure of a thousand mines
> To wond'rous shapes by stubborn labour wrought?
> (III, 555–8)

In a footnote he calls attention to the passage in which Virgil has said how impossible it is to try to ennumerate the different sorts of grape:

> But for the many kinds, or the names they bear, there is no numbering – nor, indeed, is the numbering worth the pains.   (II, 104–5)

The imitation has little of the mock-heroic about it because there is insufficient disparity between the two subjects: it is rather a question of the parallel forcing itself upon Jago's attention as he is in the process of composition, a chiming which is quite accidental from the thematic point of view, but which Jago feels gives an added interest to the surface of the writing. It recalls Fielding's comment on the burlesque diction of *Joseph Andrews*, that it was put there for the entertainment of 'the classical reader'.

On a similarly generalized level Jago, when he writes on the diseases of sheep, directs attention to Virgil's passage on the plague:

> Then on every side amid gladsome herbage the young kine die or yield up sweet life by their full folds . . .
> (III, 494–5)

but his supposed imitation is not really very close:

> they the professed dainty lothe
> And death exulting claims his destin'd prey.
> (IV 301–2)

'The mob of gentlemen...'

Here the intention of the reference is not so much to signal an actual borrowing as to point to a general parallelism of subject-matter. It reminds the reader that this is a traditional topic and the lines to some extent a variation on a theme. There is perhaps some significance in the citation of Virgil rather than Lucretius: it suggests, certainly, that Jago regarded his poem from a Georgic standpoint.

These imitations are good examples of the variety of eighteenth-century practice, but there are two references that go deeper than those discussed so far. In describing the work of an iron foundry, Jago says

> See, how they strain
> The swelling nerve, and lift the sinewy arm
> In measur'd time; while with their clatt'ring blows
> From street to street the propagated sound
> Increasing echoes, and, on every side
> The tortured metal sheds a radiant shower.
>
> (III, 527–32)

and he quotes in a footnote his Virgilian source:

> (The Cyclops) with mighty force, now one, now another, raise their arms in measured cadence.
>
> (IV, 174–5)

These lines are from Virgil's description of the labours of the bees, and from one of his most clearly mock-heroic passages in which he compares the activity of the hive with that of the Cyclops' forge. 'If little things with great we may compare', he says, then we can liken the exertions of the Cyclops in their forge, 'while Aetna groans under the anvils laid upon her', with the work of the insects. The comparison brings into play a characteristic element of sympathetic satire, and Jago's recollection of Virgilian mock-heroics at this point gives a very precise indication of his own attitude to his subject. When he writes:

> Now Cyclopean chief!
> Quick on the anvil lay the burning bar,
> And with thy lusty fellows, on its sides
> Impress the weighty stroke
>
> (III, 524–7)

there is not the same degree of discrepancy as there is in Virgil's comparison of the cyclop and the bee, but some measure of incongruity (and again the blend of sympathy and satire) is certainly present, and this incongruity is developed and used when Jago discusses the various functions to which steel may be put:

> See there the glitt'ring knife
> Of temper'd edge! The scissors double shaft,
> Useless apart, in social union joined,
> Each aiding each! Emblem how beautiful
> Of happy nuptial leagues! The button round
> Plain, or imbost, or bright with steely rays...
>
> (III, 544–9)

The facts, the exaggerated moral, the sensuousness and the literary reference combine to create a mélange of the grave and the ludicrous which is perhaps the only possible treatment for the subject. The Virgilian reference helps to establish an appropriate tone and to avoid the unintentionally ludicrous.

Another important reference, but of a rather different character, occurs in the same section of the poem, where Jago says that

> The rough file grates: yet useful is its touch...
> How the coarse metal brightens into fame
> Shap'd by their plastic hands! what ornament!
> What various use!
>
> (III, 539–44)

He points as his source to the lines in the first *Georgic* in which Virgil refers to the discovery of iron and the invention of the saw. Again they are important lines. Just as the passage analysed above is associated with the phrase 'so little things with great we may compare' (a phrase influential in indicating Jago's attitude) these lines immediately precede and refer to the *labor omnia vicit* tag, and in so doing help to establish the philosophical basis of the passage. Birmingham is a centre of industry and as such symbolizes the moral triumph of British prosperity. With the knowledge of this success behind him, and the feeling that Britain is emulating the achievements of Augustan Rome (or at least faithfully following a path that would have been approved by Virgil) it is appropriate for Jago to exclaim, as he does a few lines later), 'Hail native ore!', and to follow this with lines which echo Virgil's praise of

Italy, although on this occasion Jago does not feel any need to acknowledge a debt:

> We envy not Golconda's sparkling mines,
> Nor thine Potosi! nor thy kindred hills,
> Teeming with gold.
>
> (III, 476–9)

By this series of references, some comparatively trivial and some of a more fundamental significance, Jago establishes the predominantly Georgic character of his poem. The citation of parallels in the footnotes makes it clear that they are not adventitious, but are elements in the meaning of the work as a whole, stressing that Jago's attitude towards his subject matter is a blend of all the elements associated with the Georgic tradition. An analysis of one or two of the poem's leading *motifs* shows the nature of the debt.

In his account, for example, of the origins of the earth and the early history of mankind (an account which, in its geological emphasis, owes something to the Virgilian desire to understand the causes of things) Jago utilizes the traditional opposition between the Golden and the Iron ages, but places it in a specifically Christian context. After the Creation the earth was a shapely sphere 'of sea and land harmonious form'd', a 'sweet interchange of hill and dale',

> But man, ungrateful man! to deadly ill
> Soon turn'd the good bestow'd with horrid crimes
> Polluting earth's fair seat, his maker's gift!
>
> (I, 119–21)

The corruptions of nature and consequently the hardness of life are Man's responsibility: the assertion of that corruption at the very beginning of the poem echoes the similar assertions by Virgil and Thomson, and in each case it is an important element in the subsequent treatment of the natural scene.

In this context it is inevitably earth's fruitful nature that is most celebrated. As in Pope and Thomson it is the harvest scene that appeals most strongly, when 'cultivation spreads her height'ning lustre', and the merely natural scene gives way to a man-made order and abundance:

> Over all her horn
> Fair plenty pours ...

The English Georgic

>   See, beneath her touch
> The smiling harvests rise, with bending line,
> And wavy ridge, along the dappled glebe
> Stretching their lengthen'd beds ...
>
> (II, 43–8)

The image is a cliché, but it is a cliché which retains its emotional power. It is traditional, but with the weight of a tradition which is fundamental to human experience.

Another traditional aspect of Jago's attitude to the countryside is seen in his pleasure in moralizing, as his title suggests, the rural prospect:

>   Thus, from the rural landscape, learn to know
>   The various characters of time and place ...
>
> (I, 394–5)

What one learns by examining the landscape is, above all, to appreciate 'fair liberty, and freedom's generous reign'. A passage which is clearly indebted to *Cooper's Hill* and *Windsor Forest* begins with a description of the castle of Beaudesert with its 'moated hall' and 'pensile bridge', but Jago soon turns to a contrast between the darkness of Norman rule and contemporary enlightenment. In the past the nobles

>   o'er defenceless tribes, with wanton rage,
>   Tyrannic rul'd; and, in their castled halls
>   Secure, with wild excess their revels kept.
>
> (I, 380–2)

The landscape of the past, with its isolated pockets of humanity surrounded by hostile forces, is seen as a reflection of the political and social situation. Similarly the landscape of Jago's day reflects contemporary political stability. We can learn

>   To hail, from open scenes, and cultur'd fields,
>   Fair liberty, and freedom's gen'rous reign
>   With guardian laws, and polish'd arts adorn'd.
>   While the portcullis huge, or moated fence
>   The sad reverse of savage times betray –
>   Distrust, barbarity, and Gothic rule.
>
> (I, 397–402)

'The mob of gentlemen...'

This contrast between past and present conditions and the note of self-congratulation is, as we have seen, typical of the Georgic form in a wide variety of developments.

Jago's treatment of the transitoriness of glory also echoes the handling of that theme in Denham, Pope and Thomson. A picture of desolate ruins displays 'the melancholy tale of pomp laid low in dust':

>   But regal state
> And sprightly mirth, beneath the festive roof,
> Are now no more.
>   All, alas, is gone,
> And silence keeps her melancholy court
> Throughout the walls; save, where in rooms of state,
> Kings once reposed! chatter the wrangling daws,
> Or screech owls hoot along the vaulted isles.
>   (II, 307–14)

Obviously this is not an exclusively Georgic theme. In English it occurs, after all, as early as the Anglo-Saxon *Wanderer*. But it is a theme which comes with particular potency in a genre which celebrates Man's achievements. There is a very marked contrast between Man's ability to subdue Nature to his purposes in so many directions and his inability to combat death. 'The melancholy tale of pomp laid low in dust' cuts across the basic optimism of the genre as it does, of course, very importantly in the *Georgics* itself. Jago himself provides an echo of the passage in which Virgil thinks of the farmer turning up rusty weapons with his plough or marvelling 'at the giant bones in the upturned graves':

> Still as the ploughman breaks the clotted glebe,
> He ever and anon some trophy finds,
> The relics of the war – or rusty spear,
> Or canker'd ball; but from sepul'chral soil
> Cautious he turns aside the shining steel,
> Lest haply at its touch uncover'd bones
> Should start to view and blast his rural toil.
>   (IV, 513–19)

This sort of awareness provides a substratum to the celebration of human triumphs which is the central theme of the poem.

That theme itself is expressed most extensively and consciously in the section on Birmingham, with its praise of British industry, the mock-heroic aspect of which has already been touched upon. The *Argument* gives the subject-matter of the section:

> Bremicham. Its manufactures. Coal-mines, Iron-ore. Process of it. Panegyric upon iron.

The dominant emotion is one of wonder. The coal-mine which

> echoes with the noise
> Of swarthy slaves and instruments of toil
> (III, 437-8)

rouses Jago's imagination, and its dangers – 'the flood . . . drowning the nether world', or the 'kindling flames by pitchy vapours fed' excite his awe. He feels a similar mixture of emotions in the iron foundry amidst the 'fierce heat' and the 'impetuous rage' of the furnace where, despite the 'noise and hurry' objects of the utmost delicacy are produced:

> who can count the forms
> That hourly from the glowing embers rise?
> (III, 552-3)

Jago does communicate a sense of excitement and, although his enthusiasm sometimes appears naive in the light of the later developments of industrialization, his basic position is a sound one. British prosperity does depend upon coal and iron. His scornful rejection of exotic golden ages is deeply-felt and understandable:

> Would ye your coarse, unsightly mines exchange
> For Mexiconian hills? to tread on gold
> As vulgar sand? with naked limbs to brave
> The cold, bleak air? to urge the tedious chase,
> By painful hunger stung, with artless toil,
> Through gloomy forests, where the sounding axe,
> To the sun's beam, ne'er op'd the cheerful glade,
> Nor culture's healthful face was ever seen!
> (III, 613-20)

A study of *Edge-Hill* as of *The Chase* is most interesting in showing how valuable a poetic tradition could be in helping a not particularly talented poet to develop a viable attitude towards his subject matter. *Edge-Hill* is an extremely wide-ranging poem thematically

– it is, as we have seen, concerned with historical and philosophical matters as well as having an extensive descriptive intention – and it shows an awareness of the complexity of the subject. That Jago succeeds in imposing order upon this range and this complexity is due to the fact that he can draw upon a traditional mode. In the Georgic attitudes which, as he makes clear, govern the poem, Jago finds a way of approaching his material without having to be over-explicit or over-simple. There are many weaknesses in the execution of *Edge-Hill*, but in its grasp of the material and in its use of the topographical framework it is remarkably successful.

In the work of a succession of 'nature' poets then, from Denham to Jago, the Virgilian influence is at work, giving shape and a traditional validity to the interpretation of country life. But *Edge-Hill* is the last descriptive poem of this kind in which the Georgic influence has a controlling power. When one turns to Cowper's *Retirement* and *The Task* there is a decisive shift.

It is not that Cowper is unaware of the Virgilian tradition: indeed there are frequent passages which show the characteristic *motifs* of Georgic writing. There is even one passage of practical horticultural instruction which is very close, stylistically, to the didactic parts of *Cyder* or *The Fleece*. This is the section on growing cucumbers in which Cowper has need to describe the proper building of a dungheap, and does so in a flamboyant Miltonic pastiche:

> The stable yields a stercoragceous heap,
> Impregnated with quick fermenting salts
> And potent to resist the freezing blast ...
>
> (III, 463–5)

As so often happens with this kind of writing Cowper seems to be interested both in giving information and in stylistic manipulation. His own comment on gardening is, *mutatis mutandis*, an apt one:

> Strength may wield the ponderous spade,
> May turn the clod and wheel the compost home,
> But elegance, chief grace the garden shows,
> And most attractive is the fair result.
>
> (III, 636–9)

Apart from this extended piece of practical instruction one is most often reminded of the Georgic tradition in lines which echo earlier passages either of scientific philosophizing or the praise of retired life. In *Retirement*, which has an epigraph from *Georgics* IV, for example, Cowper writes on how the observer of insect life may

> trace in Nature's most minute design
> The signature and stamp of power divine,
> Contrivance intricate expressed with ease,
> Where unassisted sight no beauty sees,
> The shapely limb and lubricated joint,
> Within the small dimensions of a point ...
>
> (53-8)

A similar theme is taken up, but much more critically, in *The Task*. The scientist who seeks God through His works (of whom Newton is the type) is praised, but most scientists suffer from a pride which is atheistical:

> Some drill and bore
> The solid earth, and from the strata there
> Extract a register, by which we learn,
> That he who made it, and revealed its date
> To Moses, was mistaken in its age.
>
> (III, 150-4)

In expressing these doubts Cowper is moving away from the traditional interpretations of Virgil's *rerum cognososcere causas* passage, and the pessimism about Man's potentialities which is at the root of his changed emphasis perhaps explains why the *Georgics* could not serve him as a model as it had served Thomson. Virgil's poem is in some ways a bleak one. Man is subject to unforeseeable calamities and life demands unremitting labour, but still the Virgilian view, as we have seen it constantly in this chapter, is that life with all its difficulties must be confronted, and that if it is confronted Man can dominate his environment. In the work of Denham, Pope and Thomson this confrontation is explored at various levels – political, commercial, personal – and diverse facets of human experience are seen in relation to one another. In Cowper, on the contrary, this very important element of confrontation is missing. For Cowper retirement from the active world is not one aspect of life (and one that must be reconciled with many other aspects): it is a central, dominating necessity. Virgil had pictured himself passing his days in Naples while Augustus thundered in war on the banks of the Euphrates, but he sympathized with military and political greatness. Cowper, partly for personal reasons of health and temperament but partly because of the age in which he lived, wished for total seclusion from the world.

Conclusion

Eighteenth-century writers were much exercised by the notion of formal categories, and Addison's *Essay on the Georgics*, together with the work of such men as Trapp or Warton, can be seen as part of a continuous critical effort to define the structure and prescribe the style of the various kinds of literature deductively. Addison clearly feels confident in stating both the scope and the limitations of the form. Pope's *Discourse on Pastoral Poetry* (published in 1717 with the *Pastorals*, but written according to Pope in 1704) is an example of similar critical assumptions. He begins with a precise definition of the genre:

> A Pastoral is an imitation of the action of a shepherd, or one considered under that character. The form of this imitation is dramatic, or narrative, or mixed of both ... the fable simple, the manners not too polite nor too rustic: the thoughts are plain, yet admit a little quickness and passion, but that short and flowing: the expression humble, yet as pure as the language will afford; neat, but not florid, easy, and yet lively. In short, the fable, manners, thoughts, and expressions are full of the greatest simplicity in nature.
>
> The complete character of this poem consists in simplicity, brevity and delicacy; the two first of which render an eclogue natural, and the last delightful.

Pope is concerned to make the nature of his chosen kind as definite as possible, and at the end he can add that 'it is by rules like these that we ought to judge of pastoral'. The rules themselves are not, of course, purely theoretical. They are drawn from 'the practice of Theocritus and Virgil. (the only undisputed authors of pastoral)' and they therefore carry authoritative weight.

The most striking, because least expected, example of the eighteenth-century preoccupation with categories is Fielding's theorizing about the novel. He begins his Preface to *Joseph Andrews* as Addison had begun his essay on the *Georgics*, by saying that he is dealing with a topic that has been virtually ignored in the past. But this does not prevent him from citing authorities. He discusses epic and romance, refers to Aristotle, Homer and *Telemachus*, and soon concludes that the book he is offering to the public is related to the epic kind. He then gives rules for the proper conduct of the action, fable and diction of this new form. It is a matter of bringing the novel into the literary commonwealth, establishing its status and the criteria for judgement. If the critical framework that had been developed to deal with epic could be related to the novel, then the most dangerous argument against the new form, that it was a species of anti-literature, formless and unregulated, would be countered.

The impression made by these and similar discussions is almost inevitably one of critical rigidity. The persistent wish to establish 'rules', the regard for authority, and the apparent intention of limiting experiment all seem to point in the direction of narrowness and inflexibility. And in no form does it seem more likely that the expectation of rigidity will be fulfilled than in the Georgic, a genre whose re-emergence appears on the face of it to have depended entirely on a reverence for classical precedent, and whose moral and didactic weight is so considerable. Yet the energy of inventiveness which characterizes eighteenth-century literature in general, and which makes it an exceptionally exciting period of formal development, in spite of critical preoccupations which appear to be narrowing, is certainly also present in the Georgic form.

The essential reason seems to have been that the poets on the whole were not primarily concerned with formal imitation for its own sake. Some, of course, were, and in *Cyder*, *The Fleece*, *The Hop-Garden* or *Sugar-Cane* the element of pastiche is strong. But three of these poems occur late in the history of the genre, and none of them is particularly vital today. The interest that they now offer is historical. Examination of the chronological development from Denham shows clearly, however, that the initial impulse towards the adoption of formal features of the *Georgics* came from the poets' choice of subject-matter and their movement towards a particular interpretation of it. Denham turned to Virgil because he saw a way of exploiting some lines from the passage on Italy so as to lend authority to his own patriotism and to his praise of trade. The echo in Denham seems to be fortuitous; certainly its importance is thematic. But once the link had been perceived and used the significance of the parallel became inescapable for subsequent poets in similar contexts, more especially since *Cooper's Hill* established itself as a minor classic. That similar contexts did occur was made inevitable by the conditions of political and commerical life after the Restoration. The wealth of the country was seen increasingly to depend on trade, and it would have been extraordinary if this realization had not been reflected in the poetry, as indeed it was in Waller or Dryden. And it continued to be reflected at first through relatively limited Virgilian echoes.

But once the *Georgics* had been used by Denham in this particular way the wider significance of the poem for the period as a whole was plainly there to be grasped. The *Georgics* sprang, as we saw, from the national situation of pre-Augustan Rome and this paralleled in many ways the situation of late seventeenth-century England. Virgil celebrates the order, stability and fruitfulness of farming in contrast to the disorganization, insecurity and destruction of the decade which followed Julius Caesar's death: the same dangers had faced England, and the same values were, in consequence, felt to be important. When Pope came to write *Windsor Forest* he turned inevitably to Denham's poem as a model, and then developed brilliantly the implications of the Georgic elements which he found in that work. The poem is an intepretation of English history in the light of Virgil's ideals, imitating also many of the central passages of the *Georgics*. It is not in any way a pastiche, but a recreation in which, if the reader wishes, he can ignore the influence of the model, although it remains an extremely important factor in controlling the structure.

The driving force behind *Windsor Forest*, which is expressed in the themes of the opening section, is the fragility of political order and the precariousness of civilization, two of the leading ideas of Virgil's work. Thomson's *Seasons*, the most complex and far-reaching of all the Georgic imitations is conerned with these themes, but it also explores, to a much greater extent than *Windsor Forest*, the social, psychological and moral implications of disorder. The exploration takes place through Thomson's use, at many points in *The Seasons*, of the Golden-Iron Age myth and his development of the theme of rural retirement – both, in his handling, profoundly Virgilian concepts which can be most fully understood in relation to the *Georgics* and the philosophy of life which that poem presents.

Conclusion

So far this summary suggests that the most significant factor in the development of English Georgic poetry was the correspondence between the situations of pre-Augustan and post-Restoration England, and it is certainly true that that correspondence is of great importance and is deeply felt. Imitation begins on the thematic and develops to a formal level. But with Pope, and even more Thomson, it becomes clear that, although imitation of the *Georgics* was first inspired by historical factors, its continuation involved much wider sympathies between eighteenth-century writers and Virgil.

In the discussion of Dryden's translation it was said that the *Georgics* is a *montage* involving sudden shifts of subject and mood so that a pattern of comparisons and contrasts is built up which defies easy explanation. The horror of the plague cannot be reconciled with scenes of abundant fertility. There is no attempt to blur the sharp outlines of the problem and Virgil does not provide any formula of explanation: he leaves the contrasts to speak for themselves. There is a brilliant lecture on 'The Philosophy of Virgil' in which Professor R. S. Conway argues that the antithetical way of thought that is illustrated in this way on a large scale in the structure of the *Georgics* is fundamental in Virgil:[1]

> Virgil was rarely content to see a fact, or a feeling, or an event, in which he was interested, as something which stood by itself. He instinctively sought for some parallel event, some complementary fact, to set beside the first.

Conway illustrates this Virgilian variability of standpoint with a great deal of detailed analysis, involving sometimes a single phrase, sometimes a whole episode, and the case that emerges is an extremely impressive one. The more local analysis is often of great interest to a reader who is concerned with the multiple viewpoints so frequent in eighteenth-century work, and it is well worth giving an example. In his fourth book Virgil had warned the beekeeper not to put his hive too near the nests of swallows because the swallows would carry off the bees to feed their young:

> ore ferunt dulcem nidis immitibus escam
>
> (IV, 17)
>
> they carry them off in their mouths, a sweet morsel for their cruel nestlings

Conway discusses the unexpectedness of the word *dulcem* ('sweet') rather than *facilem* ('easy') which 'would have enforced the point, namely, the greediness of the baby swallows and the consequent danger to the bees'.

> What has Virgil done by choosing *dulcem*? We shall see at once, if for the word *immitibus* ('cruel') we substitute a more common epithet of young birds, say *crepantibus* ('twittering, clamorous'). What should we have then? 'A sweet morsel for their clamouring (that is, hungry) young.' If Virgil had written that, you would have seen clearly that he was expressing sympathy with the swallows and that he had forgotten to be sorry for the bees. But by using both the word *dulcem* and the word *immitibus* – 'a sweet morsel for their cruel nestlings' – Virgil expresses his sympathy, first with the swallows and then with the bees, in one and the same line.

Conway suggests that in cases like this Virgil practices 'a kind of brief quotation ... he describes part of the scene for a moment, as it appears to one of the actors in it', but without, of course, relinquishing the authorial viewpoint. On a larger scale the same thing happens in the narrative structure of the *Aeneid* where 'the action is continually shared by two leading characters at a time, each presented to us with almost equal sympathy', as conspicuously happens in the story of Dido and Aeneas.

This analysis has a striking relevance for anyone interested in the eighteenth-century Georgic tradition. One thing that consistently emerges from the poetry dealt with in this book is the authors' fondness for the exploration of multiple viewpoints. Even in the relatively low-powered writing of John Philips or James Grainger there are frequent shifts of mood and tone in the juxtaposition of the various aspects of the subjects. In Pope or Thomson a similar pattern of contrasting attitudes is established with a degree of technical accomplishment that allows for a far greater complexity. But it is clear that one of the qualities in the *Georgics* that made an instinctive appeal to eighteenth-century writers is precisely the one that Professor Conway analyses. Nothing about the period is felt so strongly as its fondness for antithesis and balance. It has often been suggested that the popularity of the couplet form itself is a reflection of an antithetical

Conclusion

habit of mind. Within the couplet the frequent counterpoising of one idea by its opposite is almost inevitable, and it is clearly the perfect vehicle for a dialectical presentation of argument. It is easy to see the Johnsonian sentence, with its constant tendency towards syntactic balance, as the development of a similar order in prose. In the intellectual climate that laid such stress upon potentially antithetical forms of writing the structure of the *Georgics* had a distinct potentiality which, as we have seen, was continuously exploited. It is perhaps this above all that accounts for the popularity of the genre.

But one should couple with this the opportunities which the form presents for the exploration of experience through different levels of style. It was argued in the first chapter that Dryden's use of a mock-heroic style in parts of his translation was entirely consonant with Virgil's intentions. Certainly the authors of subsequent imitations seem to have felt so. One of the most characteristic devices of the genre is to make the style stand in opposition to the subject in such a way that more than one attitude is expressed. Style, however elaborate, is seldom merely decorative: it is used to put the subject in new lights and so dispose it for sceptical scrutiny. Gay pushes the experiment to its furthest point in *Rural Sports* and *Trivia*; but all the Georgic imitations show the same kind of stylistic self-consciousness, and even the minor writers assume a very sophisticated response on the part of their audience.

It is the combination of a natural sympathy with Virgil's preoccupations and his moral and political assumptions, together with an admiration for the structural and stylistic means that he used to express those assumptions, that guides the diversity of Georgic imitation in the eighteenth century.

Note

1. R. S. Conway *Harvard Lectures on the Virgilian Age* (1928), p. 99.

Select Bibliography

(a) *The 'Georgics': Text and Translation*

The most convenient text is in the 'Loeb Library'; *Virgil With an English Translation*, by H. Rushton Fairclough. Volume 1: *Eclogues, Georgics, Aeneid* I–IV. (revised edition 1935). The third book of Dryden's translation of the *Georgics* appeared in *The Annual Miscellany* (1694), and the complete poem in *The Works of Virgil: Containing his Pastorals, Georgics and Aeneis Translated into English Verse* (1697). The translation is available in the World's Classics series of reprints (with an Introduction by James Kinsley), and is included in Dryden's *Poetical Works*, edited by G. R. Noyes (revised edition 1952). Modern verse translations include those by C. Day Lewis (1941) and Palmer Bovie Smith (1956).

(b) *English Georgic Poetry*

Poems discussed in this book are listed here and references given to modern editions where appropriate. Much of the material can be most conveniently studied, however, in one of the standard collections of English poetry. See especially:

R. Anderson *Poets of Great Britain*, 13 Volumes (1792–95)
A. Chalmers *The English Poets*, 21 Volumes (1810)

DENHAM, JOHN: The first edition of *Cooper's Hill* in 1642 was unauthorized and incomplete. The first authentic text appeared in 1655, and the last version to appear in Denham's lifetime was published in *Poems and Translations* (1668). The standard modern edition is by T. H. Banks (1928), and there is an easily accessible reprint in *Poetry of Landscape and the Night: Two Eighteenth-Century Traditions*, edited by Charles Peake (1967).

DYER, JOHN: *The Fleece: a Poem in Four Books* (1757). There is a reprint in *Minor Poets of the Eighteenth Century*, edited by H. I'A. Fausset (1930) for the Everyman Library.

Bibliography

GAY, JOHN: *Rural Sports, a Poem* (1713); extensively revised version *Rural Sports: a Georgic* (1720). *Trivia: or, the Art of Walking the Streets of London* (1716). The standard edition is *Poetical Works*, edited by G. C. Faber (1926).

GRAINGER, JAMES: *The Sugar-Cane: A Poem. In Four Books with Notes* (1764).

JAGO, RICHARD: *Edge-Hill, or the Rural Prospect Delineated and Moralized. A Poem in Four Books* (1767).

PHILIPS, JOHN: *Cyder: A Poem in Two Books* (1708). The most recent edition is *The Poems of John Philips*, by M. G. Lloyd Thomas (1927).

POPE, ALEXANDER: *Windsor Forest* was first published in 1713, and numerous revisions were incorporated when the poem appeared in Pope's *Works* (1717). The standard modern text is in Vol. I of the 'Twickenham Edition', and is edited by E. Audra and Aubrey Williams. A manuscript of the poem which dates from 1712 and which differs in many ways from the published text is reproduced in facsimile in Robert M. Schmitz's *Pope's Windsor Forest, 1712, A Study of the Washington University Holograph* (1952).

SMART, CHRISTOPHER: *The Hop-Garden* was first published in *Poems on Several Occasions* (1752). The standard modern edition is in *The Collected Poems of Christopher Smart, with an Introduction and Critical Comments*, edited by Norman Callan (1949).

SOMERVILLE, WILLIAM: *The Chace: a Poem* (1735). *Hobbinol, or the Rural Games. A Burlesque Poem, in Blank Verse* (1740).

THOMSON, JAMES: The first edition of *Winter* appeared in March 1726, and the second, enlarged, revised and with a Preface, in the following June. *Summer* was published in 1727, *Spring* in 1728, and *Autumn* appeared in 1730 as part of the first edition of the collected *Seasons*. The *Hymn* was first published in 1730. The best modern texts are *Thomson's Seasons: Critical Edition, being a reproduction of the original texts with all the various readings of the later editions, historically arranged*, edited by Otto Zippel (1908). Palaestra LXVI, and *The Complete Poetical Works of James Thomson* edited, with notes by J. Logie Robertson (1908). Robertson's edition also provides an extensive textual apparatus.

WALLER, EDMUND: *A Penegyrick to my Lord Protector* (1665); *To the King, upon his Majesty's Happy Return* (1660).

Bibliography

(c) Contemporary criticism

ADDISON, JOSEPH: *An Essay on the 'Georgics'* was published as a Preface to Dryden's translation in 1697. It is reprinted in *Eighteenth-Century Critical Essays*, edited by Scott Elledge, Two Volumes (1961). The essays on the Pleasures of the Imagination were published in *The Spectator*, 411–421, in June and July 1712. See *The Spectator*, edited with an Introduction and Notes by Donald F. Bond, Four Volumes (1965).

COWLEY, ABRAHAM: The Preface to the *Pindarique Odes* was published in *Poems* (1656). The standard modern edition is by A. R. Waller (1905). It is included in Abraham Cowley *Poetry and Prose* edited by L. C. Martin (1949).

DRYDEN, JOHN: Prefaces to *Ovid's Epistles, Translated by Several Hands* (1680) and to *Sylvae: or the Second Part of Poetical Miscellanies* (1685). See John Dryden *Of Dramatic Poesy and Other Critical Essays*, edited with an Introduction by George Watson (1962).

FELTON, HENRY: *A Dissertation of Reading the Classics* (1713).

JOHNSON, SAMUEL: *The Lives of the English Poets* were published between 1779–81. See especially the lives of Denham, Dryden, John Philips, Gay, Somerville, Pope, Thomson and Dyer. The standard edition is by G. Birkbeck Hill, Three Volumes (1905).

POPE, ALEXANDER: *Peri Bathous, or the Art of Sinking in Poetry* (1728). There are modern editions by E. L. Steeves (1952) and by Bertrand A. Goldgar (1965).

TRAPP, JOSEPH: *Praelectiones Poeticae*, Two Volumes, (1711–15). Translated into English as *The Oxford Lectures on Poetry*, by W. Clarke and W. Bowyer (1742).

WARTON, JOSEPH: *A Discourse on Didactic Poetry*, published with his edition of *Virgil* (1753).

(d) Recent criticism

ARMENS, SVEN: *John Gay, Social Critic* (1954).

BROWER, R. A.: *Alexander Pope: the Poetry of Allusion* (1959).

COHEN, RALPH: *The Art of Discrimination. Thomson's 'The Seasons' and the Language of Criticism* (1964).

CONWAY, R. S.: *Harvard Lectures on the Virgilian Age* (1928).

Bibliography

DOBRÉE, BONAMY: *English Literature in the Early Eighteenth Century, 1700–1740*. 'The Oxford History of English Literature', Volume VII (1959).

DURLING, DWIGHT: *Georgic Tradition in English Poetry* (1935).

FORSGREN, ADINA: *John Gay: Poet of a Lower Order. Comments on His Rural Poems and Other Early Writings* (1964).

IRVING, W. H.: *John Gay, Favorite of the Wits* (1940).
John Gay's London (1928).

KNIGHT, W. F. JACKSON: *Roman Virgil* (1944).

PRICE, MARTIN: *To the Palace of Wisdom: Studies in Order and Energy from Dryden to Blake* (1964).

RAND, E. K.: *The Magical Art of Virgil* (1931).

RØSTVIG, MAREN-SOFIE: *The Happy Man: Studies in the Metamorphoses of a Classical Ideal*. Volume I: 1600–1700 (1954); Volume II: 1700–1760 (1958).

SPACKS, PATRICIA: *The Varied God* (a study of Thomson's *Seasons*: 1959). *John Gay* (1965).

SUTHERLAND, J. R.: 'John Gay' in *Pope and His Contemporaries*, edited by J. L. Clifford and L. A. Lands (1949).

WASSERMAN, E. R.: *The Subtler Language: Critical Readings of Neo-Classic and Romantic Poems* (1959).

Index

Absalom and Achitophel (Dryden), 29, 30
Actium, Battle of, 5, 7, 8, 10
Addison, Joseph, influence on didactic poets of, 17;
   Essay on the Georgics by, 17–21, 29, 30, 32, 72, 206;
   on poetic style, 19, 33;
   on dignity of words, 19–20;
   on Hesiod, 20;
   and Virgil, 20–1;
   on 'loves of the beasts', 21;
   on mock-heroic in *Georgics*, 27–8, 30;
   Philips and, 40–1;
   Essay in *Spectator* by, 41;
   Thomson and, 125;
   Gay, and 172;
   on burlesque, 189
Aden, John M., 144, 179 n. 4
Aeneid (Virgil), 78, 172, 180
L'Allegro (Milton), 90, 93, 147
Anne, Queen, 45, 72, 79, 80, 81–2, 85, 86, 141, 142
Annus Mirabilis (Dryden), 71
Antony, Mark, 5, 6, 7,
Aratus, 18
Arber, Edward, 179 n. 10
Argument (Thomson), 131
Argument (Jago), 202
Aristotle, 207
Armens, Sven, 178
Art of Discrimination, The (Cohen), 139 n. 2
Art of Poetry (Horace), 64 n. 1

Augustus Caesar, 5, 6, 7, 8;
   Virgil and, 4, 8–10, 24, 83, 123, 160, 204;
   Smart and, 49;
   Grainger and, 64
Autumn (Thomson), see *The Seasons*

Background to Thomson's Seasons (McKillop), 93, 139 n. 4
Blake, William, 69, 89 n. 7
Boileau, Nicolas, essay on La Fontaine by, 190
Book of Job, 113
Boswell, James, 57, 58
Britannia's Pastorals (Browne), 135
Brooks, Harold, 64 n. 1
Broughton, Dorothy, 156, 179 n. 11
Browne, Sir Thomas, 111, 135
Brutus, 5
Butler, Samuel, 190

Caesar, see Julius Caesar
Cassius, 5
Cato, 114
Cervantes, 1
Chase, The (Somerville), 95, 124, 180;
   preface to, 180;
   origins of, 180;
   and history of hunting, 180;
   influence of *Georgics* on, 181;
   patriotism in, 181;
   and exotic hunting scenes, 185;
   stag-hunt in, 186;
   Hobbinol and, 188;
   style of, 191;
   Milton's influence on, 192;
   breeding of hounds in, 192;

Chase, The—contd.
  sociological justification of, 194;
  poetic tradition and, 202
City Shower, A (Swift);
  influence of Virgil on, 168;
  Juvenalian style of, 168;
  Trivia and, 167–9;
  negation of Georgic values in, 169
Cohen, Ralph, 139 n. 2, 140 n. 14
Colonel Jacque (Defoe), 12, 15 n. 9
Compleat Angler, The, or the Contemplative Man's Recreation (Walton), 151, 179 n. 5, 179 n. 6
Complete Husbandry, 5
Complete Works of William Diaper, The (ed. Broughton), 179 n. 11, 179 n. 12
Complete Writings of William Blake, The (ed. Geoffrey Keynes), 89 n. 7
Conway, Professor R.S., 15 n. 4, 209, 210, 211 n. 1
Cooper's Hill (Denham), 17, 66, 72;
  Dr. Johnson's comment on, 67;
  social and political aspects of, 67, 208;
  scorn of London in, 69;
  themes of patriotism and progress in, 72;
  its influence on Pope, 81, 82, 83, 87;
  publication of, 88 n. 1;
  stag-hunt in, 186;
  Jago and, 200
Corycian swain, old, 26;
  The Sugar-Cane and, 62
Cotton, Charles, 179 n. 5
Cowley, Abraham, 35;
  adaption of Pindar by, 34;
  preface to first two Pindarique odes by, 34;
  cited in *Windsor Forest*, 85;
  and method of translation, 35
Cowper, William;
  Virgilian tradition and, 203;
  on cucumbers, 203;
  and the scientist, 204;
  pessimism of, 204;
  his central theme of retirement, 204–5

Cox, Richard, 184
Cromwell, Oliver, 70
Cyclops, 28
Cyder, (Philips), 1, 36, 46, 51, 55;
  practical purpose of, 37;
  mock-heroic passages in, 40;
  complexity of, 45;
  influence of Virgil on, 45, 66;
  publication of, 45, 72;
  Thomson and, 92, 97;
  Cowper and, 203;
  pastiche in, 207
Cynegetica (Nemesianus), 159, 161, 179 n. 14
Cynegeticon (Grattius), 158, 162

Dacier, André, 191
Defoe, Daniel, 12, 13, 14, 15
Denham, Sir John, 17, 85;
  and *Cooper's Hill*, 66, 88 n. 1;
  moral preoccupation of, 66;
  discursiveness of, 67;
  Dr. Johnson's comments on, 67;
  and Ben Jonson, 67;
  social and political ideas of, 67–8;
  Virgil's influence on 68, 71, 72, 141, 207, 208;
  his utilitarian view of Thames, 68;
  patriotism of, 68, 207;
  and belief in trade, 68–9, 207;
  Blake and, 69;
  his scorn of London merchants, 69;
  views on commercial life, 70;
  Waller and, 70–1;
  his influence on Pope, 72, 83, 85, 208;
  Thomson and, 93, 127;
  Somerville and, 186;
  Jago and, 201, 203;
  his belief in Man, 204;
Dennys, John, 149, 153;
  his use of Georgic motifs, 153–4, 156;
  and mythology, 154;
  advice on angling by, 154;
  praises retirement, 154–5;
De Rerum Natura (Lucretius), 101–2, 140 n. 9, 159

Index

Diaper, William, 156;
  interpretation of Oppian by, 157
Discourse on Didactic Poetry, A (Warton) 33 n. 2
Discourse on Pastoral Poetry (Pope), 206
Dissertation on Reading the Classics, A (Felton), 88
Dromore, Bishop of, 58
Dryden's Aeneid and its Seventeenth-Century Predecessors (Proudfoot), 33 n. 7
Dryden and the Art of Translation (Frost) 33 n. 7
Dryden, John,
  translation of Virgil, 10, 27–32, 39, 43, 62, 71, 72, 74, 85, 140 n. 13, 169, 171, 209;
  publication of translation by, 17;
  his emphasis on mock-heroic, 21–4;
  and patriotism of, 24;
  on Virgil's epic passages, 26;
  emphasis on civil war by, 29;
  and dignity of agriculture, 30–1;
  his views on *Georgics*, 31;
  preface to *Ovid's Epistles, Translated by Several Hands* by, 34, 65 n. 1;
  on translation, 34–5;
  and 'imitation', 35–6;
  his poetic treatment of trade, 71;
  and moral approach to animal world, 157;
  his translation of Juvenal, 165–6;
  Philips and, 190;
  Somerville and, 193;
  importance of trade for, 208;
  mock-heroic style of, 211
'Dryden's Translation of *The Georgics*' (Hooker), 33 n. 7
Duff, J. Wright and Arnold M, 179 n. 14
Dunciad, The (Pope), 11, 12, 15
Durling, Dwight, 93, 140 n. 6, 216
Dyer, John, 1;
  and formal Georgic, 36;
  The Fleece by, 51–5;
  glorification of subject by, 52;
  his use of history and mythology, 52;
  patriotism of, 53;
  belief in trade of, 53, 54;
  self-mockery of, 54;
  as a poet, 54;
  elevated style of, 54, 55;
  Grainger and, 55, 56, 59;
  Dr. Johnson and, 59;
  Virgil's influence on, 64

Eclogues (Virgil), 7, 87, 105–6
Eclogues of Virgil, The (Rose), 15 n.6
Edge-Hill, or the rural prospect delineated and moralized (Jago), 180, 195–203;
  social value of, 195;
  patriotism in, 195;
  footnote references in, 195–7;
  section on industrial Birmingham in, 201–2;
  and value of poetic tradition, 202–3
  complexity of, 202–3
English Garner, An: Ingatherings from our History and Literature (Arber), 179 n. 10
English Writings of Abraham Cowley, The (ed. Waller), 64 n. 1
Epistle to the Right Honourable Richard Earl of Burlington (Pope), 2, 3, 15 n. 1;
  emphasis on prosperity and utility in, 3
Essay on the Georgics (Addison), 17, 206

Fairie Queen (Spenser), 101
Felton, Henry, 88, 123
Fielding, Henry, 1, 78, 196;
  Smart and, 51;
  views on novel, 206–7
First Satire of the Second Book of Horace Imitated, The (Pope), 65 n. 4;
  Advertisement to, 36
Fleece, The (Dyer), 1, 36, 51, 55;
  heroic treatment of subject in, 52;
  and poetic quality of, 55;
  criticism by Dr. Johnson of, 59;
  Thomson and, 92;
  Cowper and, 203;
  pastiche in, 207
Forsgren, Adina, 179 n. 1

Four Books of Husbandry (Heresbachius) 151, 179 n. 9
Frederick, Prince of Wales, 181, 184, 186, 187, 192, 194
Frost, W., 33 n. 7

Gay, John, 1, 45, 89 n. 10;
and *Rural Sports*, 78, 141;
Pope and, 72, 78, 142;
theme of 'loves of the beasts' and, 124;
Thomson and, 127;
political attitude of, 141–2;
his praise of rural life, 142, 143;
and wide range of themes, 142;
and retirement, 143;
Virgilian mood of, 141, 143, 144, 145, 158, 162, 170, 172;
Nemesianus and, 145, 158, 162;
individualistic style of, 145, 147, 152, 211;
his relation with subject-matter, 146, 147, 148, 169;
Milton's influence on, 147, 149;
description of fishing by, 147–51, 156, 158;
his love of detail, 149;
use of comic element by, 149, 176, 177;
and theme of temptation, 150;
moral attitude of, 150, 152;
complexity of, 153;
Denny's influence on, 153, 155;
Oppian and, 156, 157;
hunting poetry of, 157, 158, 162;
and humanitarianism, 157, 158;
his urban descriptions, 163, 168–9;
and nostalgia for Golden Age, 164;
eye for detail of, 164;
emotional and moral conflict of, 165;
Juvenal and, 166–7;
Swift and, 167–9;
use of imitation by, 170, 171, 172;
and fusion of literary and actual, 171;
praise of his own work by, 173;
his version of Aristaeus legend, 174–6;
and use of irony, 177;
patriotism of, 178;
adaptability of, 178
Gentleman's Recreation, The (Cox), 184
Georgics, The (Virgil), significance of, 1;
Pope and, 3, 4, 74, 76, 78, 82, 83, 87, 208, 209;
content of, 4;
and association with Octavian, 9;
political background to, 5–8, 10, 24;
influence on eighteenth century of, 12, 13, 15, 78, 141, 210;
Dryden's translation of, 17;
affinities with preceptive poetry of, 18;
Addison's *Essay* on, 17–21, 206;
epic use of natural description in, 25;
and struggle of man and nature, 26–7;
mock-heroic in, 21–4, 27–8, 36;
and contrast of mundane and heroic, 26–7, 36;
Book IV of, 27–9;
theme of husbandry in, 32, 184;
praise of Italy in, 25, 37, 43;
and influence on Philips, 39, 43, 44, 46;
and trade, 53;
Grainger and, 62, 63;
Denham and, 68, 208;
as model for descriptive poetry, 72;
popularity of, 72;
account of plague in, 76;
Influence on *The Seasons* of, 92, 93, 94, 95, 112–14, 208, 209;
complexity of, 104–6, 123, 209;
theme of retirement in, 112, 119;
and pursuit of science, 113–14;
'loves of the beasts' theme in, 124, 125;
Gay and, 144, 153, 158, 162, 169;
breeding of animals in, 158–9;
theme of progress in, 158–9;
Grattius and, 162;

220

Georgics, The—contd.
  'signs of the weather' section in, 169, 171;
  theme of active virtue in, 177;
  influence on *The Chase* of, 181, 185, 188, 192, 193, 194, 195, 201;
  as model for *Edge-Hill*, 195;
  Cowper and, 204;
Georgic Tradition, The, in English Poetry (Durling), 140 n. 6
Goldgar, Bertrand A., 33 n. 4;
  and Dyer, 55
Googe, Barnaby, 179 n. 9
Grainger, James, 55–64;
  and formal Georgic, 36;
  The Sugar-Cane by, 55;
  utilitarianism of, 55;
  and 'terms of art', 55;
  use of mock-epic by, 56, 58, 59, 60;
  Boswell's criticism of, 57, 58;
  his control of subject-matter, 59;
  and theme of man against nature, 60;
  his use of epic style, 60, 61, 64;
  and Miltonian imagery, 61;
  poetic merit of, 61;
  Virgil and, 62, 64, 66;
  contrasting views of, 210
Granville, 72, 85, 87
Grattii Falisci Cynegetica, 179 n. 14
Grattius, belief in progress of, 158;
  influence of *Georgics* on, 162;
  hunting theme of, 162, 180, 182;
  date of, 179 n. 14;
  influence on *The Chase* of, 192
Gray, Thomas, 11, 12
Great Chain of Being, The (Lovejoy), 140 n. 15

Halieutica (Oppian), 156, 161;
  Virgil's influence on, 157
Happy Man, The, Vol II: Studies in the Metamorphoses of a Classical Ideal 1700–1760 (Røstvig), 89 n. 8, 139 n. 5
Harley, Robert, Earl of Oxford, 45
Harvard Lectures on the Virgilian Age (Conway), 211 n. 1

Hazlitt, William, 90, 139 n. 3
Hengist, 47
Heresbachius, 151, 152
Hesiod, 17;
  consideration of, by Addison, 20;
  influence on Smart of, 46
Hinchliffe, William, 127
Hind and the Panther, The (Dryden), 32
History of Love, The (Hopkins), 72
Hobbinol (Somerville), 188;
  Hogarth and, 188;
  levels of style in, 191, 192;
  Milton's influence on, 192
Hogarth, 188
Homer, 58, 114, 207
Hooker, H.M., 33 n. 7
Hop Garden, The (Smart), 36, 46, 51, 55;
  local patriotism in, 46;
  tribute to Sidney in, 46;
  range of conventions, 48;
  and mock-heroic, 50;
  Miltonic imitation by, 46, 51;
  pastiche in, 207
Hopkins, Charles, 72
Horace, 34, 64 n. 1, 190;
  Thomson and, 93;
  adaptation by Cowley of, 34;
  method of translation of, 35;
  as source of imitation, 36;
  Pope and, 36, 84;
  Gay and, 143

Iliad (Homer), 175
Imitation, concept of, 34;
  Dryden on, 35;
  as creative writing, 35–6;
  ' "Imitation" in English Poetry, The, Especially in Formal Satire Before the Age of Pope' (Brooks), 64 n. 1
Impromptu on Lord Holland's Seat (Gray), 11
Irving, W.H., 179 n. 16

Jago, Richard, 180;
  social approach of, 195;

Index

Jago—*contd.*
    Virgilian tradition of, 195, 201, 203;
    Philips and, 195;
    his friendship with Somerville, 195;
    imitation of Virgil by, 196–7;
    sympathetic satire of, 197–8;
    patriotism of, 198;
    his theme of corruption of nature, 199;
    view of countryside of, 200;
    and transitoriness of glory, 201;
    basic optimism of, 201;
    and praise of industry, 201–2;
    his use of poetic tradition, 203
John Gay: Favorite of the Wits (Irving), 179 n. 16
John Gay: 'Poet of a Lower Order' (Forsgren), 179 n. 1
John Gay: Social Critic (Armens), 178
Johnson, Dr. Samuel, 19, 54, 59, 65 n. 3, 67, 88 n. 4, 92;
    his comments on Somerville, 180, 194
Jones, John, 156
Jonson, Ben, 67, 88 n. 5
Joseph Andrews (Fielding), 196;
    preface to, 206–7
Journal of the Plague Year, A (Defoe), 13, 15 n. 9
Jubilate Agno (Smart), 46
Julius Caesar, 5, 7, 8, 10, 37, 39, 109, 208
Juvenal, as model for eighteenth-century poets, 36;
    Gay and, 143, 165–7;
    and theme of retirement, 165;
    his hatred of town life, 166

Kent, William, 90
Knight, W.F. Jackson, 15 n. 3

La Fontaine, Jean de, 190
Lectures on the English Poets (Hazlitt), 90, 139 n. 3
Lectures on the Virgilian Age (Conway), 15 n. 4
Lepidus, 5, 6, 7,

Lives of the English Poets (Johnson), 19, 65 n. 3, 67, 88 n. 4, 180, 194
Lucius, 6
Lucretius, 18, 25, 197;
    Thomson and, 101–3, 104, 106, 140 n. 9;
    attitude to progress of, 158

McKillop, A.D., 93, 139 n. 4
Maecenas, 8
Magical Art of Virgil, The (Rand), 33 n. 1
Mair, A.W., 179 n. 13, 179 n. 15
Marlborough, Duke of, 141
Martyn, Colonel, 55
Marvell, Andrew, 66
Medal, The (Dryden), 29, 30
Metamorphoses (Ovid), 103, 140 n. 10
Milton, John, 23, 26;
    Philips and, 38–9, 42, 65 n. 5, 190;
    influence on Smart of, 46, 47, 48, 50, 51;
    Dyer and, 55;
    Grainger and, 61;
    influence on Thomson of, 90, 91, 92, 99, 100, 111, 127;
    Gay and, 147, 149–50.
Minor Latin Poets (Duff), 179 n. 14
Miscellaneous Poems and Translations (Pope), 88 n. 2
Moral Essays (Pope), 36

Nemesianus, 159, 160, 161;
    Gay and, 145, 158;
    Virgil's influence on, 160, 162;
    and hunting theme of, 159–60, 180;
    patriotism of, 160;
    his praise of country life, 160–1;
    date of, 179 n. 14;
    influence on *The Chase* of, 192, 193
Newton, Isaac, 204

Octavia, 6
Octavius Caesar, *see* Augustus
Ode to Solitude (Pope), 84
Of Dramatic Poetry and other Critical Essays (Dryden), 65 n. 2

'Of the Use of Riches', see *Epistle to Burlington*
Oldham, 34, 35, 64 n. 1
Oppian, 156;
  use of moral analogy by, 156, 157;
  Nemesianus and, 161;
  use of hunting theme by, 161, 162, 180, 182;
  and 'loves of the beasts', 161;
  Somerville and, 185;
  influence on *The Chase* of, 192
Oppian, Colluthus, Tryphiodorus (tr. Mair), 179 n. 13
Ovid, 140 n. 10, 179 n. 14;
  Pope and, 82;
  his influence on Thomson, 100, 101, 103, 104, 106;
  Dennys and, 154
Ovid's Epistles, Translated by Several Hands, preface to (Dryden), 34, 65 n. 2
Oxford Lectures on Poetry, The (tr. Clarke and Bowyer), 33 n. 2

Palace of Wisdom, The (Price), 174, 179 n. 17
Panegyric to My Lord Protector of the Present Greatness and Joint Interest of His Highness and this Nation, A (Waller), 70
Paradise Lost (Milton), 23, 26, 33 n. 6, 42, 91, 93, 100, 150, 169
Pastorals (Pope), 88 n. 2, 127, 206
Penseroso, Il (Milton), 93
Percy, Thomas, *see* Bishop of Dromore
Pere Labat, 55
Peri Bathous, or the Art of Sinking in Poetry (Pope), 19, 33 n. 4
Perusia, 6
Philippi, 3, 6, 8, 9
Philips, John, 1:
  and formal Georgic, 36;
  Cyder by, 36, 37–46;
  Virgil's influence on, 37, 38, 39, 43;
  'signs of the weather' and;
  Milton and, 38–9, 42;
  epic style of, 38;
  on value of agriculture, 39–40;
  and mock-heroic element, 40, 42–3;
  on manuring, 40, 41;
  patriotism of, 40, 43, 44–5;
  his skill as poet, 41;
  and wasps, 41–2;
  his use of parody, 42;
  passage on apples, 42, 43;
  Milton's influence on, 42;
  political views of, 45;
  imitation of *Georgics* by, 45–6;
  Smart and, 46, 47, 48;
  Grainger and, 55, 56, 59;
  Pope and, 72;
  Thomson and, 97, 127;
  Edmund Smith's praise of, 190;
  Butler and, 190;
  contrasting attitudes of, 210
Pindar, 34
Pindariques Odes (Cowley), 34, 64 n. 1
Pleasures of the Imagination (Addison), 41
Plutarch, 6
Poem in Memory of Mr. John Philips, A (Smith), 189
Poems (Cowley), 64 n. 1
Poems and Letters of Andrew Marvell (ed. Margoliouth), 88 n. 3
Poems and Translations (Denham), 88 n. 1
Poems of Alexander Pope ('Twickenham Edition', Vol. I, ed. Audra and Williams), 88 n. 2, 89 n. 9
Poetical Works of John Gay (ed. Faber), 179 n. 2
Pope, Alexander, and Horatian epistles, 1;
  Windsor Forest by, 1, 3, 4, 66, 72–88;
  and his *Epistle to Burlington*, 2, 3;
  satiric imagery of, 2;
  his views on agriculture, 2, 3;
  Virgil and, 3, 72, 74, 88, 141;
  influence of *Georgics* on, 4, 72, 74, 76, 208, 209;
  and man's responsibility, 12;
  Horace and, 36;
  Grainger and, 66;
  patriotism of, 72, 74, 79;
  and views on trade, 72, 74, 86, 87;

223

Index

Pope—*contd.*
  Denham's influence on, 72, 208;
  political preoccupation of, 72, 80;
  description of Windsor Forest by, 73;
  and theory of 'balanced tensions', 75;
  mock-heroic tone of, 75;
  passage on Norman desolation by, 76;
  his contrasting visions of life, 76–7;
  hunting scenes of, 77–82;
  he compares hunting with war, 79;
  ambiguity of, 80;
  Queen Anne and, 72, 79, 80, 81–2, 85, 86;
  use of mythology by, 82;
  his views of commerce, 83;
  and retirement, 83, 84;
  Ode to Solitude by, 84;
  his scientific enthusiasm, 84;
  praise of famous men by, 84–5;
  passage on civil war by, 85;
  and praise of Thames, 83, 85;
  Thomson and, 93, 127, 130;
  Gay and, 87, 142, 145, 157;
  Jago and, 201;
  his belief in man, 204;
  definition of pastoral by, 206;
  contrasting attitudes of, 210
Praelectiones Poeticae (Trapp), 33 n. 2
Price, Martin, 174, 179 n. 17

Rand, E.K., 33 n. 1
Rambler, 33 n. 3
Rape of the Lock, The (Pope), 59, 65 n. 8, 172, 187, 188
Religio Laici (Dryden), 32
Retirement (Cowper), 203–4
Reynolds, Sir Joshua, 57
Richard II (Shakespeare), 140 n. 11
Richardson, Samuel, 194
Robinson Crusoe (Defoe), 12, 14, 15, 15 n. 9
Roman Virgil (Knight), 15 n. 3
Rome in the Augustan Age (Rowell), 15 n. 5
Rose, H.J., 15 n. 5

Røstvig, Maren-Sofie, 69, 89 n. 8, 139 n. 5;
  comments on *The Seasons*, 93
Rowell, H.T., 7, 15 n. 5
Roxena, 47
Rural Sports (Gay), 45, 78, 140 n. 7;
  Virgil's influence on, 72, 141, 145, 162;
  Thomson and, 97, 127;
  theme of 'loves of the beasts' in, 124;
  political content of, 141–2;
  and returning peace, 142;
  publication of, 142, 153;
  1713 and 1720 versions of, 142, 144, 145;
  individual style of, 145;
  relation of poet to subject in, 147, 148, 169;
  passage on fishing in, 148–51;
  moral parallel of animals and man in, 152;
  Dennys' influence on, 155;
  epigraph to 1720 edition of *Rural Sports*, 162;
  complexity of, 163;
  fusion of literary and actual in, 169;
  flexibility of style in, 178; 211;
  Somerville and, 181;
  Jago and, 199

Sarbiewski, Casimire, 93
Scriblerus Club, 33 n. 4
Scribonia, 6
Seasons, The (Hinchliffe), 127
Seasons, The (Thomson), 1;
  publication of, 90, 121, 139 n. 1;
  complexity of, 90, 92, 100;
  sublime passages in, 91;
  and man's insignificance, 91;
  pastoral mood of, 91, 135;
  and stylistic diversity, 92, 134, 135;
  weak structure of, 92;
  theme of commercial expansion, 145;
  Virgil's influence on, 45, 94–7, 104–11, 112, 141;
  Røstvig's comments on, 93;

224

Seasons, The—contd.
  agricultural aspects of, 96;
  three central themes of, 98;
  vision of Golden Age in, 100;
  Miltonic reflections in, 100–1;
  and Ovid, 100;
  pastoralism linked with progressivism in, 106–7;
  patriotism in, 109–11;
  and theme of retirement, 112–24;
  cyclical aspect of, 128, 130;
  and nature's abundance, 128, 129;
  destructive and creative elements in, 131–3, 208;
  contrasting themes of, 134;
  and heroic style, 136–9;
  'realistic' character of, 139;
  'A Check List of Editions of *The Seasons*' (Cohen), 139 n. 2
  Spring, 87;
    Milton's influence on, 90–1, 101;
    reflections of *Georgics* in, 94, 97;
    pastoral scene in, 91;
    and fishing, 96;
    praise of agriculture in, 98;
    jingoistic patronage in, 99, 126;
    Ovidian sections in, 103;
    and praise of wealth, 106;
    idealization of nature in, 111, 116, 129, 130, 133;
    theme of retirement in, 117, 126;
    and description of Hagley Park, 121;
    theme of virtuous love and marriage in, 122, 125–6;
    and insect pests, 124, 137;
    virtue of labour and reason in, 126;
    and abundance in nature, 129–30;
    creative element in, 131;
    and variation in style, 134–5;
    catalogue of flowers in, 135;
    and mock-heroic element, 137;
  Summer, 91;
    tale of Celadon and Amelia in, 91, 132–3;
    influence of *Georgics* on, 95, 109;
    patriotism in, 99;
    and sheep-shearing scene, 106;
    description of tropics in, 107;
    paraphrase of Virgil in, 109–10;
    retirement and progress linked in, 115;
    destructive element in, 131, 132, 133;
    varied styles of, 135;
    Damon and Musidora episode in, 138–9;
    and mock-heroic in, 138–9;
  Autumn, Virgilian paraphrase in, 95;
    influence of *Rural Sports* on, 97;
    Cyder and, 97;
    Lucretian influence on, 102;
    idealization of nature in, 111;
    retirement and progress linked in, 113, 118;
    and moral influence of nature, 117;
    creative element in, 131;
    theme of harvest in, 133;
    tale of Palamon and Lavinia in, 133;
    Hunt scenes in, 136;
    and use of mock-heroic, 136–7;
  Winter, 90, 93;
    sublime mood of, 91, 127–8;
    Virgil's influence on, 96;
    and theme of retirement, 96;
    life of Lapps and Russians in, 107–9;
    retirement and progress linked in, 112–13, 114, 118;
    Preface to June 1726 edition of, 127, 128;
    destructive element in 131, 133;
    contrasting themes of, 134;
    descent of wolves in, 135–6;
Second Epode (Horace), 84
Secrets of Angling, The (Dennys), 149, 179 n. 10;
  publication of, 153;
  Gay and, 156;
Sextus Pompeius, 6, 7
Shaftsbury, Earl of, 116
Shakespeare, William, 110, 111

Index

Sidney, Sir Philip, 46
Smart, Christopher, and formal Georgic, 36;
  poetic works of, 46;
  publication of *The Hop Garden* by, 46;
  influence of Virgil on, 46, 64;
  idealization of Kent by, 46–8;
  epic element in, 47, 48;
  Miltonic pastiche of, 47, 48, 49;
  varied styles of, 48;
  and sexual imagery, 49;
  mythological treatment by, 49;
  and pastoralism, 49;
  his views on the Navy;
  and Augustus;
  his use of mock-heroic;
  experimental style of, 51;
  Grainger and, 55
Smith, Edmund, 189, 190
Socrates, 114
Somervile, William, 95, 124;
  Dr. Johnson's comment on, 180;
  hunting poetry and, 180;
  self-consciousness of, 181, 188, 192;
  patriotism of, 180, 183;
  and nostalgia for Golden Age, 182;
  Virgil's influence on, 182, 185, 186, 193;
  Grattius and, 182, 183;
  Oppian and, 182;
  his knowledge of hunting, 183;
  and theme of retirement, 183, 184;
  his sentimentalizing of Virgil;
  patriotism linked with hunting by, 184;
  social attitude of, 184;
  Georgics as model for, 184, 194;
  account of stag-hunt by, 186;
  Denham and, 186;
  inversion of mock-heroic by, 187;
  praises Prince of Wales, 181, 184, 186, 187, 192;
  his awareness of hidden irony, 188;
  Hogarth and, 188;
  style of, 189–91;
  use of burlesque by, 189;
  Miltonic style and, 189;
  Edmund Smith and, 189;
  approach to rhyming of, 189–90;
  Boileau and, 190;
  Dacier and, 191;
  his use of sources, 193;
Song to David, A (Smart), 46
Spacks, Patricia, 100, 140 n. 8
Spectator, 151;
  essay by Addison in, 41, 65 n. 6, 189
Spenser, Edmund, 101, 187
Splendid Shilling, The (Philips), 38, 41, 65 n. 5, 190
Spring (Thomson), see *The Seasons*
Statius, 81
Steeves, E.L., 33 n. 4
Strafford, Thomas Wentworth, Earl of, 67
Subtler Language, The (Wasserman), 89 n. 12
Sugar-Cane, The (Grainger), 36;
  emphasis on utility of, 55;
  Boswell's criticism of, 57;
  and Dr. Johnson, 59;
  influence of Virgil on, 63, 66;
  patriotism in, 63;
  element of pastiche in, 207
Summer (Thomson), see *The Seasons*
Surrey, Earl of, 85
Swift, Jonathan, 1, 122
  Gay and, 167–9
  Juvenalian style of, 168;
  satiric caricature of town by, 168

Task, The (Cowper), 203–4;
  theme of scientist in, 204
Telemachus, 207
Temple of Janus, 7
Theocritus, 206
Third Satire (Juvenal), 143, 165
Thomson, James, 1, 45
  Smart and, 49;
  Grainger and, 60, 62;
  publication of *The Seasons* by, 90;
  Hazlitt's comment on, 90;
  complexity of subject matter of, 90, 106–7, 108–9, 131–3, 139, 208, 210;

Thomson—*contd.*
  sublime mood of, 91, 127, 128;
  and sense of pastoral in, 91;
  moralizing character of, 92;
  Dr. Johnson's comment on, 92;
  Røstvig's comments on, 93;
  and McKillop's views of, 93;
  Virgil's influence on, 93, 94–7, 100, 104–6, 125, 141, 209;
  his view of country life, 95;
  and retirement, 95, 112–24, 126, 208;
  theme of agriculture and, 96, 106, 124;
  and English Georgic tradition, 97;
  three central themes of, 98, 126;
  his use of syntax, 99;
  Spack's criticism of, 100;
  Golden/Iron Age myth and, 100–7, 123, 208;
  Milton's influence on, 100;
  Ovid's influence on, 100;
  comment on sheep-shearing by, 106;
  nostalgic progressivism of, 109;
  patriotism of, 109, 111, 126;
  his account of British heroes, 110;
  and idealization of nature, 111, 129;
  association of nature and science by, 113–17;
  and poetic rapture, 115;
  his image of virtuous man, 115, 204;
  and social aspect of retirement, 120, 123;
  his belief in virtuous love, 122;
  and marriage, 125–6;
  and theme of 'loves of the beasts', 124;
  his belief in harmony of world, 125, 129;
  and value of labour, 126;
  and man's psychological disharmony, 126;
  his love of seasonal cycle, 128, 130;
  and abundance of nature, 128;
  theory of 'vital scale' and, 129;
  his varied style, 134, 138;
  pastoral writers and, 135;
  dislike of hunting by, 136;
  heroic mood of, 136, 138;
  mock-heroic style of, 136–8;
  self-irony of, 138;
  Jago and, 199, 201;
Thomson's Seasons: Critical Edition (ed. Zippel), 139 n. 1
To The King, Upon His Majesty's Happy Return (Waller), 71
To Penshurst (Jonson), 67, 88 n. 5
Trapp, Joseph, 17, 33 n. 2, 206
Tristram Shandy (Sterne), 92
Trivia, or the Art of Walking the Streets of London (Gay), 1, 45
  theme of town pleasures in, 163;
  Juvenal's influence on, 166;
  Swift and, 167–9;
  relationship of poet and subject, 169;
  imitative element in, 169, 170, 177;
  description of London scene in, 170;
  fusion of art and real life in, 171;
  Georgics and, 172, 173;
  last episodes of, 173;
  versatility in, 174, 178;
  patriotism in, 178;
  and style, 211
Turnus, 27
'Twickenham Edition', see *Poems of Alexander Pope*

Upon the Hill and Grove at Bilborow (Marvell), 66
Utrecht, Treaty of, 72, 86, 141

Van Dyck, 187
Varied God, The: A Critical Study of Thomson's 'Seasons', (Spacks), 140 n. 8
Virgil, and influence on Georgic writing, 1–2, 3;
  and comparison with Pope, 3, 76;
  complexity of, 4–5, 104–6, 209, 210;

Virgil—contd.
  and First *Eclogue*. 8;
  social purpose of 8–9, 10;
  and Octavian, 8–10, 24;
  and Roman civilization, 10;
  influence on eighteenth century of, 12, 15, 45–6, 64, 66, 211;
  Defoe and, 13–14;
  and *Essay on the Georgics*, 17, 20, 30;
  Hesoid and, 17, 20;
  and 'loves of the beasts', 21–3, 124;
  epic description of nature by, 25–6;
  Dryden on, 26;
  and struggle between man and nature, 27;
  mock-heroic attitude of, 27–8, 211;
  political attitude of, 29, 83;
  and husbandry, 30–2, 119, 127, 208;
  imitation of, 33, 64;
  contrast of mundane and heroic of, 26–7, 36;
  epic narratives by, 36;
  Philips and, 37, 38, 39, 43, 44, 45;
  and 'signs of the weather', 37;
  on wine, 44;
  Smart and, 46, 48;
  Dyer and, 52, 53;
  Grainger and, 62;
  influence on Denham of, 68, 72, 141, 207;
  and Waller, 70;
  patriotism of, 70, 78, 109, 111;
  and poetic treatment of trade, 71;
  praise of Italy by, 71, 74, 86, 109, 178;
  his influence on Pope, 3, 72, 76, 77, 81, 82, 83, 84, 85, 86, 87, 88, 141, 195, 198, 209;
  and belief in Man, 74, 104–5, 204;
  and mock-heroic war of bees, 77;
  his scientific enthusiasm, 84, 112–13;
  influence on *The Seasons* of, 92, 93, 95, 96, 97, 100, 104, 105, 106, 109, 110, 114, 116, 117, 120, 123, 125, 126, 141, 208, 209;
  themes of retirement and knowledge of, 112–24, 158;
  his influence on Gay, 141, 142, 143, 144, 170–3, 176, 178, 179;
  Dennys and, 153, 154, 155;
  Oppian and, 157;
  hunting themes of, 158, 180;
  Nemesianus and, 160;
  Swift and, 168;
  his version of Aristaeus legend, 174–5;
  theme of active virtue of, 177;
  Grattius and, 179 n. 14
  Somerville and, 181, 182, 184, 185, 188, 193, 194;
  influence on Jago, 195–9;
  Cowper and, 204;
  pastoral poem and, 206

Wakefield, 72, 89 n. 11
Waller, A.R., 64 n. 1;
  Denham's influence on, 70;
  patriotism of, 70;
  Charles II and, 71;
  Virgil's influence on, 71;
  and theme of trade, 208
Walton, Izaak, 149, 151, 152, 153, 179 n. 5
Warburton, 77;
Warton, Joseph, 17, 33 n. 2, 206
Wasserman, Earl R., 74, 89 n. 12
Windsor Forest (Pope), 1, 3, 4, 45, 66;
  imitative element in, 72;
  political aspect of, 72, 142;
  Virgil's influence on, 74, 84, 208;
  and Groves of Eden, 74;
  desolate landscapes in, 75;
  hunting section of, 77–82;
  and function of hunting, 77;
  social and political elements in, 80;
  in praise of famous men, 84;
  conclusion of, 87;
  publication of, 87, 88 n. 2, 90;
  Introduction to, 88 n. 2, 89 n. 9;
  Thomson and, 130–1;
  fowling section in, 157;

Index

Windsor Forest—contd.
  Somerville and, 181;
  influence on Jago of, 200
Winter (Thomson), see *The Seasons*
Winter's Tale, The (Shakespeare), 135
Wordsworth, William, 92

Works (Pope), 88 n. 2
Works (Diaper), 156

Xenophon, 180

Zippel, Otto, 97, 139 n. 1

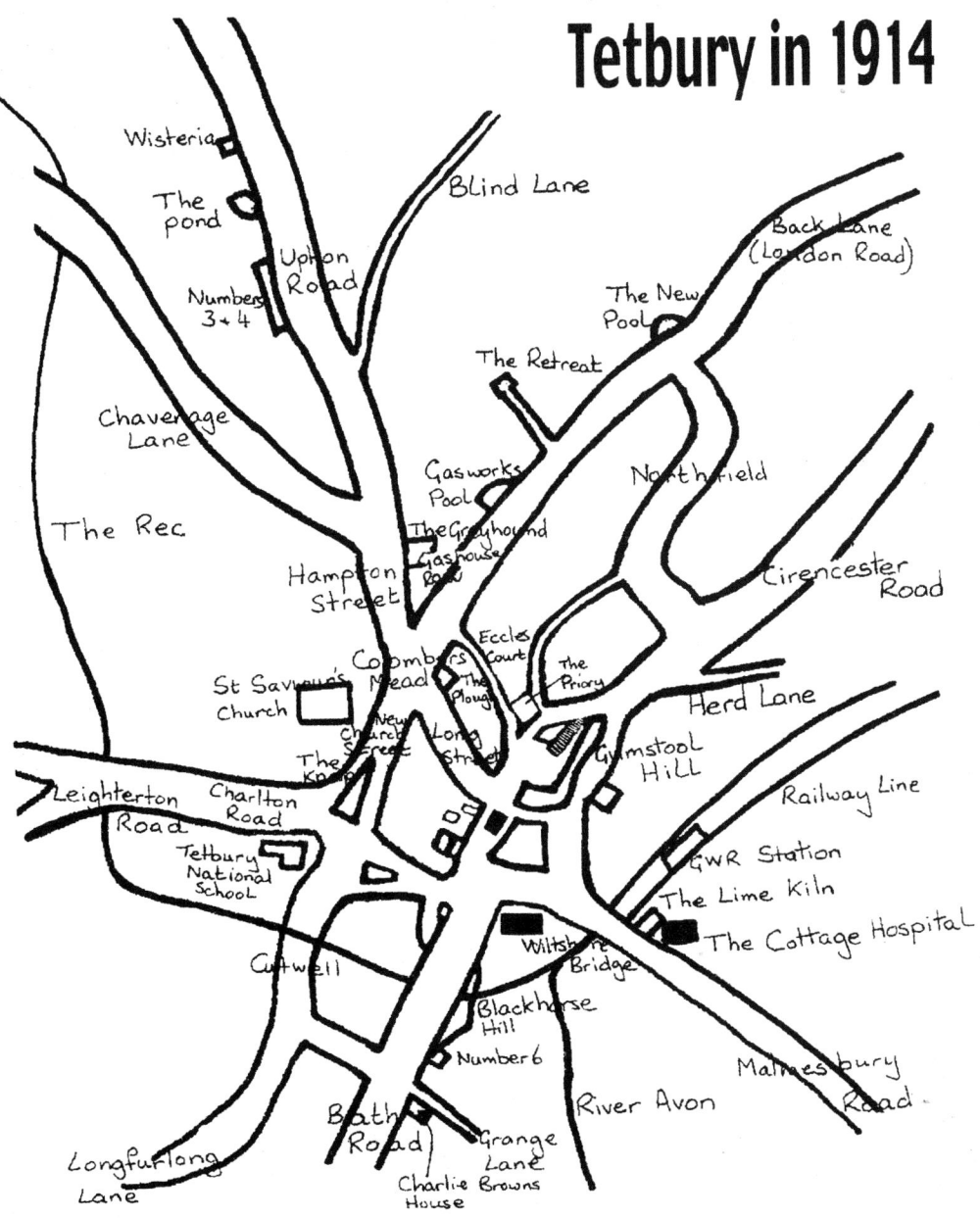

A Boy in Tetbury

by

FRANK PETERS

JOURNEYMAN BAKER, 1905-2000

© Copyright Frank Peters 1996-99

Published by John Peters, The Woodcock Press, 2002